Job Search

Job Search
The Total System

Second Edition

KENNETH M. DAWSON

SHERYL N. DAWSON

John Wiley & Sons, Inc.
New York • Chichester • Brisbane • Toronto • Singapore

Library of Congress Cataloging-in-Publication Data:

Dawson, Kenneth M.
    Job search : the total system / Kenneth M. Dawson, Sheryl N.
Dawson. — 2nd ed.
      p.   cm.
    Includes index.
    ISBN 0-471-14590-4 (pbk. : alk. paper)
    1. Job hunting. I. Dawson, Sheryl N. II. Title.
HF5382.7.D38   1996
650.14—dc20   95-46091

Printed in the United States of America

10 9 8 7 6 5 4 3 2

This book is dedicated to:

*Our sponsoring companies who have
entrusted their employees to us;*

*Our individual clients who have proven
that our system works;*

*Our staff who serve as a model of the
qualities and techniques that create success;*

*Our parents who taught us to excel
and encouraged us to achieve;*

*Ourselves for believing in each other
and making our dreams reality.*

Foreword

Hugh R. James

President
Tenneco Gas Australia
Pty Limited

As a former client of the Dawsons, I am especially honored to contribute this Foreword to the second edition of *Job Search: The Total System.* Having personally witnessed the success of the Dawsons' advice and proven techniques, I am eminently qualified to tout its effectiveness.

As a former vice president of a major international engineering and construction company, I thought that my own success record, credentials, and expertise were adequate to insulate me from corporate reorganization, reengineering, and downsizing. I could not have been more wrong. No one is invincible in today's business environment. That's the bad news. But the good news is that *Job Search: The Total System* provides the success philosophy, marketing techniques, and practical applications to help anyone who is organizationally displaced or who chooses voluntarily to make a job or career change, and to do so with optimal results.

Fortunately, my former company recognized the value and importance of the Dawsons' professional outplacement service. Skeptical initially, I quickly realized that for all my experience in organizations—in consulting and in operating my own business—there were many lessons to be learned from *The Total System.* The first critical lesson was that seeking help from outplacement experts was not demeaning or in any way suggestive of personal or professional inadequacy. Seeking the Dawsons' help in their area of expertise was one of the smartest things that I have ever done. Their advice saved me many hours that would have been expended had I pursued my search independently. There was no need to "reinvent the wheel" as I implemented my job search campaign because *The Total System* is a sophisticated process that really works. And, I am convinced their advice increased my negotiated compensation package with my new employer by tens of thousands of dollars. Though I had negotiated many multimillion dollar deals for former employers and clients, *The Total System* taught me negotiating as it relates to personal compensation. Applying those principles will result in literally millions of dollars in increased future compensation.

Having used the first edition to achieve my goals, I envy those who will have the privilege to apply the second edition of *Job Search: The Total System.* You will benefit from many new examples, cases, and sample resumes, updated forms, expanded advice, and additional techniques. I am impressed with how the Dawsons' have shown readers, regardless of their backgrounds, organizational levels, or functional and industry expertise, how to successfully apply *The Total System* techniques to their unique situations.

I will always be grateful to my former company, to the Dawsons, and *The Total System* for the opportunity to advance my career as a result of my encounter with corporate displacement. Having applied the lessons not only to my job search but in my new company, I have since been promoted and assumed new challenges that will maximize my future career potential and opportunities.

You, too, can experience job search and career success by applying the principles of *The Total System.* Keep reading, believing, and implementing these proven techniques and you will achieve a better job, with a better company, for better pay—I did!

Donald C. Vaughn

Executive Vice President, Dresser Industries
Chairman, President and Chief Executive Officer,
M.W. Kellogg Inc., Houston, Texas

Success in today's intensely competitive business world, more than ever before, depends on careful preparation and effective presentation. The M. W. Kellogg Company is well known as a progressive engineering and construction firm, an international leader in its field. Yet we don't take our reputation for granted. Each prospective new project calls for extensive information gathering, careful attention to detail, and our very best sales effort.

The same rules must apply to those seeking successful job placement and subsequent advancement. Certainly, applicants cannot depend on simply presenting a resume of past activities and waiting for someone else to do something about it.

Job Search: The Total System is written expressly for those seeking positions in today's highly competitive job market. It is designed to prepare an individual to be a winner in that environment. The formula is based on the professional knowledge and proven experience of Ken and Sheryl Dawson. As management consultants, they have worked with major corporations in the outplacement field and in developing corporate and executive excellence programs. I know first hand of their expertise through their association with the M. W. Kellogg Company as consultants.

The major skills addressed in this book are important not only in finding new employment but also in achieving career advancement. Professional commitment, interpersonal skills, and expertise in negotiation are qualities that any business prizes in its employees.

Job Search: The Total System is an especially valuable resource because job seekers must prepare so diligently for their task. Mergers, acquisitions, and cost cutting have eliminated many jobs and made many professional positions even more demanding. Business has become leaner and more streamlined. The job candidate must take the same approach. Technical competence, education, experience, and individual accomplishment are of great importance. But they are not necessarily enough to land a sought-after position. Before knocking on the door, you must learn a great deal about the firm you seek to join. Who are the clients? What are the company's needs and opportunities? Where could you fit into the organization? Employers are looking for a high level of commitment and interest. They want prospective employees to be knowledgeable about the firm's business objectives and standards. These factors are as important as the degree of technical competence.

Because business has become increasingly competitive, companies must do their homework as never before in looking for prospective employees. Every single job applicant must be evaluated not only in terms of technical knowhow but also in terms of how he or she will fit into the culture of the organization.

Recognizing that the employment process is a two-way street, progressive companies require prepared job seekers. Thus, our firm welcomes pertinent questions from the job candidate and makes every effort to respond as fully as possible. Remember, too, that input from the job seeker can be of great value to a company in assuring that the right person is placed in the right job.

M. W. Kellogg makes every effort to prepare individuals for advancement and success. At the same time, we greatly value individual initiative and a strong sense of accountability in our employees. In the final analysis, it is your own responsibility to take control of your career. This is true regardless of whether you are currently an employee of a firm or are looking for a position in a new company. *Job Search: The Total System* can be a great ally as you take control of your career. I wish you every success as you explore its contents and put its valuable lessons to work.

Preface

The second edition of *Job Search: The Total System* is your guidebook to your next profitable, successful, and rewarding position. If you are unemployed or are dissatisfied with your present position, or if you are merely thinking about making a job change, this book will prepare you to achieve your ultimate career goal.

We are the Dawsons. As outplacement specialists, we have assisted individuals at all organizational levels, in a wide spectrum of functional areas, and across many industries with excellent results; our clients' average time-to-placement is 3.2 months, almost half the industry average of six months. The advice and techniques we recommend to our clients to achieve *a better job, in a better company, for better pay* are contained in this book. We are not a search firm and we do not find jobs for our clients, but their successes have proved that the assistance we provide is far more valuable.

Since publishing the first edition of *Job Search: The Total System,* our clients and thousands of others applying the techniques presented in *The Total System* have proven their power to enhance one's ability to achieve a better job, with a better company, for better pay. The vast majority of our clients at all levels and functions have, in fact, achieved their job search goals and taken the next step in their career progression or career change.

While the basic techniques of *The Total System* are unchanged, this second edition presents many more examples and illustrations, revised forms and exhibits, new strategies in every step of the process, a vastly expanded interviewing chapter, and all new and improved resumes, representing an increased number of backgrounds, functions, and industries. Throughout the second edition, the application of *The Total System* techniques for new graduates, return-to-work situations, military transitions, and other special situations is explained. Whatever your circumstance, *The Total System* is your ticket to success in job search as well as career transition and advancement.

Every job search technique that we teach relates to the concept of *psychological leverage*. At each step in your job search, you must be mentally a step ahead. Psychological leverage enables you to be proactive, better prepared, more aware, always anticipating your next action. Begin now to build psychological leverage by making up your mind to take control of your job search. When you realize that placement is up to *you*, the job hunter, this book will become an indispensable guide. *Job Search: The Total System* provides the tools for your successful job search.

With companies restructuring because of acquisitions, mergers, divestitures, re-engineering, right sizing, and other organizational changes, it's a fact of life that job security has gone the way of the dinosaurs. The phenomenon of the dual-career couple also has made it increasingly difficult for individuals to plan their careers in only one organization, which may frequently demand relocation for promotion. Rapid technology advancements and the wholesale shift in employment opportunities from agricultural and manufacturing to service-oriented and information-oriented jobs has made job and career change a way of life for virtually every employee. A generation ago, an individual may have looked for a job only once in a career; now, however, job and even career changes may occur several times throughout one's working life.

The techniques and skills presented in this book apply to any job seeker, whether an executive, manager, professional, new graduate or an ambitious employee seeking that first supervisory opportunity. The earlier in your career that you develop effective job search skills, the more quickly your career will advance. For the senior executive who thinks that his or her needs are unique, consider the fact that whereas once only 40 percent of executives responded to search firm inquiries, now only 10 percent dare ignore such calls. This book will enlighten you to the fallacy of relying strictly on executive search firms and will provide a dynamic system for you to take control of your next job search.

As professional career counselors and management consultants, we have helped thousands of employees to develop their careers within organizations and to find new jobs and career opportunities when their current employers presented them with pink slips. In case such services are new to you, the latter is called *outplacement*. Although getting a pink slip used to be a notice of incompetence, and being jobless was the same as wearing a badge of dishonor, today unemployment is an accepted reality of a constantly changing work force. Corporate conscience has motivated many organizations to recognize that it is their responsibility to hand out more than just pink slips. As part of their severance packages, terminated employees are provided professional assistance to find new employment in another company, a consulting opportunity, or their own business. Key phases of outplacement include career assessment and counseling, professional resume preparation, job search organization, networking and interviewing skill development, as well as spouse and financial counseling. In addition, a comprehensive range of support and administrative services for executives, managers, and professionals is provided in a positive and professional environment. The objective of outplacement is to assist the displaced employee in finding *the right position within the shortest period of time and with a minimum of trauma.*

Because our services are offered only through corporate sponsorship, we have felt at a loss to help individuals who are not sponsored by corporations in their job searches. These individuals are at a disadvantage in the job marketplace because they lack the proper skills and knowledge to conduct a job search effectively. *Job Search: The Total System* solves that deficiency and provides a means for us to help, cost-effectively, the vast majority of job seekers who lack company sponsorship in outplacement programs.

In case you are contemplating a passive approach to your job search, bear this statistic in mind: Only 10 to 20 percent of jobs are secured through classified ads or placement agencies. Unless your propensity for risk is to accept ten-to-one odds against you, this book is for you. On these pages we will challenge you, stretch you, force you into an eyeball-to-eyeball confrontation with yourself. To that end, we are unyielding, unrelenting, and dogmatic in our approach to teaching job search techniques. There is good reason for such a demanding regimen—today's job market is a Darwinian environment. In our Houston outplacement facility, we've created a system that gives our clients an advantage in the survival-of-the-fittest challenge. Only the committed, however, make the cut.

Believe this, and you've taken a giant step toward survival in job search: Short cuts, gimmicks, and dramatic innovations simply do not exist. No doubt, you'll find charlatans peddling a variety of search techniques with the promise that they will simplify and expedite your job campaign. We stand on our previous statement. Information is out there in abundance, but much of it is misinformation. In terms of helping your search for a new position, much of it is pure tripe.

Make no mistake about this—you'll not find any "warm fuzzies" or meaningless "feel-goods" on these pages. Suggestions such as "Take a couple of weeks off to rest and let your psyche heal" or "Go to the beach, sit on a pier, and watch the tides; contemplate where you want to go next" are commonplace in the job search world.

We won't challenge the idea that you need time for reflection and assessment; you have an important decision in your immediate future. However, you don't arrive at realistic solutions by sitting at the end of a pier, awaiting a message in a bottle to wash in with the tide. You prepare for important decisions by researching, planning, analyzing, and networking.

In any high stress or difficult situation, we all must rely on our subconscious minds for guidance and direction. But understand this: You get out only what you put in. Unless you spend time putting valid information in, you won't get any substantive conclusions in return. The most valid information about job search is traditional, time-tested. The tactics that work best today are those that have worked for 50 years and will continue to work best for 50 years into the future. *Dedication, discipline, courage, preparation, self-confidence, consistency, and professionalism* stand as the drive wheels for success in any phase of career or life. But their importance expands geometrically during job search, when emotions are taut, time is pressing, and second chances are few. As a result, we seek—*demand*—an intensive short-range time and energy commitment from you, coupled with a pledge to plan and use your time efficiently.

And we guarantee that those who won't buy into our principles, who can't make a commitment without reservations, will simply be screened out by natural selection. That's the toughest news: We can help only the strong, or those who would be strong. But the good news is that survival in the world of job search—unlike in nature—isn't based on intrinsic qualities or good fortune. Everything you need to know to be fit for survival is learnable. And we are the teachers. As the student, all you need to do is continue reading and follow our guidelines to job search success.

Note: Throughout *Job Search: The Total System,* we provide examples to illustrate specific techniques. All names used in our examples have been changed to respect the confidentiality of our clients.

KENNETH M. DAWSON
SHERYL N. DAWSON

Contents

CHAPTER 1

Setting the Stage: Where You've Been, Where You Are, Where You're Going

In the pages of this book, you'll learn more about the nuances of job search and your career than you ever thought existed. To categorize the information, we can say that all we know, all we teach, fits under the umbrella of our two great commandments of job search. If you have a stone tablet handy, carve these down: *linkage* and *positive thinking*.

THE FIRST COMMANDMENT: LINKAGE

Typically, job search is approached as a series of freestanding, unrelated events. Resume writing, networking, interviewing, and negotiating are generally written about or taught as a series of independent occurrences. This is not so. By adopting our principle of linkage and putting it into action, you'll begin to see job search as a series of interlocking steps, each inexorably linked to the previous event and the subsequent one.

Linkage means that you approach your job search with a specific game plan. A series of unrelated plays, no matter how great, is not likely to result in a win. Linkage requires that each step in your job search be thought through and carefully planned, for itself and in relation to the other steps, just as athletes look at each play as part of an overall strategy to win the game. A great resume may get you an interview, but if you are unprepared to back up your accomplishments with solid evidence during that interview, you've failed to use linkage. Or if you've obtained a reference letter from a former employer but didn't prepare him for a reference check by a potential employer, you've failed to use linkage. In effect, linkage in job search is a tightly structured plan of action to achieve a specific career objective or objectives. Nothing is left to chance as you take control of your job search game plan.

For example, although you want to impress a potential employer during the interview that your skills and strengths are limitless, your answers to interview questions don't come from a box of Wheaties—they come from your resume. Likewise, when you wonder what one of your references might say about you, stop wondering and use linkage to take control: Prepare a draft of a reference letter and submit it to your former employer for the appropriate signatures.

When you're negotiating compensation, you don't throw a number on the table and expect the employer to go after it like a famished German shepherd. Your *research* should have already firmly established your negotiating position as fair, reasonable, and consistent with industry and company norms. Moreover, your interviewing *performance* will have so impressed the hiring authority that you are being aggressively pursued as a valuable member of the team. Consequently, you will have psychological leverage to negotiate a mutually satisfactory compensation package.

THE SECOND COMMANDMENT: POSITIVE THINKING

If you do not think positively, you will not succeed at job search. We exercise autocratic authority in this regard at our outplacement facilities. If you can't maintain an upbeat, positive attitude, you're just not welcome there. Those who want to bathe in negativity must do so at home, where they can screw up only their own job search, no one else's.

We recognize that losing a job can be a tough blow psychologically. Typically, a termination will drag you through a five-step process:

1. *Denial*—This can't be happening to me.
2. *Anger*—How can they do this to me when others do only half the work I do?
3. *Bargaining*—Can I take another job at lower pay?
4. *Depression*—No one's hiring; there's no use trying.
5. *Acceptance*—OK, they cut me loose. Where do I go from here?

For a few people—generally those with serious disorders predating their career disruption—that process is a steep slide downhill. They never rise to step 5. For those cases, we recommend a therapist or a psychologist to help sort out the problems. But for the rest of us—the vast majority of people—we can reach the point of "Let's get moving." This is a problem of *attitude,* and it's controllable. We believe your attitude can be controlled as surely as your behavior can be controlled. We stress to clients that there are three time periods to life: the past, the present, and the future. Two of those you can control, but the past is history. So why get depressed and confused for weeks following termination? Certainly, you can work through the five-step process, but we believe that's a task measurable in hours or perhaps days, not weeks or months. Go beyond the past—deal with the present and your future.

Don't lay more psychological weight on this event than it need carry. Have you ever experienced the death of a child, a spouse, a best friend, or a parent? Those are truly devastating psychological traumas; each could be a life-shattering event. Moreover, they are irreversible. Not so your job loss—that is a salvageable situation. Remember, you've lost your job, not your talent or your career. How many other cities can you target your skills toward? How many other industries might use your talent and background in an area you haven't yet investigated? Don't get depressed, get busy. That's the best cure for any attitude problem. Don't allow yourself to wallow in self-pity. Don't get angry, get assertive. When you do, you begin to build momentum, which begets positive thinking, which begets hard work and effort, which begets success.

We watch the scenario unfold every day in our facility. In fact, we see it happen so often that we like to suggest to just-terminated clients: *Rather than the worst thing, this could be the best thing that's every happened to you.* . . . If you follow our system and advice!

We base that belief on the notion that termination is seldom a surprise. If indeed you're shocked by it, it's probably an indication you just haven't been aware of what's happening around you. More important, however, we have the evidence; we see a consistent pattern of placement that verifies our proposition. Our clients who utilize these principles of job search do land better jobs, in better companies—for more money. The application of our principles of positive thinking and hard work boosts these displaced workers to their next career step—frequently without a hitch. Often that next step is another (usually better) job. Occasionally, a person who is released from a position will decide to become an independent business owner or a consultant, or change careers completely.

Witness the experiences of three former clients in our facility, who represent very different but typical examples. They entered our program weighted down with fear and uncertainty about their future.

Joe Williams, an introverted engineer in his early 40s, was so paralyzed over the prospect of making cold calls to seek out job opportunities that he had trouble picking up the phone, let alone talking into it. Initially, Joe came to us to ask if we'd be willing to place that first, tough telephone call to break the ice for him.

Hank Turner, a former operations vice president over 60, was conditioned to believe that he'd have to slide into retirement after his termination because no one, anywhere, was being hired in his area of expertise—and especially not people over 60. The market was too overpopulated with young hotshots for that to happen.

Tracy Miller was a recent college graduate with a computer degree. All of her work experience was unrelated to her chosen field and performed in short-term spurts to help put herself through school. Tracy was concerned people would not take notice of her, especially with competition from foreign candidates.

Rather than succumbing to the deceptive warnings of many so-called experts who say that it will take one month of searching for every $10,000 you earn, let's look at the facts instead as they relate to our three clients:

Joe Williams applied himself fully to our program, bought into our concepts, bonded with our staff, and within two months was working the phones as though he'd done it all his life. More important, within another month he'd generated three fine job offers. Incredibly, Joe orchestrated the pace and timing of those offers so that all three were on the table on a Friday afternoon—every *t* crossed and every *i* dotted, ready for his evaluation and final answer. He took the weekend to discuss the offers with his family, came back on Monday and said yes to the company he thought offered the best opportunity with significantly more money.

This was a textbook case—in three months, he'd progressed from ground zero to the top 1 percent of all job hunters. Joe transformed the worst event of his life into a turning point in his life—for the better. Now he's living in a community of about 20,000 people—just what he and his family had wanted. He's working for a small engineering company, which he preferred over a multinational corporate giant. And he's working in municipal construction, where business and the new company is booming—away from the strangling atmosphere of an industry in transition.

Hank Turner, the former operations vice president, took his search in another direction but nonetheless generated similar positive results. Cut loose from his firm, Hank spent the first 45 days networking, reestablishing contact with people all over the world. Ultimately, he didn't have to accept early retirement. Instead, he was placed in a senior operations consulting role with a foreign steel manufacturer.

The startling part of Hank's story is that his new employer had an absolute, international hiring freeze in force. Yet Hank networked his way into the firm, leveraged his contact—in this case, the chairman of the board—to the limit, and got the offer. So not only did he get another job, but it was a better job, with more responsibility and more money and with a better company. Even the term *better job* doesn't touch upon the magnitude of his accomplishment, however. What Hank created was his *ideal job*. He analyzed what the steel company needed in order to get where it had to go. Then he built a scenario detailing how his skills could help it get there, by utilizing our requirements/qualifications letter (see pages 186–187). When he was ready, he sold the idea to the chairman. He created his own new job, structuring for himself a position of duties that included those he had always enjoyed performing while eliminating those he didn't enjoy. What might have been the end of his career had been transformed into an opportunity to make the last five years of his career the best years of his career.

One aside: During his job search, Hank kept hearing one objection repeatedly, "You're too experienced." Of course, that's a polite and legal way of telling an applicant "You're too old." So Hank conceived the best answer we've ever encountered to the underlying objection. When he sensed that the interviewer was building toward the stock objection, he would preempt it by saying, "Well, I have thirty-five years of operations experience and that's what you need. The fact is, if you want someone with thirty-five years' work experience, you're going to have to hire an older person." Not only was his response clever, it met the test of any selling statement. Rather than trying to shield or minimize a negative perception, Hank faced the potential objection head-on and diffused it by transforming it into a positive with a bit of humor. And he sold the chairman by demonstrating, through his accomplishments on his resume, what his five-year contribution to the bottom line would be.

In our third client example, Tracy Miller followed our advice outlined in Chapter 3 on presenting her work experience in the most favorable light. While unrelated to her chosen field, it showed many other desirable attributes and skills. Tracy was conscientious and hard working and had demonstrated her willingness to perform any task necessary to get the job done. She was thorough and cared about the quality of her work. Finally, her resume reflected the skills she had acquired through school, not only her technical computer skills, but her writing and problem-solving skills. Tracy was surprised that employers cared about her background and skills. As a result of her networking, she received two offers, one with a small computer marketing firm and one with a larger computer applications development company. After considering the pluses and minuses of each offer and negotiating the best offer with each, she selected the marketing firm position because she felt it would give her the greatest exposure to multiple roles; it would be her best first professional experience. In addition, it was for considerably more money than she expected!

All three of these former clients met our test of what makes people succeed in job search. They, along with thousands of other clients we've helped over the years, organized and implemented a personal assault on the job market. We take considerable pride in contributing to that success. All were placed within a three-month period. But we don't presume to take all the credit, because we didn't conduct their job searches for them. We push, pull, lead, and counsel—whatever is most needed. The individual does the work, investigates the company, conducts a needs analysis, then devises a sales presentation designed to convince the company that he or she can solve their problems.

Just as these clients did it, you can do it. We can't tell you the precise words to say, because it's *your* background you're selling. We can't tell you which companies are hiring or which to use as networking contacts—that's your job. If you do it well, you'll have access to those jobs a step ahead of the rest of the job search world. You'll catch those jobs before they "go public" with listings in state employment services, search firms, and newspaper ads.

You will have identified the company's needs, you will have orchestrated a scenario establishing that your skills and background can benefit the company in an area of need, and you will communicate those facts in your networking, cold-calling, and interviewing opportunities. This is how you find jobs. In subsequent chapters, we'll discuss extensively how each element works. But prepare yourself to accept the fact that *you* must do the work. We'll put up some signposts, guardrails, and speed limits to help you through the tough parts and keep you on course.

It's central to our philosophy of job search that you take on this responsibility for your own campaign. Remember, *you will find a job.* Anyone can do that—almost everyone does eventually. That's not an issue in your search. *What* job you find is an issue. Now we're getting into variables. What job you get and how long your search takes are controlled primarily by you, not by market conditions. It doesn't take a mathematical genius to figure out that if you work five hours a day and find your new position in six months, you might find that same position in three months if you work ten hours a day. What you do with those hours is as important as the basic decision to use them for work. For example, during prime business hours, you work the telephone, networking and cold-calling. In the evenings and on weekends, you read, research, answer newspaper ads, and otherwise use the time when you won't be able to reach most people by phone. That's how you build a winning job search formula. And that's how you achieve placement in record time.

THERE'S NO MAGIC FORMULA

We know our principles work. They work so well, in part, because they're so old. Like bad cars, bad ideas never have a chance to get old. Don't assume that you must "reinvent the wheel" to find a job. People search endlessly for the final solution—some hi-tech innovation that will beat the traditional methods of job search. The fallacy of this approach, however, is that there's nothing wrong with the traditional steps. People fail with them not because of the methods but because of the implementation. In other words, they don't find new positions because they don't work hard and long enough and because their ability to communicate their skills and attitude aren't yet ready for a nose-to-nose and toes-to-toes session with an employer.

In contrast, you can build your own cycle of success. If you work hard, you'll take pride in what you're doing. When you're proud, you're confident. And when you're confident, you become more proficient at job search and more attractive to employers. That's *linkage* in action. You eliminate negative attitudes because you're busy locating job openings or networking into new companies. If you follow our advice to the letter, you'll start your search a step ahead of about 99 percent of all job hunters.

Let's look briefly at some concerns with which job hunters must deal.

Separation Benefits

You negotiate going into a job, so don't think it out of place to negotiate when you go out. You should initiate discussions with your immediate superior and provide a list of what you need to make the transition to your next position easier. At the top of most lists would be salary continuation and health insurance coverage. Often, the use of company office space and administrative support is suggested as part of the package, but we don't recommend that. If you're history at that company, don't hang around. You're striving for psychological leverage in your job search, and using the office of a former employer is not conducive to that attitude. Instead, you can get those benefits much more effectively, along with other essential services, from a quality outplacement service. Outplacement is one of the most valuable negotiable separation benefits—ask for it.

Budget

You probably already have a workable budget for your household. If you don't, institute one immediately. You'll need it now, more than ever, during your job search. For your current purposes, however, you don't use a budget simply to monitor income and outgo. During job search, your budget becomes a key player in the goals and time periods you establish for each step in your campaign. For example, if your budget calculations indicate that your household can continue operating for six months on reduced income, you can plan on establishing a six-month job search campaign. Like every other phase of our instructions, your budget links with the time frame you've set to regulate your entire job search calendar.

Goal-Setting

We're assuming that you've utilized goal-setting as an important component of your professional success to this point. Don't abandon it now. Like all goals, your job search goals should be realistic, specific, timed, and measurable. (To assist you in goal-setting from the beginning of your job campaign, Exhibit 1.1 provides a form for getting started. As you read the chapters that explain the tasks outlined on the form, set your goals for completion and monitor your own progress.)

SPECIAL SITUATIONS

In addition to these concerns, following are suggestions for applying *The Total System* to a diversity of career and life situations. Whatever your particular circumstance, the techniques throughout this book can be adapted to ensure your success whether or not the following situations apply to you.

New College Graduate

As we learned from Tracy Miller's case described earlier, the new college graduate has more to offer than he or she usually realizes. While it may seem that experience in minimum wage and part-time jobs, as well as in co-curricular activities and organizations, is impossible to translate into skill-based accomplishment statements, it is not. And doing so is essential to properly and effectively market or sell yourself to an employer. Your resume at the kick-off of your career is just as important as it will be at midcareer and in your preretirement years. Take time to evaluate your work history in terms of employers' needs and requirements and you will be surprised at

EXHIBIT 1.1
Personal Marketing Plan: Getting Started

TASKS TO COMPLETE	GOAL	DATE COMPLETED
1. ASSESSMENT		
A. Evaluate career goals	A. _____	A. _____
B. Explore independent business options	B. _____	B. _____
2. RESUME		
A. First draft	A. _____	A. _____
B. Second draft	B. _____	B. _____
C. Final draft	C. _____	C. _____
3. GENERIC LETTERS		
A. Cover	A. _____	A. _____
B. Search Firm	B. _____	B. _____
C. Ad response	C. _____	C. _____
4. REFERENCE LETTERS		
A. Boss	A. _____	A. _____
B. Boss's boss	B. _____	B. _____
C. Peer and others	C. _____	C. _____
5. NETWORKING		
A. Personal/professional contact list	A. _____	A. _____
B. Target companies initial list	B. _____	B. _____
i. A priority high		
ii. B priority medium		
iii. C priority low		
6. SEARCH FIRM LIST	_____	_____
7. IDENTIFY AD RESPONSE SOURCES	_____	_____
8. PRACTICE INTERVIEWING	_____	_____
9. IMPLEMENT PERSONAL MARKETING PLAN	_____	_____
10. PLACEMENT (NEW POSITION)	_____	_____

your own capabilities. Also respond to the assessment questions in this chapter to assist you in this evaluation. Finally, review the sample accomplishment statements for new graduates in Chapter 3 and in the Appendix as you draft your resume.

Enhancing Credentials

If you have reached a plateau in your career, or lack skills or requirements essential for continued advancement in your industry or functional responsibility, now may be the time to consider enhancing your credentials. Taking certification courses, completing skills training, or entering a degree program may be just the boost you need to energize your career. Check with your manager and/or human resources department to identify what learning opportunities are available internally, what the educational reimbursement policy is, and what other training or support resources are available. Plan carefully to ensure that the programs you select will enhance your credentials for the long term as well as the short term.

Once you have completed the training and educational plan, use your accomplishment as one more negotiating tool for advancement within your company and to market yourself when you are job searching. Be sure to include credentials, education, and training on your resume. You may also wish to highlight recent enhancements of credentials in your resume summary and/or in your cover letter. The point is, when you are better qualified, your value to a company increases along with your psychological leverage.

Early Retiree

Whether you voluntarily opt for an early retirement package or are faced with separation that includes an involuntary retirement option, if you still want to work and financially need to work, then you can work! With the aging of the American population, companies are learning to take advantage of this growing segment of the workforce. To prepare for the inevitable—no one can stop the clock—follow these recommendations:

- Keep your skills current—continue to learn.
- Do not allow yourself to become complacent in a job, "coasting to retirement."
- Keep your network current, including younger contacts.
- Maintain your health and fitness.
- When job searching, emphasize your maturity, experience, energy, work ethic, and flexibility.

- Consider contract/consulting options as an "early retirement" career opportunity; if benefits are not a concern to you, then let companies know—it will build your leverage with them.

Age is not a problem unless you think or act "old." We have had clients in their seventies who successfully placed because they followed these tenets for remaining marketable at any age.

Returning to the Workforce

The fear and lack of confidence felt by a just-terminated employee is often insignificant compared to that felt by the individual returning to the workforce after raising a family or returning to school for a degree. Out-of-step with the workforce for a number of years, the returning candidate feels that he or she is no competition for seasoned workers or younger graduates. If you are in that circumstance, take heart! You too have more to offer than you think. First, is your maturity. Yes, that is a plus and you should use it to your advantage as you present yourself. Whether or not you've just received a degree, you must take stock of your skills, both technical as well as interpersonal, and your organizational skills. Do not overlook experience in the nonprofit or volunteer association arenas. While you may not have been compensated for these roles, no doubt you did make significant contributions and developed skills. In particular, communication, organizational, presentation, fund-raising and team building skills are often highly developed through such associations and assignments. Just because they were achieved part-time or were uncompensated makes them no less valuable to an employer. Some examples of return-to-work successes follow.

> Martha had raised her family and traveled extensively as her husband pursued his career. She had been active in PTA as well as volunteer organizations, including the Red Cross and a hospital. She sought to begin a career in health care by emphasizing her exposure to this industry through her volunteer activities. Martha's resume reflected excellent communication and leadership abilities, which were demonstrated by her accomplishments in various volunteer projects. Her contacts in these various organizations were also very helpful as she networked into a position in the patient relations department of a hospital. Her international travel and exposure to other cultures was also an asset in obtaining the job offer since many patients were from other countries.

> After teaching for several years following graduation, Connie had focused her energies on her family for many years. She was ready to

return to work, but was terrified of the prospect because she had not participated in any significant activities outside the home since her teaching years. She developed a resume from her early teaching experience and began to contact her seemingly limited network. To her surprise, a friend suggested contacting the school's credit union where she successfully interviewed for a part-time position. Her confidence boosted, Connie began working. She discovered that her organizational and communication skills were well-developed compared with her younger co-workers. Connie quickly became a full-time employee and after establishing an excellent performance record and learning the credit union's procedures, she was promoted within 18 months to a supervisory role.

Examine the return-to-work and nonprofit sample resumes in the Appendix for examples of how to present these experiences. If you were not involved in these activities and primarily focused on family needs, then your sales task is a greater challenge. But if you want to work or must work, you can. First, believe in yourself, then evaluate your capabilities through the assessment following in this chapter, and finally utilize the techniques throughout the book to get off to the best start possible as you return to work. Once working, you can rebuild your experience, prove yourself to your employer and move on to bigger and better opportunities in the future using the same techniques.

Changing Careers

Career change is certainly a viable option for someone coming out of a stagnant industry. But be sure that you comprehend the parameters. If you have grown tired of petroleum engineering because there has been too little engineering and too much petroleum, and you are thinking of electronics or computers, think again. That's usually not a profitable or wise career change. Jump from a slow industry if that's best for you, but be certain that you pick a landing spot that can best utilize your skills. Otherwise, you'll walk into a lineup with the rest of the rookies. Build on what you've done, and what you can bring to the bottom line in terms of results and accomplishments as presented in your resume. Don't hastily chuck it all just because of a transitory economic slowdown.

On the other hand, if you have in mind a change of careers for other personal reasons, then building on past experience may not be as relevant. For instance, if you have been in manufacturing operations for many years, have grown tired of the repetition of your work, and now would like to enter health care, your technical manufacturing skills will probably not help you make the transition. This type of career change may require additional training or degree work and may necessitate beginning at the entry level to make the transition. This is a personal choice only you can make, but researching the alternatives and evaluating your potential for success based on your self-assessment and discussions with others in your field of interest are essential before making the change.

To assist you in evaluating the possibility of changing careers, answer these questions:

- What specific careers hold the most appeal for me?
- What are current market conditions in those careers?
- Are there related occupations I need to learn about?
- Whom do I know in this field? Whom do they know?
- What about other options—independent business, entrepreneurial organization, consulting?

Industry/Function Transitions

The key to changing industries or functional areas is transferable skills. If you desire a change or the marketplace necessitates a change, use self-assessment to identify your skills. Then research viable areas to which your skills are transferable and build your job search campaign strategy around them. Using linkage, highlight those skills in your resume, cover letter, networking, and interviewing. Be sure to do your homework on the industry, function, and companies that you target. Reading the literature of the industry or function and talking with professionals in those areas is essential to learning the unique language of the field, understanding its goals and needs, and identifying how your transferable skills apply.

Military to Civilian

Making the change from the military to the civilian workforce is similar to the career change process, but can be even more challenging and perhaps disconcerting. The questions relating to changing careers outlined earlier should be answered initially. Use the self-assessment section in this chapter and research the fields and industries of primary interest to you or to which your skills most readily apply as the next essential steps. Translating your military experience into language that civilian employers can understand and relate to is critical to a successful transition. Your technical and management training and experience coupled with the military's strong results-oriented focus are highly marketable attributes to emphasize. Be prepared too for very different relationships between employee and employer, manager and subordinate. No longer will there be a rigid chain-of-command and strict structure to the workplace. But, while the civilian workplace has more informal structures, you may have much to offer in terms of valuing teamwork and applying team principles to achievement of organizational goals. Be sure to emphasize these assets as you present your skills to employers. An example of a military transition follows.

> Howard was a pilot who had completed his service and was floundering in presenting himself to civilian employers. His father-in-law suggested he visit with us. He applied the total system from restructuring his resume to networking to interviewing. Emphasizing his work ethic, strong technical skills, maturity, and professionalism, Howard landed a position with a commercial airline. Within two years, he realized that he was ready to change careers and continued to apply *The Total System* principles. Howard successfully made another job transition to purchasing.

Be sure to examine the military-to-civilian sample resumes in the Appendix when writing your resume as recommended in Chapter 3.

ASSESSING STRENGTHS AND WEAKNESSES

Ideally, career assessment should be done professionally. Frequently, universities and colleges have assessment centers where you can complete a professional career assessment very cost-effectively. If you must do it yourself, first make a list of your likes and dislikes. When you've identified a potential direction, then the work really starts. Do your research and networking to discover the career possibilities in the chosen area.

SELF-ASSESSMENT

To evaluate *where you've been, where you are,* and *where you're going,* complete the following self-assessment questionnaires. They are designed to help you focus on the factors that are important in targeting your job search.

9. What topics do you enjoy reading and talking about?

10. What must you achieve during your lifetime in order to consider your-self a success?

11. What are your short-term personal goals (for the next 1 to 5 years)?

12. What are your long-term personal goals (for the next 6 to 20 years)?

Past Career Assessment

Also critical to this process is a self-analysis of what you've done in the past. This is a good time to separate personalities from actual occupational problems. For 10 years, you might have thought you were out of place as a computer programmer. Now, in retrospect, you might discover that programming is fine—it's the ingrate you worked for all those years that made your life miserable. Part of our conviction that job search is a positive experience is rooted in the idea that this is the perfect time to sort out all these emotions. Evaluate all the data, then set a new course.

1. Why did you select the career opportunities or jobs you have held in the past?

2. Have you been doing what you felt you wanted to do or what you had to do?

3. List the titles of the jobs you have held throughout your career, in order, from the first job to your most recent.

4. Do you feel you were well suited to your most recent position? (Why or why not?)

5. What did you like about your most recent position, job, or other activity, such as volunteer work or co-curricular associations?

6. What did you dislike about your most recent position, job, or other activity, such as volunteer work or co-curricular associations?

7. What skills or personal qualities have you been complimented on by previous employers, professors, or association affiliations?

8. What, to your knowledge, have employers, co-workers, and/or subordinates found fault with? Did more than one person have the same complaint?

9. Have you held a position in the past that you would describe as your ideal job? (If so, what was this position and what characteristics of this job made it ideal for you?)

Future Career Assessment

1. Which of the following occupations or functions are of special interest to you? (Circle your choices.)

Accounting/bookkeeping

Acting

Administration

Advertising

Agriculture

Anthropology

Archeology

Architecture

Art (fine, commercial)

Athletics

Aviation

Banking

Biomedical technology

Biological Sciences

Building, construction and
 maintenance

Business development

Communications systems/technology

Community service

Computer technology

Consulting

Customer relations/service

Dancing

Data processing

Decorating

Dentistry

Distribution

Domestic and personal services

Ecology/natural sciences

Economic analysis

Education

Electronics

Engineering/technical specialties,
 industrial applications, design

Entertainment

Environmental technology

Finance

Financial planning

Fine manual work

Firefighting

Food/restaurant

Forestry

Geology

Government contracts/relations

Government and public service

Graphic arts

Health care

Health and safety

Home economics

Human resources

Information systems

Insurance/risk management

Landscaping

Languages

Law

Law enforcement

Library

Machine operation and repair

Maintenance

Management

Manufacturing

Mathematics

Mechanical design and
    construction/repair

Medicine

Military

Ministry

Music

Non-profit associations

Oceanography

Operations

Organization planning

Packaging

Performing arts

Photography

Physical services

Policy development

Product/process design,
    development

Production (planning, scheduling
    controls)

Psychologist/counselor

Public relations

Publishing and printing

Purchasing/procurement

Quality control/assurance

Real estate

Research/investigation

Retail/merchandising

Safety/housekeeping

Sales/marketing

Scientist

Securities

Security

Social services

Social work

Strategic planning

Systems analysis (methods, procedures, control)

Taxes

Teaching

Technical services

Technician

Telemarketing

Therapy

Training

Transportation

Travel and leisure

Warehousing/inventory

Waste management

Wholesaling

Word processing/clerical

Writing/journalism

Other: _____

_____

_____

_____

2. How do you rank the following in terms of importance to you? (Rank the most important as 1 and the least important as 12.)

_____ Earnings

_____ Working conditions

_____ Tasks of the job

_____ Status of the job

_____ People I'd work with

_____ Chance to do important work

_____ Supervisor I'd report to

_____ Job security

_____ Opportunity for advancement

_____ Benefit program

_____ Opportunity to use abilities and interests

_____ Opportunity to learn

3. How would you describe your ideal job today?

4. Which of the following *skills* and *abilities* do you have that would make this an ideal job for you? (Circle your choices.)

Analyzing/synthesizing

Artistic design

Communications/verbal (speeches, presentations, teaching, languages, writing, etc.)

Conceptual

Controlling

Coordinating

Creative

Data/details (figures, records, systems, controls, research)

Decision making

Idea generation (ingenuity, original thinking)

Interpersonal (people sensitivity)

Intuitive

Innovative

Judgmental

Leadership (directing, motivating)

Listening

Making money

Management/supervisory

Mechanical/manual

Memory

Negotiating

Observant

Organizational

Planning

Problem identification/solving

Resourcefulness

Teamwork

Technical

Other: _____

_____

_____

5. What special *knowledge* and *experience* do you have that would make this an ideal job for you? (Circle your choices.)

Accounting/bookkeeping

Acting

Administration

Advertising

Agriculture

Anthropology

Archeology

Architecture

Art (fine, commercial)

Athletics

Aviation

Banking

Biomedical technology

Biological sciences

Building, construction and maintenance

Business development

Communications systems/technology

Community service

Computer technology

Consulting

Customer relations/service

Dancing

Data processing

Decorating

Dentistry

Distribution

Domestic and personal services

Ecology/natural sciences

Economic analysis

Education

Electronics

Engineering/technical specialties, industrial applications, design

Entertainment

Environmental technology

Finance

Financial planning

Fine manual work

Firefighting

Food/restaurant

Forestry

Geology

Government contracts/relations

Government and public service

Graphic arts

Health care

Health and safety

Home economics

Human resources

Information systems

Insurance/risk management

Landscaping

Languages

Law

Law enforcement

Library

Machine operation and repair

Maintenance

Management

Manufacturing

Mathematics

Mechanical design and construction/repair

Medicine

Military

Ministry

Music

Non-profit associations

Oceanography

Operations

Organization planning

Packaging

Performing arts

Photography

Physical services

Policy development

Product/process design, development

Production (planning, scheduling controls)

Psychologist/counselor

Public relations

Publishing and printing

Purchasing/procurement

Quality control/assurance

Real estate

Research/investigation

Retail/merchandising

Safety/housekeeping

Sales/marketing

Scientist

Securities

Security

Social services

Social work

Strategic planning

Systems analysis (methods, procedures, control)

Taxes

Teaching

Technical services

Technician

Telemarketing

Therapy

Training

Transportation

Travel and leisure	Wholesaling
Warehousing/inventory	Word processing/clerical
Waste management	Writing/journalism

Other: _____

_____

_____

_____

6. Which of the following *personal qualities* do you have that would make this an ideal job for you? (Circle your choices.)

I am:

Accurate	Decisive
Alert	Dedicated
Analytical	Deep thinking
Assertive	Deliberate
Authoritative	Dependable/reliable
Calm	Diligent
Cautious	Direct
Charismatic	Discreet/tactful/diplomatic
Compassionate	Easy to converse with/share with
Competitive	Economical
Concept-oriented	Effective communicator
Conceptual	Empathetic
Confident	Energetic
Consistent	Enterprising
Content to be alone	Enthusiastic
Cooperative	Extroverted
Courageous	Fair
Creative	Flexible/adaptable

Friendly

Gregarious

Growth-oriented

"Hard-nosed"

Humorous

Idealistic

Independent

Individualistic

Ingenious

Innovative

Insightful

Inspiring

Intelligent

Introspective

Introverted

Intuitive

Knowledgeable

Likeable

Logical

Long-range planner

Lucky

Magnetic

Methodical

Objective

Open/flexible

Organized

Original/imaginative

Participative

Patient

Perceptive

Persistent

Persuasive

Practical/realistic/pragmatic

Professional

Prudent

Punctual

Quality conscious

Rational

Receptive

Reflective/quiet

Responsible

Resourceful

Results oriented

Sensitive to others

Solid/unwavering

Sparkling

Spontaneous

Stabilizing

Thorough

Uncomplaining

Understanding

Versatile

Well-organized

Other: _____

_____

_____

I can:

Anticipate problems

Appreciate excellence

Commit to cause

Cut through emotional
    smokescreens

Delegate well

Develop systems

Draw out feelings

Follow through

Get things done

Get to the core of the problems

Impose high standards

Increase cooperation/teamwork

Keep current (knowledgeable)

Keep others informed

Meet deadlines

Resolve conflicts

See inter-relationships

See the "big picture"

Strive for excellence

Take calculated risks

Take and give orders

Take responsibility

Think quickly

Use time effectively

Value ideas

Weigh alternatives

Work well under stress

Work with minimal supervision

Other: _____

_____

_____

I have:

Energy/drive,

Initiative

Preference for people, variety,
    action

Rich friendships

Sense of timing/priorities

Other: _____

_____

7. What additional capabilities, experience, or educational qualifications
   would you need to acquire in order to be well prepared for your ideal job?

8. What are your greatest strengths which apply to the job?

9. How can these strengths benefit an employer?

10. What are your potential weaknesses which apply to work?

11. How can you eliminate these potential weaknesses or turn them into a benefit for an employer?

12. What is your long-term career goal (for the next six to twenty years)?

13. What is your short-term career goal (for the next one to five years)?

14. How do your career goals relate to the career and life goals of your family members?

15. Do you believe that your ideal job is attainable today? (If so, please explain.)

16. If not, what major obstacles stand in the way?

17. Can you overcome these obstacles to achieve your career goals? (If not, please explain.)

18. Would you relocate for the right career opportunity? (If so, where are you prepared to relocate?)

19. What specific jobs have you targeted for your employment search?

20. Are the jobs you have targeted realistic career goals, given the nature of the current marketplace?

21. Do you prefer a small, medium, or large firm?

22. Do you want to work in a highly charged environment or a more evenly paced one?

23. What leadership style is compatible with yours?

24. Are you willing and able to risk joining a relatively new company?

25. Have you targeted specific companies you would like to join? (If so, list these companies and state the factors that attracted you to them.)

26. How hard would you be willing to work to join one of these companies?

27. Do you want to explore consulting, independent business, or other opportunities? (If so, why?)

28. Using the pie diagram, how would you divide your level of interest in three options:

   a.   Company position/employment
   b.   Consulting/Contract Work
   c.   Independent Business

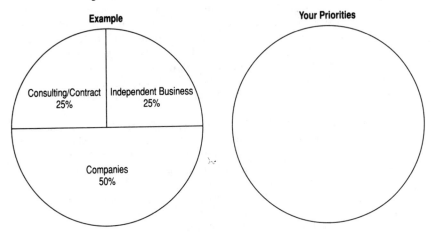

29. Based on your priorities, how do you plan to allocate your research/networking time among these three options?

   a.   Company position/employment _____ %
   b.   Consulting/Contract Work   _____ %
   c.   Independent Business   _____ %

30. Have you set a personal goal regarding when you expect to be employed or earning income from consulting or a business venture? (If so, what is the date? If you have not set a date, please explain.)

31. How many hours per week do you plan to work to achieve this goal?

SET YOUR GOAL

Having completed your self-assessment, review it carefully and set your goal for the position or independent opportunity you desire. Illustrations of how important goal setting is to achieving the right job for you follow:

> Vance was a new graduate who wanted to go on to medical school. Unfortunately, he had not yet been accepted, so he needed work. He was depressed about his situation, but we encouraged him to target medical research institutions to strengthen his ability to gain acceptance in medical school. He was skeptical about his marketability, but after putting a winning resume together and identifying institutions to target, he found employment in 6 weeks with a research institute.

> Phillip had progressed from technical positions to vice president of business development when a merger eliminated his position. At 57, he wondered what he could do as a next step in his career. After reviewing the self-assessment, he realized that he could market himself either for another corporate position with a medium-sized firm or pursue consulting opportunities. He chose to explore both simultaneously, dividing his networking time equally initially, but remaining flexible to reallocate his time as opportunities arose.

These are just two examples of how the assessment process links to the job campaign. If Vance had merely looked in the classifieds or took the first job that was available, he probably would have settled for a job unrelated to his degree or career aspirations. For Phillip, pursuing multiple objectives gave him greater flexibility and increased his ability to market his capabilities. Setting a goal based on your assessment is an essential step in landing not just a job, but the *best* job for you and your career.

CAUTIONS

Although we set world records for emphasis on positive thinking, a few *don'ts* can help eliminate grief and streamline your search.

- *Don't take time off.* You don't deserve a reward until you have accepted your new position—then take the time you need before you start.

- *Don't assume that your closest networking contacts know all there is to know about you.* Even your best friend may have misconceptions about what you can do and where you've done it. You must tell them explicitly what you're aiming toward and what you want them to do for you.

• *Don't take rejection personally.* It's a normal by-product of job search. Learn to transform an initial no answer into a positive conclusion for you. Obviously, the majority of the contacts you make will not have an opening, and if you stop there you will be wallowing in negative feedback. We insist that your contact shouldn't stop with a *no.* Push the phone call forward. If you can't get a job offer or a lead, get additional names you can contact. In that way, almost every call becomes positive. One of the job search theories we dislike most is the Mickey Mouse exercise called "the rule of no's." The idea is to write the word no on a piece of paper several hundred times, then write yes at the bottom, and paste the paper on your wall. Then, each time someone tells you no, rejoice and cross one no off, because you're even closer to your yes. We dislike that because it's a cop out. If your phone calls are all ending in no's, the problem is you. Learn to cold-call (Chapter 7), improve your technique, and meet your goals. If you won't be satisfied with a *no,* we guarantee you won't hear it as often in your job search.

• *Don't count on one hot lead working out.* The most encouraging network contacts—the hottest leads—turn up stone cold more often than not. Never sit by the phone waiting for one contact to bear fruit. Keep working and keep making your contacts. Remember, you don't have a job, and your search isn't completed until you have an offer, have accepted it, and have started working in your new position.

• *Don't expect search firms, classified advertisements, other job listings or resume data banks to do all your work.* Combined, these sources account for at most 10 to 20 percent of jobs. Yet most people spend 100 percent of their time working these sources. When you read about rejection, depression, and endless searches for new jobs, the victimized people are almost without exception the people who rely on search firms and ads. That is the easy way, the lazy way. But it usually doesn't work, because you're competing with the whole world. Also, be aware that when you use a search firm, although you're dealing with someone who professes to be able to assist you, in reality he's an agent of the employer and is looking out, first, for the interests of the company. The people who network and cold-call are the people who get the best jobs first.

• *Don't keep the bad news to yourself.* If you've been terminated, don't be embarrassed about telling close friends and family members. They can help in two ways. During the initial period, when you're dealing with your emotions, they are your best support system. Then they become the first names on your networking lists.

• *Don't call a lawyer.* We teach job search as a win-win proposition. Filing suit against your former employer violates every rule of positive thinking and smart planning that we teach. By engaging in a lawsuit, you're focusing on the past. Remember, that's beyond control. Even if you win a lawsuit—and ten years from now get back pay, reinstatement, or a settlement—so what? You've wallowed in bitterness and anger for all those years, and that's not any way to live and work. Termination isn't a disaster; it's an opportunity. Get on with your future. Let your former employer be an asset to your future through an excellent reference.

Now for the last caution before you begin structuring your job search:

• *Don't fall prey to the snake oil artists.* Be careful! Don't touch the ink on this page. If our passion about these guys has been transmitted through the printing process, it may be poisonous—dangerous to your health. Even if the ink is toxic, however, it's not nearly as hazardous as the charlatans who are waiting out there to rip you off. Anyone who wants your money up front for job placement or counseling services is suspect in our view. Frequently, they are called career counselors or retail outplacement firms, but whatever their title, they share a common bond. If they want your money first, stay away from them like the plague—because that's just what they are.

Everyone has to make a living. Our firm is funded by the sponsoring corporations of the individual clients. A legitimate employment agency or reputable search firm is paid by the company listing a job. In some cases, the individual job hunter pays the freight—but only after services have been rendered and you have a job. There are other ways to spend money—needlessly, we think—on resume preparation, for example. Resume services will likely not give you a professional resume, but we won't suggest that they're crooks. Beware, however, of any others who want to take your money up front for job search advice or services. Don't get hooked up with some charlatan who'll give you a resume and a computer printout, plus a stack of pamphlets with acronyms for titles. Typically, you'll take a hit of between $2,000 to $10,000 for these "services." They'll get rich. You'll get little or nothing.

Your only protection is to keep your money in your pocket. If you're tempted by a sales pitch, first contact your local Better Business Bureau, your state attorney general's office, or any other consumer protection agency in your area to inquire about their track record or potential complaints.

Now that your income has stopped, you need to monitor your cash flow more than ever. It would be tragic to blow it on some thief who will not help your job search. We recall one client whose experience sums it up best:

> After completing our outplacement seminar as a corporate-sponsored client, Bill Brown commented that several years before, he'd fallen prey to one such job search consulting service. The experience cost him nearly $6,000. Bill told us, "You people actually do what they promised they would do. I spent all that money and got nothing but a half-baked resume in return. I'm really ashamed to admit I did that. I'm a lawyer and I'm supposed to know better than that."

If you would like professional assistance from a reputable career counselor or outplacement firm, the following criteria distinguish the pros from the peddlers:

1. Seek good, solid references, credentials, and a proven track record of success.
2. Review services carefully; they should be clearly defined with samples of resumes, letters, and materials.
3. Evaluate whether services promised can be met by their staff, facilities, and credentials.
4. Beware of firms that claim to do search and outplacement—there is an inherent conflict of interest between the two.
5. Evaluate the environment and sales approach—if it makes you feel pressured and uncomfortable, leave!
6. Avoid high-pressure techniques or psychological hooks which make you feel inadequate. You should be encouraged, motivated, and energized by professional and knowledgeable assistance.

Now, with the main issues and cautions on the table, let's move on to the first actual step of job search—deciding if *a job* is really what you want!

Before You Search:
Explore Independent Options

It's only Chapter 2, and already we're telling you not to look for a job—at least not yet. (We promised this wouldn't be run-of-the-mill career advice.) The fact is that we want everyone who's looking for a new position to consider contract, consulting, or entrepreneurial ventures first, before plugging into the traditional employee environment. We don't want to push anyone into a field for which he or she is not suited, but it's imperative that you look at entrepreneurship now, if you've ever had an interest in it. After you're in a new position, you'll only be second-guessing whether you might have succeeded independently. So stop now and analyze whether or not your skills and personality might successfully drive a small business, consulting operation, or contract work relationship. Whether you are faced with a voluntary or involuntary change, military-to-civilian transition, return to work, early retirement, or other work change scenarios, do not skip this chapter.

Independent work options are becoming increasingly important in our changing economy. The advent of the information age has changed the way work is done and forced companies to restructure, reengineer and redefine their missions. As a result, the contingent workforce has grown dramatically. Part-timers, self-employed, temporary workers, freelancers, consultants, leased employees, and independent contractors may represent as much as 35% of the U.S. workforce by 2000. That suggests, whether or not you prefer independent options, you may be forced to consider them. Taking control of your career and planning for your next inevitable change is more important than ever to your career success.

BE YOUR OWN BOSS

Self-reliance and individualism are values that the new work trend promotes. Adapt them to your career and you will discover a whole new realm of possibilities opening up before you. If you seek only a traditional job, given the contingency work trend, you've eliminated about one-third of work alternatives! To help you adapt to being your own boss, acquire or develop the following:

1. Ability to identify the value of your work to an organization in terms of bottom line results.
2. Ability to demonstrate your value in each work situation you find yourself.
3. A view of yourself as an external vendor, rather than a traditional employee—if you become a contingent worker, you will be anyway!
4. A perception of being in business for yourself. Even if you are an employee, consider that your company has "outsourced" certain responsibilities to you.
5. A commitment to career-long self-development. Look for ways to develop your skills, expand your responsibilities, and learn new functions.
6. Responsibility for your health insurance, retirement funds, and negotiating your compensation as your work situation changes (whether an employee or independent worker).
7. Ability to work effectively in teams, to be flexible, to work without a clear job description and without close supervision, and to handle multiple tasks. (Sounds like a small businessman or entrepreneur!)
8. Self-marketing skills to promote yourself internally and externally. *The Total System* is your textbook to develop these skills.

If these recommendations are uncomfortable for you or seem risky, or too demanding, you are not alone. While change is never easy, the alternative can be far worse—becoming obsolete, stagnated, bored, or simply jobless!

INDEPENDENT CONTRACTING

This option has become very viable in today's contingent workforce. While once the domain of low level, repetitive functions, contracting is common in virtually all functions and all levels.

Katherine wanted to begin a family and continue to work part-time. As a public relations manager, she decided to market herself as an independent. She used her extensive network to present her capabilities and services. Operating out of a home office, she succeeded in developing a number of ongoing relationships and, by referrals, accepted short-term assignments as she had time.

Even executives are sought for temporary or contract assignments. Organizations may have a project that requires short-term leadership, or restructuring may have left holes in various functions, or an organization may seek to test the abilities of a new executive prior to offering a permanent role. Interim contracts for executives are on the rise.

Outsourcing is another trend that has fueled the need for contract workers. Beyond basic support services, companies are outsourcing functions more critical to operations such as internal auditing, management of computer systems, benefits, and even manufacturing. While a major company may outsource a function and downsize, job opportunities are created by the firm that wins the contract for providing the services outsourced. If you have the skills and capabilities to perform the outsourced function, it may also be an opportunity for you to be an independent contractor!

Kevin had managed the computer operations of a large firm for five years when they decided to outsource the operation. In negotiating with several alternative companies to take over the function, he decided he could best meet the company's needs for the least cost. He prepared a proposal and negotiated an arrangement with his company in which he provided the services required as an independent business. When the transition took place, there was minimal disruption to operations or personnel. Everyone won.

We won't attempt here to outline and clarify all the legal, financial, and technical elements of creating your own business. Rather, we will share our ideas on the personality and motivational aspects of life as a free agent. Our hope is to give you a better understanding of what you're looking at—why some people succeed and others fail—when you consider independent options.

Before all else, however, you'd best discover if you have the personality suited to an independent career. That's what we'll attempt to help you sort out first.

Consider the following traits you'll need to be a successful contractor, consultant, or entrepreneur:

- *Enthusiasm and energy level:* Success as a consultant, contractor or entrepreneur may require that you have the stamina to work long hours for sustained periods.

- *Self-reliance:* You need self-confidence, a belief in your ability to achieve goals, and a sense that events in your life are determined primarily by you.
- *Calculated risk-taking:* Entrepreneurship is generally equated with risk-taking, and properly so. You don't have to act like a riverboat gambler, but much of the dependability regarding income and benefits will be eliminated from your professional life, at least for the short term.
- *Aiming for high goals:* You need the ability to set and reach goals and objectives that other people might consider too challenging.
- *Enjoyment of problem solving:* You must have an intense and consistent desire to drive toward completion of a task or solution of a problem.
- *Long-range commitment:* You must be able to commit yourself to completing projects that will require two to five years of intermittent work.
- *Ability to set the tempo and take charge:* You need the desire to seek and assume initiative and to put yourself in the middle of situations in which you are personally responsible for the success or failure of the project.
- *Growing from setbacks:* You must be able to use failures as learning experiences. Setbacks must not discourage or frustrate you.
- *Maximum utilization of talent:* You must be able to effectively identify and nurture the expertise of others. You can not be so intent on meeting your goals and independent accomplishments that you fail to delegate responsibility.
- *Optimism:* If you can't be totally positive about yourself, your skills, and your business idea every day, why in the world would you want to be an entrepreneur? Starting and running a new business successfully is one of the most difficult propositions you'll ever face in your professional life. You must believe in yourself without equivocation before you start and every day you operate your business.
- *Sales skills:* You must either have sales skills or learn them if you expect to succeed in any venture. Businesses don't survive unless someone is selling the products or services. And make no mistake—when you're independent, that someone is you.

Those are only a sampling of what's required to operate independently. We suggest that you approach any assessment of your personality more thoroughly than any book can profile you. For example, part of the outplacement counseling process in our Houston facility is a thorough personal assessment. Our clients receive a professional, accurate, introspective look at how they work at work. With this comprehensive assessment, they can go forth confident that they've picked the best of the three options available—another company, independent business, or consulting/contracting.

But you're making a fatal error if you assume that only your personal characteristics, attitudes, and aptitudes dictate success as an independent business operator. You must also look at the marketplace potential before you jump. For example, our favorite illustration of a marketing disaster in the flesh is the story of a geologist who opened a fishing camp because he liked to fish. And then there was the systems analyst who bought into a hot dog restaurant franchise because he always loved to eat hot dogs. That is not proper targeting in the marketplace, let alone market research. Use all your networking contacts (Chapter 5) and your cold-calling skills (Chapter 7) to learn how your ability and background will sell in the marketplace before you venture out.

As for the specific building blocks of a small business, you can find volumes of information in the library—enough books and government pamphlets to fill a warehouse—all to guide you through the creation and operation of a business. That's why we've elected not to compete with those books. So do your homework—and be as certain as possible before you make a decision.

FINDING HELP

For guidance in the mechanics of going into business for yourself, we recommend that you consult an attorney, an accountant, and other professionals concerning legalities, accounting, financing, taxes, patents, contracts, copyrights, and the like. Do not rely on books as your sole source of information. That would be like performing a triple coronary bypass with a scalpel in one hand and a medical text in the other. If you expect to succeed in your new business, get a legal eagle to advise you as well as a number cruncher who can make the dollar signs sprout on trees.

Then utilize all the educational materials. This is when the books can help, as a supplemental source of information. Remember, also, that most chambers of commerce have small business or entrepreneurial committees that sponsor workshops and business lead sessions. Moreover, the Small Business Administration conducts frequent seminars for independent business owners. For perhaps the first time, you will have ultimate responsibility for finance and accounting, marketing, sales, production, managing growth, human resource administration—in short, every event that comes up in small business (and then you come to the second hour of the day). Given the fact that four out of five new enterprises go out of business in the first year because of mismanagement or undercapitalization, commit yourself, first, to doing the necessary research to get your embryonic business off of the ground and running in the proper direction.

If you feel that you fit the mold thus far, perhaps you're ready to consider some of the positives and negatives of contract work, consulting, or entrepreneurship.

SOME POSITIVES

- It is a chance to be truly your own boss, with minimum involvement in organizational politics and red tape.
- It can allow you to control your time—the number of hours you work and the time of day or night you work.
- It presents the opportunity for varied work settings and travel.
- Consulting can require minimal capital investment.
- It does not have a mandatory or traditional retirement age.
- It has great potential to be financially very lucrative.

SOME NEGATIVES

- Because it is so attractive, the competition is intense.
- Because you are on your own, you do not have the support system of an organization.
- Because you are outside the power structure of an organization, you lack the authority to impose solutions on others.
- Because you can control your time, you do not have the aid of a regimen or schedule with which you must conform.
- Because your time is your own, you may find that the distinction between working time and leisure time is lost; your time may actually become your client's time.
- Because financial resources are frequently difficult to obtain, cash flow can be a serious problem in a small business.
- Because of the risks, job security is very low and the potential for failure is high.

BASIC SKILLS

In addition to weighing the pluses and minuses of contract work, consulting, or entrepreneurship and considering whether your personality traits match those of successful independent professionals, you must bring to the table a basic set of skills before you bet your career on independence. We like to consolidate them into the following four categories.

Interpersonal Skills

You must be able to relate well to the client or customer and to his or her staff. Your communications skills must be sufficient to persuade the client that your analysis, problem identification, and proposed solution are valid and worth acting upon. You must assume responsibility for reducing any friction in the client's office or plant that results from your presence, positioning yourself as a problem-solver who will benefit the company and its employees. Finally, you must communicate effectively in the jargon of the industry and the company, and you must be prepared to do this at all levels of the organization.

Marketing Skills

You must have confidence in yourself and in what you're doing. And it's imperative that you communicate that confidence always, everywhere. As an independent consultant or entrepreneur, you not only maintain a formal marketing program for your company and utilize sales skills to generate new business, but you also become a spokesman for your business in every phase of your life. Whenever and wherever you meet people—at parties, conventions, or professional meetings, or across a backyard fence—they become potential clients or leads to potential clients.

Technical Skills

Your skills in a professional discipline are, of course, the basis for your confidence and marketability. Quite naturally, these skills should be a given for anyone opting for independence. But, be aware that if your employment background portrays you as a *generalist*—the type of person whose versatility and flexibility are invaluable to organizational efficiency—perhaps corporate life is just where you belong. Your potential client most likely doesn't need a generalist. Someone like that is probably already on staff. You must have specific technical skills—preferably on the cutting edge of technology—to be able to attack the client's problems successfully.

Consulting Skills

At first glance, a requirement for consulting skills may seem a redundancy. Actually, however, consulting skills and technical skills can differ dramatically. For example, simply because you're the finest reservoir engineer in the world doesn't mean that you're worth a three-legged alley cat as a consultant.

The difference lies in the consultant's communications skills, leadership, problem-solving ability, and personal motivation. A consulting engineer's area of concern is not just the reservoir—how much is there and how to get it out—but in focusing that expertise on how it relates to the client's company and strategy.

Following are just two examples of how the independent business option can breathe new life into a career and expand one's financial prospects.

> Bert had decided that being outsourced was a signal to take control of his career. He evaluated his options and decided a small business was his best route. He researched the purchase of a number of going concerns and settled on a franchise operation. A thorough review of the market and financials further convinced him that he was ready to become a small businessman.

> Matthew had been an architect with major companies for many years and was considering starting his own business. However, he was unsure of how to get established since his financial resources were limited. Involving his family, he developed a plan of action based on his research and assessment. The family agreed to reduce their standard of living and relocate to the desired location. Matthew marketed himself for short-term consulting opportunities to meet immediate cash flow needs. In the interim, he developed his business plan and began marketing his new business service. Within 6 months, he had relocated and begun implementing his plan. After 2 months, he projected matching his old salary within a year and achieving significantly increased revenues thereafter.

MAKING YOUR DECISION

We've given you a great deal to evaluate before you leap to independence. Although much of the information we've provided may seem like pitfalls, we don't mean to discourage you from considering the independent/entrepreneurial/consulting option. Much of the advice you'll encounter from consultants and networkers will be negative, but you should consider the source carefully. In some cases, successful consultants may be reluctant to provide you with a favorable picture of their operation—for obvious competitive reasons. So don't be scared off, but do evaluate fully what you're walking into before you take the first step. Remember that the correct answers for your life and career aren't in this book or any other book. Nor are they found in what the members of your network advise. Until you've been through a professional assessment of your attitudes and aptitudes, you're not ready to hang out your shingle. Until you've worked in conjunction with a lawyer and an accountant or financial analyst, you're not ready to unlock the door under that shingle.

If all signals are go, however, we'd like to share with you—as a potential cornerstone of your fledgling business—our custom-designed consulting proposal. Quite naturally, we like it because we created it, but also because it's simple, it works, and it has contributed to the success of many of our clients.

The necessary elements of a consulting proposal include:

- A brief heading used as a title.
- A synopsis of the client's problem, supported by a brief analysis of your documentation.
- A brief outline of your proposed solution.
- A statement of the benefits the client will realize as a result of following the course of action you recommend.
- An outline of the first step of the solution, which should be simple and should involve you personally.
- An estimate of the time to completion for the first stage of the project.
- A full description of your ongoing role—gathering further information, overseeing the first stage of the solution, diagnosing other manifestations of the problem, analyzing results following completion of your suggestions, and so on.
- A statement of your fees.

Our clients have successfully used straightforward, bottom-line proposals to begin their consulting careers and so can you. Here's just one example:

> Theresa had been restructured out of her job in health care manufacturing. Two months later, she was tempted to take her first job offer which would have involved a lateral move and relocation. Recognizing her talent and marketability, we cautioned her to go more slowly and consider a consulting option. Using the consulting proposal model, she approached the firm that had extended her the offer with the idea of meeting their needs as a consultant. Rather than losing her, they accepted, and it was only the beginning of Theresa's successful independent business.

See Exhibit 2.1 for an example of a consulting proposal which will get a company's attention and commitment.

Whether your answer is yes, no, or maybe to the contract/consulting or independent business option, don't stop reading. Whether you're a consultant, a small business owner, or a corporate employee, you'll need a resume. Turn one more page, and you'll discover a new world of resumes—resumes

EXHIBIT 2.1
Consulting Proposal

NAME
Address
City, State Zip
Phone #

Consulting Proposal
Date:

- **Objective:**

  To provide a management consulting service to DELTA HEALTH CORP., a new health equity resource company.

- **Synopsis of requirements and needs:**
  Based upon my initial understanding, I recommend three (3) areas of concentration:

  (1) Providing needed consulting services to develop a business plan for Delta Health Corp.
  (2) Assisting in presentations to potential clients with the Delta Health Corp. team.
  (3) Providing technical coordination and evaluation of potential facility programs in support of analysis.

- **Proposed solution:**
  Based upon the above stated problems, I recommend an initial 6-month contract as Health Care Consultant to provide the necessary consulting services to identify and solve any problems related to 1, 2, and 3 above.

- **Benefits the client will realize as a result of following the course of action recommended:**
  At the conclusion of a 6-month time frame, the client will have a completed business plan with a five year strategy plan; plus, a marketing effort that produces awarded projects to initiate the capitalization of Delta Health Corp.

- **First step of the solution:**
  My first step of the solution will involve working in various locations convenient to your team to review the concept and develop a proposed schedule and plan to resolve these problems for your review and approval and to assist in contracting with your funding source.

- **Completion time for the first stage of the project:**
  My estimated time frame for the first stage of the consultant work will be 6 months, which can then be monitored and extended as necessary.

- **Ongoing role:**
  My ongoing role will be determined during the development of the business and strategy plan.

- **Fees:**
  My monthly consultant fee is $7,000 per month, which amounts to $42,000 for the initial 6 month period. In addition, all expenses will be reimbursed at cost.

Accepted by: (company)   Accepted by: (consultant)

_____   _____
Name   Name

_____   _____
Title   Title

_____   _____
Date   Date

which get results, to be precise. We are confident that our approach to resumes is the best in the entire job market because we have thousands of success stories to prove it!

Likewise, whoever you are, wherever you go, you'll need our networking, cold-calling, interviewing, and negotiating skills. Although you may already be a world-class consultant or a proven, fast-tracking corporate employee, over the next eight chapters you will become a world-class job campaigner.

CHAPTER 3

Beyond Resume Platitudes: The Foundation for Goal Setting

Before you even think about writing a resume, do yourself a favor. Purge from your mind any advice you've ever heard or read about the subject—how to write a resume, how to avoid writing one, how to get a better job without one. When you put pencil on paper to create a resume, make sure your brain is free of clutter.

Almost every piece of advice you've ever received about resumes is useless. When you go looking for any kind of information in books, you're going to find some good, some not so good, and a small percentage downright bankrupt. With resumes, the bankrupt advice dominates the field. As the reader, your greatest responsibility is to discern quality advice from the garbage being peddled by unemployed hucksters. If you've learned a bunch of "trendy" junk from such pseudo-career counselors, exorcise it from your brain and your library.

If you've done any serious research on conducting a job campaign, you're familiar with the verbal effluent with which many "authors" or "consultants" flood the job marketplace. The theories parallel this line of thought: Resumes don't work. . . . Corporations get hundreds, or thousands, every week. . . . Yours won't be read, . . . so don't use one. The rationale continues that a "savvy" job hunter makes direct contact with the hiring authority, uses an alternative marketing letter to generate interviews, and never sends a resume to the company.

There's a grain of truth in that scenario: It acknowledges the value of networking. But networking doesn't replace your resume; they are two tools that complement one another. So if you swallow that trendy line and follow it, you're not as savvy as you think. You're listening to people who don't understand resumes, who probably have never written or read a truly good resume, and who can't even conceive of the multiple benefits an effective resume can produce for your job campaign. In short, our conviction is that *your resume drives your entire job search.* Certainly, it will if you'll agree to do it our way. Any other suggestion will not provide legitimate guidance for your campaign. In fact, it's not really job search advice at all. Most likely, it's intended to generate book sales, lecture tours, and television talk show appearances for the purveyors.

HOW THE RESUME WORKS FOR YOU

Honor your resume; understand that it summarizes your work life and charts your future. A resume is not just a calling card. That's one of its important functions, but many people limit it to that. Nor does the resume simply attract the employer's attention and allow you access to the hiring authority, although that is one of its primary jobs.

More important, however, the procedure you use for creating an effective resume reinforces the process of self-evaluation and goal setting. Your resume sets the tone and direction for all that you do in your job search. When you complete the preparations for creating a resume, you will have on paper how your skills and experience can benefit both you and your next employer.

Properly prepared, the resume will introduce you and sell your skills. Moreover, it will be an ally that will never fail you in any facet of the job campaign. In particular, the resume will assist during interviews, provided that you write it correctly and learn how to use it.

WHY MOST RESUMES ARE OVERLOOKED

Admittedly, the platitudes many of the snake oil artists peddle are based on a truth—corporations are inundated with resumes. It's therefore logical to assume that when you submit a resume you're playing a numbers game, with the odds stacked against the job hunter. In fact, only four or five out of every hundred resumes survive the corporate cut. The problem, though, isn't with the concept. It's not the pieces of paper that render a resume ineffective. Nor is it the competition from hundreds of other resumes on the same desk that makes yours get lost in the shuffle.

What renders resumes useless is what's in them. The world of job hunting may be smothering in a choking cloud of resumes, but it's a cloud of bad resumes. In general, they are as poorly written and ill-conceived as the "expert" advice that tells job hunters to eschew them. The one overriding reason that 95 out of 100 resumes don't work is that 95 out of 100 aren't worth reading. Here's an example:

> Recently a company downsized their procurement department, sending three of their professionals at various levels to our outplacement program. Having developed their resumes in our recommended format, they began to market themselves with confidence. All three learned of a job opening and separately submitted their resumes. All three were selected to be interviewed. During the process, the interviewer revealed that over 200 resumes had been received for the position, and that 6 were selected for interviews. It's no coincidence that our three clients were among the 6. Chances are that of the 200 applicants they were not really in the top 3% of candidates in terms of credentials and skills. Yet, because of the strength of their resumes, they were interviewed.

This is just one illustration of the importance of an effective resume. Can you buy into our approach? Can you commit the next two or three days of your life to writing the best resume you've ever seen? That's just what you'll get from this chapter. But if you can't follow our advice by burying all the disinformation about resumes you've heard previously, our relationship, writer to reader, is in deep trouble for the rest of this book. Without an effective resume, built according to the formula provided on the following pages, nothing works. Our approach to job search is driven by our approach to resume writing.

THE GOSPEL OF RESUMES: THERE IS ONE WAY, ONE TRUTH, ONE RESUME

- *The format is chronological order* (most recent experience first).
- *The resume is two pages long.* (On occasion, new graduates, entry levels, administrative support people, or workers in a trade can fit their professional lives into a one-page resume.)

End of resume alternatives.

Beyond that single exception, never deviate from the formula. You could probably list many different resume formats—most people say five or six. Some "resume services" offer a menu with choices of ten or twelve different styles. Please, don't fall into the trap of selecting your resume from a list of alternatives. If you write any other resume format—functional, hybrid, targeted, or our favorite aberration, the "alternative marketing letter"—you're not acting in your best interest.

Beware: All variations in format are designed to accomplish one goal—to smokescreen weaknesses in your background. A termination? A new job at a reduced salary? A cut in responsibility? Job hopping? A gap between jobs? A functional resume, for example, can effectively create the illusion that you had management experience with IBM, when in fact it was as a board member of a PTA school group. On the surface, that's great. But guess what? The person who reads resumes in companies isn't an idiot. The reviewer's first thought upon picking up a functional or targeted or hybrid resume is, "Let's see what we're hiding here."

Aside from resumes with different formats, there are the gimmick resumes. You know the scenario. A candidate wants her resume to stand out from the others and wants to catch the employer's eye, so she sends it inside a tiny coffin, with the note, "I'm dying to get this job." Or a guy sends a resume rolled up inside a shoe, with a note on the sole, "I'd walk miles to get this job." Don't waste your time. Those are gadgets. They have no place in a professional job search. More ominously, they suggest to the employer instantly that you are a promoter who needs to embellish the facts on your resume to compete with other, more qualified, candidates. A resume introduces and sells you to the employer, so a gimmick won't work—unless you're applying for a job as a ringmaster with Barnum & Bailey or a bouncer in a Tijuana strip joint.

Remember, your resume gets only about 15 or 20 seconds of reading time. You get one chance to make a good first impression. And you do that best with a resume illustrating your experience, knowledge, skills, professionalism, and maturity. When you think about sending a resume to an employer, keep one thought uppermost in mind. It's as though the company is asking, "What can you do for us?" You can't be there to answer the question, so your resume must speak for you. To that end, a two-page, chronological format serves you best.

We won't ask you to invest time in picking a resume format. Instead, the Appendix to this book presents samples of 50 different resumes. This is not a contradiction. They're all in the same format—chronological. But each represents a different function, industry, or level in the workplace. Moreover, we are confident that they are the best examples of resumes you've ever seen.

If you're a chemist, look at the sample chemical resume. A manufacturing manager can follow one example, a computer programmer another, a corporate planner another. The point is, that's the only choice you need make. Pick the function that fits your career, shoehorn your professional information into the format, and be confident that you have a real heavy-hitter on your side in your job search. Your resume will serve as the basis for your entire campaign.

If you haven't yet referred to the sample resumes in the Appendix, do so now. Concentrate on the occupational function or level that fits you, but also check the other resumes. You'll probably be able to borrow phrases and ideas from some or all of them. Plan to spend a couple of dozen hours preparing your resume. But please, don't try to write it yet. There's more to learn. If you don't also understand how to utilize the resume in your job search, you might as well send the employer that old shoe or the miniature coffin.

Recall our *First Commandment of Job Search: Linkage.* Restated, it means that every step you take in job search ties in with the previous step you took and the next one you plan. Each phone call, each networking contact, each letter of reference, each resume you send, each interview—they are all linked. And *your resume is the key link* in this process.

FORGING THE FIRST LINK

If you think ahead to the interview as you write your resume, you will see that what you put in the resume, and how you structure it, determines how you will answer the most important questions put to you when you're sitting across the desk from the hiring authority.

Don't fail to grasp this concept. In most job searches, job hunters prepare their resumes independently of the other job search activities. Consequently they send a resume, follow up with a phone call, get an interview appointment, go to the interview and talk for an hour, and go home without an offer. That's how job search works when you don't understand linkage.

In Chapter 8, we'll discuss in detail all the facets of interviewing for a job—including, of course, the tough questions. But consider for a moment the traditional opening question in a job interview—and for many candidates the toughest—"Tell us about yourself." That's a signal for most people to launch into a rambling, disjointed biographical statement. More often than not, this response is a self-incriminating litany of every reason why no one, anywhere, would ever want to hire this person. But you can be different. When you complete your resume a couple of days from now, you'll be able to answer that opening question with a response that gets you off and winging with confidence on your interview. It's really not difficult when you link your resume to the interview.

Your answer should consist of four parts, and you should talk roughly two minutes. All you really have to do is state what's in your resume, starting from the bottom of page two and moving to the top of page one.

1. Start with your *early history*—where you were born, where you grew up. If you served in the armed forces, mention that here.
2. Part two is your *education*. Tell where you went to school and what degree you received.
3. Part three is *professional experience*—a brief description of your jobs since leaving school, explaining the transitions between jobs. Then quickly move to your most recent (or current) position, *explaining how your skills, experience, and accomplishments relate to the opening.*
4. Finally, part four is a *career plan*—a brief explanation of why you and this company would be a *good match*, reflecting facts you learned in your advance research on the firm. In closing, mention what a *first-rate company* this is and that you are *pleased to be interviewed* for a position in the firm.

Voila! Your answer is complete. You not only got through—in all likelihood, you knocked them out of their chairs. Confidence boosted, you're ready for the subsequent interview questions. It's so simple, it mystifies us why more people don't do it.

The resume will serve you equally well all through the interview. Any time you get into trouble (you will—we all do, sooner or later), count on the resume to rescue the interview, as surely as a lighthouse guides a foundering vessel to port. For example:

> Beth found herself straying from the interviewer's question. Realizing that she was losing the interviewer's attention, she said, "I've given you more detail than your question asked for, but as my resume reflects, my attention to detail has enabled me to achieve significant results." The interviewer used Beth's cue to ask his next question concerning her accomplishments.

This is just one example of linkage in action. That's how a powerful resume sets the stage for a winning interview. But enough about interviewing for now—you have a resume to write.

IT'S TIME TO START WRITING

To answer the tough questions so adroitly, you must know your resume and what's in it—forward, backward, upside down, inside out. You're dead if you try to read from it during the interview, so you must know every word that's in it by heart. Obviously, it follows that you must write it yourself. Paying some laid-off secretary or unemployed personnel clerk—or, worse yet, some resume service—to write your resume short-circuits the process and guarantees a bad start for your job campaign. It's your life, your career. And it must be your resume if you're to utilize it to full advantage.

Write it. Rewrite it. Cut it down and rewrite it again. Polish it. It's probably still five pages long, so let it cool off overnight, then cut it down and rewrite it again. If it remains more than two pages long, rest assured that it's full of information no one will read, so cut it again. Follow the models and principles set out for you in this chapter. Take the resume to a friend or colleague who's good with the language and get an evaluation, but again, steer clear of the charlatans in this consulting business who prey on job hunters. Most important, don't set sail on your job search with a bad resume or a resume written by someone else.

Thus far, this has been a chapter full of theory. But one of our bedrock beliefs about job search is that people shouldn't be overdosed on theory. Hands-on, real-world training works best. So let's get to that. Here's how to build the two-page, chronological resume that will get your job search moving in high gear.

Start at the top of page one by centering your name, mailing address, and phone numbers, with area codes. Your home number is a must; include a business number if possible, fax, pager, and E-mail numbers when available.

YOUR PHONE *MUST* BE ANSWERED

Be certain that your phone will be answered at all times, but especially during business hours. If your only contact is a home phone, and no one will be available to answer during the workday, your job search is already in trouble.

Let's assume that a company has selected your resume as one of five out of 350 to follow up on for interviews. How many times do you think they will call back if there is no answer? Your best bet is to answer the first call. When you're out interviewing or doing library research, don't allow even one caller to miss you. To that end, use an answering service, get a message recorder, personal voice mail, pager, or arrange with your spouse or a friend to cover the phone while you're gone. One excellent method is to use an executive office arrangement as your job search headquarters. Our Houston facility has individual offices for executive clients as part of our corporate outplacement service. Clients get full administrative support, with a complete library, as well as individual counseling. If you can arrange outplacement support like this through your former employer, so much the better. But whatever your circumstance, make the logistics work to your advantage.

A SAMPLE RESUME

Look at Exhibit 3.1, Sample Resume A (Paul Lee). Lee's resume identifies the applicant, tells where the company can reach him by mail or phone, then moves immediately into professional qualifications. Never include your height, weight, marital status, or any other personal information in a resume. Remarkably, some people walk around carrying an occupational death wish—*Height: 4' 10"; Weight: 210; Marital Status: Divorced mother of eight children.* Incredible, but it happens every day. You might just as well walk into an interview with a scarlet letter on your chest. The point is that none of that information has any bearing whatsoever on your ability to do a job. If information isn't job-related, it doesn't belong in your resume. Another favorite trivial redundancy is the phrase at the top of many resumes: "Resume of Qualifications." Now *that's* a revelation! You can be certain that an employer isn't going to mistake a resume for your last will and testament, so it's not necessary to label it. Your cover letter will introduce the resume anyway.

Moving along to the meat of the resume, the *Objective* tells what job Paul Lee wants to get. Period. Don't include a lot of extraneous nonsense about a "challenging career position with a dynamic, growth-oriented company." Similarly, the *Summary* is direct and to-the-point. It doesn't drag the reader through every detail of Lee's life; it simply states what he's done to qualify for the job objective stated above. It's brief, well-organized, and complete. Again, there are no extraneous words cluttering up the page and stealing time from the 15 to 20 seconds Lee has in which to grab the reader's interest.

ANALYZING THE SAMPLE

In the Lee sample resume, within 5 to 7 seconds the employer could learn the applicant's name, that he wants a job in senior executive management and

EXHIBIT 3.1
Sample Resume A

PAUL LEE, P.E.
Address
Office #
Home #

OBJECTIVE

Senior Executive Management

SUMMARY

Over twenty-three years of experience in acquisition and successful management of domestic and international project opportunities in addition to extensive operations and business development activities. Have a proven track record in managing business opportunities to achieve superior financial results. Have demonstrated ability to develop and implement strategic business initiatives, integrate acquisitions into ongoing operations, and build winning engineering, field, and sales teams which have had a significant bottom line impact on overall company operations.

PROFESSIONAL EXPERIENCE

INDEPENDENT MANAGEMENT CONSULTANT   1994 - Present

Currently under contract to Development E&C, Inc., with areas of responsibility which include: (1) advising senior management, (2) customer relations, and (3) special tasks. Agreement is non-exclusive and cancelable upon either full time employment or a full time consulting contract.

DEVELOPMENT E&C, INC. - Houston, Texas   1971 - 1994

<u>Vice President Business Development</u> (1993-1994)
Responsible for sales, marketing, and major proposals for environmental business unit with a 19 person staff and a $5.8 million budget. Environmental business unit was formed in 1993 by combining the assets of three business units. Primary focus was to capture the synergy that potentially existed with the company customer base while pursuing major program opportunities with government agencies. Participated in the development of annual business and operating plans which resulted in a restructuring of the long term strategic plan for the business unit.

- Led sales team to award of multiple contracts from first time industrial customers resulting in $60 million of additional revenue.
- Initiated marketing effort to introduce the environmental unit to industrial/commercial customers resulting in $750 million of new work prospects.
- Built sales program using national account coverage and 8 account executives to identify more than 100 prospects totaling $6 billion of potential work resulting in more than $1 billion of outstanding proposals.
- Led team which developed standards and work processes for managing major proposals with the goal to reduce proposal costs by 25% or $1 million.
- Led development and implementation of computerized common data base for tracking and reporting all aspects of business acquisition process targeted to improve competitive position with goal to increase win rate of new work by 40%.

(Continued)

EXHIBIT 3.1
(Continued)

PAUL LEE, P.E.

<u>Vice President Operations, Vice President Engineering</u> (1991-1993)
Responsible for engineering and project operations in the Houston and Mobile offices for the petroleum and chemical business unit. Managed $150 million annual segment of business with overhead budget of $12 million. Participated in steering committee overseeing the integration of acquired company into engineering operations. Directed or served as executive sponsor of projects for $1.2 billion of contracts in Texas, Illinois, Ohio, Wisconsin, Pennsylvania, Louisiana, China, Malaysia, Oman, Syria, Abu Dhabi, Ecuador, and Mexico. Served as executive sponsor for the largest remediation project ever managed by the company in the northeast U.S. and several other major projects.

- Led task force to develop standard practices for bidding lump sum projects which reduced bidding costs by 40% or $4 million.
- Instituted overhead reduction program resulting in $1.2 million savings.
- Initiated project management programs to focus on consistent execution, and standardized reporting which improved accountability, cost effectiveness and bottom line returns.
- Directed reorganization of process engineering department to provide focus for oil and gas, polymers, and specific refining capabilities. Increased department size 35% to 140 employees.

<u>General Manager Marine Engineering: U.S Operations</u> (1989-1991)
Responsible for Marine Engineering Operations in the Houston office. Directed or served as executive sponsor of projects for $1 billion of contracts for offshore Alaska, California, Louisiana, Texas, China, Egypt, Iraq, and Canada. Managed engineering staff of 400 involved in design of offshore structures, facilities, subsea pipelines, and naval architecture. Participated in development of company's global marine strategy and five year business plan.

- Managed $35 million segment of business which contributed $2.5 million to company bottom line.
- Increased backlog to greater than 1 million manhours for first time in five years resulting in $40 million of new revenues.
- Led management team which won President's Award for innovative design in offshore structures resulting in $500 thousand savings per application.
- Led acquisition teams to successful awards of $19 million in design engineering contracts. The Mobile Bay project is the largest sour gas treating plant in shallow water in the Gulf of Mexico. The Zinc Project is the first subsea completion in Gulf of Mexico using North Sea technology.
- Renegotiated master services agreement with major customer leading to 20% increase in operating margin/hour.

<u>VARIOUS POSITIONS</u> (1971-1989)
Held positions of increasing responsibility in engineering, project management, and general management.

EDUCATION

B.S., Chemical Engineering, Texas Tech University, Lubbock, Texas - 1971
Advanced Management Institute, Rice University, Houston, Texas - 1990

PROFESSIONAL REGISTRATIONS

Registered Professional Engineer in 9 states: Alabama, California,
Florida, Georgia, Iowa, Louisiana, Mississippi, New York, Texas

PROFESSIONAL AFFILIATIONS

Texas Society of Professional Engineers
National Society of Professional Engineers
American Institute of Chemical Engineers
Academy of Chemical Engineering, Texas Tech University
Industrial Advisory Board of Department of Chemical Engineering, Texas Tech University
Industrial Advisory Board, School of Engineering, University of South Alabama (1984)

that he has over twenty years' experience in engineering and construction. Always remember that the people who read resumes are busy and that yours is competing with hundreds of others for their attention. Almost every other resume either will be abysmally unprofessional or will consume all 15 to 20 seconds of reading time just to discover who the applicant is. Instantaneously, you've achieved a competitive advantage.

That advantage isn't confined to just reading time required, however. Don't you agree that the sample resume is a high-impact, professional piece of work? We're not claiming originality. Our resume format is nothing but a compendium of effective features we've encountered throughout many years of human resources counseling. Still, one of the hardest lessons to get across to applicants is that no one but their mothers enjoys reading their resumes.

In this sample, the professional data is excellent. Equally important are the ample white spaces, brief statements, plus right and left margin justification. You get this tailored look on a word processor and *only* a word processor. If you don't have access to one, go to the expense of hiring an operator on an hourly contract basis to word process your resume, but write your own! That's the only way to get a tight, professional, organized appearance.

In addition, a word processor gives the flexibility you must have at the top of a resume. The following commandment blows another resume platitude out of the water: *Don't Waste Time on a Completed Resume.*

Although a resume should be custom-designed for each job opening, redesigning your entire resume for every job lead is an absolutely stupid waste of time. Time is the ultimate, finite resource for us all. Don't rewrite a resume after you have arrived at the final, polished draft. Many misguided job hunters tailor their resumes to each job opportunity. You're supposed to be busy researching, networking, getting job leads. Wasting time on a completed resume won't accomplish anything but delay in your job search.

To custom-design a resume, all you need to do is change the *objective* and possibly rephrase the *summary*, if necessary. This is where the flexibility of a word processor is essential in producing your resume. Having produced thousands of resumes for our clients, we guarantee that the word processor will streamline your job search. Your basic resume remains intact. The operator can quickly punch in the new information to lead off the resume, and instantly you have a custom-tailored document ready to help you get that interview.

Good human resources executives can tell all they need to know about you from your resume. That's why our firm stresses the importance of the complete package, custom-designed. Beyond your professional qualifications, the employer can tell how well you'll fit the corporate culture just from the appearance of the resume. A real pro can gauge your professionalism, your maturity, how much effort you put into preparing the resume, and a myriad of other impressions that virtually jump off the page for a trained interviewer.

Most of all, the interviewer is looking for excuses to stop reading. That's why it's so important to ensure that your resume presents you as a solid professional. *That's* what complements your technical skills and experience—not some gimmick or eye-catching departure from format. For example, on the Lee resume sample, the interviewer can quickly tell that Paul Lee is a pro, just from the overall impact. Then the reader learns immediately his *Objective*—Senior Executive Management. If that objective doesn't fit the company's needs, the resume is culled. (See, now, the paramount importance of custom-designing the top of your resume?) If the objective fits, the reader moves along to the *Summary*.

The Summary must justify Lee's desire to fill his job objective. If it does that, the reader continues. If not—if the summary of experience isn't heavy enough to qualify for the position targeted—the resume is tossed aside. The summary pushes the reader along to *Professional Experience*. Quickly and cleanly, Lee tells where he worked, when, and what he did. But here's the critical part of the resume—the selling statements for Lee's skills. *It's not what he did in terms of duties, but what he did to help his company make or save more money!* Read that again, underline it, commit it to memory. That's the part of your resume that catches the employer's attention. It's what causes them to put your resume on the "good" stack rather than the "bad" one.

ANOTHER SAMPLE: SIMILARITIES AND A DIFFERENCE

Now look at Exhibit 3.2, Sample Resume B (Joseph Jenkins). Jenkins's objective and summary are presented similarly to Paul Lee's. Below that, however, the two samples differ slightly. This style variance is the only discretionary element for clients in our offices. Both resumes list the company and length of service, then break out jobs within the organization as transfers and promotions occur. (Note: Both resumes use years only, not months. Never use months on your resume. That causes the reader to focus on short-term details rather than long-range accomplishments in your career.)

The new graduate who may have a series of short-term work experiences while attending school should not be concerned, however, that these

EXHIBIT 3.2
Sample Resume B

JOSEPH JENKINS
Address
City, State Zip Code
Office #
Home #

OBJECTIVE

Sales Manager

SUMMARY

Over eighteen years' of successful technical sales and management experience including thirteen with a Fortune 200 medical diagnostics company. Have developed a proven track record in domestic and international sales of medical equipment and consumables with technical after market service. Have demonstrated negotiation, creativity and problem solving skills as well as excellent interpersonal skills emphasizing the team approach which have contributed to many successful projects and accomplishments.

PROFESSIONAL EXPERIENCE

RIDELLE BAKER & CO. Diagnostic Instrument Systems - Sparks, Maryland   1981 - Present

Regional Sales Manager - Houston, Texas (1986-Present)

- Managed one of eight regions with eight sales representatives, directing sales, technical support and customer satisfaction resulting in $10 million in annual sales.

- Directed tactical implementation of regional/divisional strategic business plan which generated capital equipment sales in excess of $2 million annually, with $8 million in after market consumables for fiscal year 1992, and doubled sales volume from $4 million to $8 million in 4 years.

- Achieved consistent market share penetration over seven years resulting in an increase in regional productivity of 11% or $250,000 annually and an increase in market share for region to 75%.

- Coordinated customer-oriented sales penetration within a very competitive marketplace by integrating desired financial acquisition methods, which resulted in consistently high gross profit margins of 25-75% and improved divisional cash flow.

- Directed an international sales, marketing and service team of ten people, to create and implement strategic business plan for new market penetration in Mexico, resulting in incremental sales of $684,700 the first year, with gross profit margins exceeding 50%.

- Recruited, supervised and developed eight sales representatives in the Southwest Region comprised of ten states. Several sales representatives were recognized for national sales achievements (Presidents Club) which was comprised of the top 20% of the sales force.

- Initiated several Corporate Multi-Divisional contracts with key teaching hospital and private reference labs supporting various company divisions creating a prime vendor focus resulting in excess of $5 million in revenue.

- Established and promoted on-going business relationships with influential opinion leaders and executives, resulting in key clinical field trial sites, successful publication of data and a significantly enhanced corporate image.

(Continued)

EXHIBIT 3.2
(Continued)

JOSEPH JENKINS

National Accounts Manager - Towson, Maryland (1985-1986)

- Initiated and restarted divisional national account program, designed policy and procedure manuals and account reference book for field sales force which significantly improved efficiency.

- Developed and instituted strategic market profile analysis to systematize a prime vendor focus which resulted in key marketing alliances with national reference.

- Initiated new national agreements and negotiated renewals with existing customers of 14 major purchasing groups throughout North America resulting in $9.5 million annual revenue.

- Built and developed key, long-term business relationships with top management through the technologist level in national reference laboratories throughout the United States.

- Attained 250,000-unit increase in one year which represented an increase of $395,000 in revenues.

- Streamlined all policies and procedures and developed sales data audit program which resulted in significantly increased productivity of the field sales force and regional sales managers.

- Coordinated national account strategy for the entire North American sales team promoting improved sales focus which resulted in increased customer compliance to greater than 90%.

- Developed divisional reference material for implementation of Corporate National Account incentive agreements for numerous institutions which provided a significant competitive advantage to the company.

- Compiled all sales information on a monthly and quarterly basis which was presented to top management contributing to effective communications throughout the organization.

Regional Sales Coordinator - Houston, Texas (1984-1985)

- Assisted Regional Sales Manager with recruiting, interviewing and in-field training. Managed active sales territory of four states with a sales volume of $1.4 million annually and growth rate of 10%.

Territory Manager - Carlstadt, New Jersey (1981-1984)

- Increased revenues and sales, through new product introduction of Radioimmunoassay diagnostic product lines, consistently averaging 20-25% growth per year in a highly competitive Northeast territory.

ALEX, INC. - Chicago, Illinois   1979 - 1981

Sales Representative

- Sold generic pharmaceutical products throughout the Northeast.

DUTTON - BAKER PHARMACEUTICALS - New York, New York   1977 - 1979

Sales Representative

- Sold pharmaceuticals to major teaching hospitals, physicians and drugstores in New York City.

EDUCATION

The Management Program - Rice University, Houston, Texas - 1991

B. S. Degree, Hospital Management, Pharmacy Minor
St. John's University, New York, New York - 1977

experiences are problematic. Summer jobs and internships are expected by employers and you should include these work experiences in your early career resume. See the Appendix for samples of new college graduate resumes.

Here is the writer's discretion: Jenkins gets right into his accomplishments and incorporates his job duties into those statements. In contrast, Lee briefly summarizes his responsibilities before listing accomplishments: "Vice President, Business Development—Responsible for sales, marketing, and major proposals," and so forth. Either format is acceptable. Both work. Just be certain that you don't clutter up the accomplishment statements with a list of duties.

Note that both resume samples address *problems* faced in their jobs, what actions they took to solve the problems, and what *resulted* from their efforts. Refer back to Lee's resume: Led sales team to award of multiple contracts . . . resulting in $60 million of additional revenue; Initiated marketing effort . . . resulting in $750 million of new work prospects; Built sales program . . . resulting in more than $1 billion of outstanding proposals.

Similarly, Jenkins's resume informs the company that he helped his previous employer by doubling sales volume from $4 million to $8 million in four years, increasing regional productivity by 11% or $250,000 annually, and achieving margins of 25-75% while improving divisional cash flow.

Two points in common are evident in the two resumes, and you should adapt the same idea for yours. Both Jenkins and Lee express their job performance or results in terms of numbers—either percentages or dollars. Those are *quantitative* accomplishment statements. If your resume doesn't have that type of forcefulness, it's not yet ready for the employer to read. There are exceptions, however. Some professions just don't lend themselves to the use of flat quantitative accomplishment statements. In such cases, use *qualitative* accomplishment statements that indicate results, such as "substantial reductions," "significant increases," "improved results," and so forth. In short, the reader should infer from your accomplishment statements that you are a walking, talking, breathing bundle of management and/or technical skills. That's what your accomplishments implicitly communicate.

If your first reaction to the accomplishment approach to resumes is "I don't have any," don't despair. Whether you are just graduating, returning to work, or transitioning from the military, you do have accomplishments and skills which, without a doubt, can be included in your resume. We have assisted hourly workers and entry level employees to draft their resumes using this approach, so trust us, you can do it too! Read on to learn how.

WHAT'S IN IT FOR THE COMPANY?

Many people can't shake loose from the concept of what they did on the job—their duties or responsibilities. But to write solid accomplishment statements, you must think in terms of *value* to the employer. The following accomplishment statements include some of the values that will push the hot button of any company and can be expressed in either *quantitative* or *qualitative* terms:

- Contributed to profit increase, cost reduction, increased sales or market share.
- Increased productivity and quality; improved product or service.
- Improved relations with customers, consumer groups, governments.
- Improved employer/employee relations.
- Improved teamwork and resolved conflict.
- Improved communications and information flow.
- Reduced operating downtime, streamlined operations.
- Developed new technology or administrative procedures.
- Anticipated a need or problem and initiated effective remedial action.
- Planned or directed in an innovative manner.
- Implemented an important program or acted with significant benefits.
- Increased return on investment.

The common denominator isn't difficult to determine in that list of accomplishments. It is, of course, the corporate bottom line. The only reason a company wants to hire you is to solve its problems and enhance its performance and profitability or for a nonprofit organization, to achieve its goals within budget. The foregoing accomplishments illustrate that you know how to do both. Generally, a true accomplishment must meet one of the following tests to aid the company:

- Achieved more without utilizing increased resources.
- Achieved the same but reduced resource utilization.
- Achieved improved operations or relations.
- Achieved a goal for the first time under existing conditions.
- Achieved resolution of problems or conflicts with little or no negative effect.

THE RIGHT WORD IN THE RIGHT PLACE

The importance of measurable results in your accomplishment statements has already been addressed. Think of the statements as flags waving at the top of a fortress. But you need a foundation for each statement—the word that starts each phrase. Without fail, that word must be a strong, active-voice verb. Look over the following lists of suggested verbs, and use them in your resume. Again, refer to the Lee and Jenkins sample resumes. The opening word of each accomplishment statement captures the reader's attention and encourages the eye to move along toward the critically important dollar, percentage figure or result that illustrates the job hunter's potential worth to the employer.

Action verbs that address your *planning* skills include:

Conceived	Formulated	Projected
Created	Initiated	Reorganized
Designed	Innovated	Revised
Developed	Instituted	Scheduled
Devised	Invented	Solved
Engineered	Justified	Systematized
Established	Laid out	Tailored
Estimated	Organized	Transformed
Experimented	Originated	
Formed	Planned	

Action verbs that address your skills in *directing* employees include:

Administered	Determined	Ordered
Approved	Directed	Prescribed
Authorized	Guided	Regulated
Conducted	Headed	Specified
Controlled	Instructed	Supervised
Decided	Led	Trained
Delegated	Managed	

Action verbs that suggest that you have skills in *assuming responsibility* include:

Accepted	Built	Doubled
Achieved	Checked	Established
Adopted	Classified	Evaluated
Arranged	Collected	Experienced
Assembled	Compiled	Gathered
Assumed	Constructed	Halted
Attended	Described	Handled
Audited	Developed	Improved

Implemented	Overcame	Sold
Initiated	Performed	Simplified
Installed	Prepared	Transacted
Integrated	Produced	Tripled
Maintained	Received	Used
Made	Reduced	Utilized
Operated	Reviewed	

Action verbs that embody an ability to provide effective *service* include:

Carried out	Explained	Provided
Committed	Facilitated	Purchased
Delivered	Furnished	Rewrote
Demonstrated	Generated	Sent
Earned	Inspected	Serviced
Exchanged	Installed	Submitted
Expanded	Issued	Transmitted
Expedited	Procured	Wrote

Interactive skills with people are suggested by the use of these action verbs in your accomplishment statements:

Advised	Coordinated	Negotiated
Aided	Counseled	Participated
Apprised	Helped	Promoted
Clarified	Informed	Recommended
Conferred	Inspired	Represented
Consulted	Interpreted	Resolved
Contributed	Interviewed	Suggested
Cooperated	Mediated	Unified

Finally, your *investigative* skills emerge with the use of these action verbs:

Analyzed	Evaluated	Reviewed
Assessed	Familiarized	Searched
Calculated	Investigated	Studied
Computed	Observed	Verified
Correlated	Proved	
Discovered	Researched	

That's only a sampling of the types of words you must include in your resume. Use these lists or use other verbs to communicate your skills and how they generated accomplishments. Just be sure that you use a strong action verb to open every statement.

HITTING THE BULLSEYE

Note the • symbols that precede the accomplishment statements in the following list as well as in all the sample resumes in the Appendix. They're called *bullets*, and your job is to see that each one of them hits the target. It will if it is followed by a winning accomplishment statement. The target is that small pile of resumes on the desk of the hiring authority that are put aside to be followed up instead of discarded.

Your completed accomplishment statements should read like these:

- Achieved a 25% cost reduction in the amount of $500,000 by creating and installing a complete accounting system by department in a large agency. (Whenever possible, include dollar amounts)
- Created a profit and loss statement, by product, resulting in substantial increase of sales in the high-profit products. (If actual numbers cannot be given, utilize the term "substantial")

(Do you recognize the categories of those first two? The first is *quantitative;* the second is *qualitative.* But they both work.)

Examples of additional quantitative accomplishment statements include:

- Participated in core team to develop strategy to expand worldwide business to more than $1 billion per year through internal growth and acquisition.
- Developed the start-up strategy for the company's entry into the Mid-East and Far East and then led efforts in all phases of the strategy. The strategy resulted in the company's first international turnkey projects contributing $5 million revenue in the first year.
- Advised a major U.S. company on the reorganization of operations and sales resulting in an increase in annual sales of $1.5 million with a 10% reduction in operating costs.
- Managed a professional group in creating a sales organization after identifying a $300 million market.
- Conceived a new management information services procedure that made vital operations reports available to management daily resulting in a savings of $75,000.

- Developed a community acceptance campaign in San Francisco (a hostile market), resulting in the reduction of processing time by nearly 25%.
- Saved millions in possible damages, and prevented embarrassment by discovering potential bankruptcy of a supplier.
- Formulated policies and procedures for the administration of zoning petitions, resulting in the reduction of processing time by nearly 25% or $50,000 annually.
- Reduced rework by 20%, eliminated schedule delays, and doubled in-house manufacturing capability through reorganization and introduction of methods and systems resulting in savings of $150,000 annually.
- Designed supporting equipment and techniques for a new process that raised product market potential from $5 million to more than $20 million per year.
- Promoted a new concept in welding procedures that reduced labor costs by $100,000 annually.
- Discovered $190,000 overstatement of a division's inventory, enabling corrective action by management.
- Reduced turnover of personnel from 17% to 9% for a savings of $165,000 per year.
- Installed a cost system for complex fabricating process, saving $75,000 per year.
- Revised shipping procedures and introduced improvements that reduced cost and shipping time by 37% or $135,000 annually.
- Instituted a wage and salary program especially tailored to improve morale reducing payroll by $40,000 annually.
- Developed and installed a unique laboratory organization that eliminated duplication, encouraged cooperation, and reduced costs by $50,000 annually.

If you've read through these quantitative accomplishments and you're still saying, "I never did any of these things," try on these qualitative accomplishments:

- Entered, edited, and revised information on computer system ensuring accurate client and case data.
- Assisted in running all office support activities resulting in smooth operations.
- Assisted students in meeting academic needs which resulted in reducing student frustration and increased retention.
- Operated cash register while providing courteous customer service.
- Resolved customer complaints resulting in increased satisfaction.

- Trained new employees on use of new computer system resulting in more efficient operations.
- Provided customers with information concerning various types of accounts and other banking services which contributed to increased business.
- Drafted for small architectural office resulting in precise and neat drawings.
- Performed deliveries and pickups for the office which ensured timely business transaction.
- Wrote executive summaries of audit findings for senior management which provided adequate information for decision making.
- Awarded corporate merit bonus for exemplary performance in the audit department.
- Established computerized standards and samples for production resulting in improved quality.
- Planned and implemented first summary energy conservation and food nutrition festival which resulted in excellent community participation and increased awareness of program goals.
- Developed a program using DBase II resulting in significantly improved tracking of manpower needs.
- Greeted potential clients providing a positive and personalized image for the organization.
- Designed and implemented in-store displays resulting in improved customer traffic and increased sales.
- Served as camp counselor, aquatic instructor, and entertainment director for exclusive summer camp, providing effective staff operations support for the administrators.

These entry-level accomplishment statements prove that whatever your work experience, the tasks you have performed and the skills you have demonstrated contribute in *some* way to an organization even if you are not able to quantify your results.

This list is intended only to get you into the right frame of mind to state your accomplishments in terms of dollars, percentages and results. Review your jobs and career and pick out your accomplishment highlights. If you're still telling yourself, "I didn't do anything like that," welcome to the crowd. That's the initial reaction of most people facing resume writing. Push beyond those initial doubts. Jot down notes and thoughts and phrases as they occur to you. This is a building process, and it takes time, reflection, and effort.

Remember, we require a couple of dozen hours of commitment as your investment in your resume for the benefit of your career. This is where you'll spend the bulk of that time. One good way to get off dead center is to go ahead and write down your duties. That's probably the only way to deal with them, because most people are so preoccupied with their responsibilities that they can't get beyond the tasks of their job to highlight their achievements. Your job or position descriptions and performance appraisals can be very useful in helping you get started.

When you have the duties down on paper, begin to think through them. Recall results and benefits to the company that your duties generated. That's what goes into your accomplishment statements. Do not attempt to translate each responsibility into an accomplishment, however. Some responsibilities may not generate any significant accomplishments, while others may produce two or three.

To help you move along with the process, divide a piece of paper into three columns. At the tops of the columns, write these headings:

Action Verb   Action Taken   Benefit to Company

In the *Action Verb* column, write a verb that indicates your intensity of effort, demonstrates the power required to achieve the result, or illustrates your level of responsibility. Be certain that you use a variety of verbs. Refer to our lists for ideas. They include more than 150 verbs, and of course you're not limited to those alone. On the contrary, be as creative as possible. And be aware that even a strong action verb becomes diluted if it is repeated in your resume. In the second column, under *Action Taken,* write what you accomplished. This should be a short, concise statement about what you did. It should not be a description of how you did it. Finally, in the column under *Benefit to Company,* write the result or impact of your achievement on the company's business. This is the payoff. This is where you use dollars and percentages at every opportunity. This is what makes you valuable to a prospective employer.

Throughout this process remember that the reader will look at each entry in your resume in one of three ways: it improves your chance to get an interview; it detracts from your chance; or it's a push, a neutral. Your primary job as a resume writer is to pack as many positives into the document as your memory, imagination, and the truth will allow.

THE TRUTH?

There's that word. In your resume, you must tell the T-R-U-T-H—as in "the truth, the whole truth, and nothing but the truth." We don't agree, however—at least not in the context of "the whole" and "nothing but." You are not under oath as you develop your resume. So we present *The Final Commandment of Resume Writing: They Don't Know What You Don't Tell Them.*

Do tell the truth always as it relates to your ability to do the job. Certainly, we're not suggesting that you ever lie, cheat, or steal to get a job. Aside from the ethical and moral questions, you'll be saddled with work you're not qualified to perform if you falsify your background or experience.

We are telling you to get smart. Leaving some point out of your resume is not lying. We all make mistakes in our professional lives. We all have elements in our personal lives that we wouldn't run up and confess to a stranger. Nonetheless, people will confess to just about anything when they're looking for a job. You're not in a confessional and you're not defending your past errors of judgment. Tell the truth—fine. But don't look for a job the way a Kamikaze pilot flies an airplane. If the information will hurt you, leave it out of your resume. Period. That's not a lie.

We've already mentioned our philosophy of using years, never months, in presenting your career history. That's a good illustration. Suppose that you worked at Space Odyssey, Inc. from November 1995 to January 1996. If you put those months in your resume, you've probably made yourself into instant history as an applicant. However, if you put that you worked at Space Odyssey, Inc. from 1995 to 1996, you're not placing yourself in dire jeopardy immediately. Make no mistake, you'll have to address your brief tenure at Space Odyssey, Inc. during the interview, but at least you haven't prematurely removed yourself from consideration with one careless entry on a resume. Did you lie? Of course you didn't. You simply told the truth in terms that make you most attractive to the employer. If your mother or your old scoutmaster doesn't like that approach, that's too bad. Do some good turns and make it up to them later. First get a job.

FIRST THINGS FIRST GETS YOU WHERE YOU SHOULD BE

Now that you understand the truth as it relates to getting a job, get back to your accomplishments. Under your most recent job, you should include several entries to demonstrate your marketability. Remember, don't try to include everything you've ever achieved in that job, just the highlights that make you an attractive candidate. With proper margin alignment and white space between each element we've discussed thus far, you should be at the bottom of page one. And that's proper—that's the way we construct a resume. Your last position and your accomplishments in that job are most critical. Your other jobs will go on page two unless your most recent position was relatively short.

Continue the same philosophy with accomplishment statements, but don't go back more than about ten years chronologically or two-thirds of the second page graphically. If you have thirty or thirty-five years' experience, just summarize in one brief statement all the work experience and your accomplishments prior to the last ten years. Refer to Lee's resume for an example of this technique. Another acceptable presentation is to list the job titles and dates.

The point is that if the information is more than ten years old, few really care about the details. Summarize information that is dated; otherwise, you'll be cluttering up your resume with entries that won't be read because they're obsolete and/or irrelevant. We recognize that you may earnestly feel that you want to include a critically important accomplishment from many years back, but believe us, it probably won't help. Summarize it, and keep your resume to two pages. On the other hand, if you have space remaining on the second page to include more detail from early experience, by all means include it to fill your two pages. (See Jenkins sample resume.)

"JUST THE FACTS, PLEASE"

Next, list your *Military* background, but only if you were an officer (this indicates leadership capabilities) or if you served in a career-related enlisted rate (this implies hands-on training and experience). For example, an MIS degree coupled with prebaccalaureate working experience on a military data processing system can enhance your attractiveness as a candidate. These entries should be brief and concise.

Cover your *Education* similarly. If you have advanced degrees, list the highest degree attained first, then any undergraduate degrees. If you graduated with honors, include your grade point average; otherwise, leave it out. Do not list training courses or seminars under *Education*. As we mentioned earlier, if you're working in a field that requires a degree and you don't have one, put in your resume that you're working toward the required degree, and give the projected completion date of your studies. (Again, don't lie. If your profession requires a college degree and you haven't completed school yet, do something about that. You're on borrowed time—enroll. Get a degree plan in action so that your resume won't be lying.)

The next resume entry is *Professional Affiliations*. Include here any societies, institutes, or other *Professional Associations* to which you belong. This shows the employer what you are when you aren't working. It implies civic involvement. Also, any certifications and registrations you have achieved should be listed here.

Finally, wrap up your resume with any other important job-related data, especially *Technical Skills* including computer hardware and software proficiency and *Language* fluency. It's also permissible to include an entry on community involvement or *Civic Associations.* But be certain that the information enhances your impact on the employer. Did you coach Little League baseball? That's great, but it doesn't belong in a resume. If you served on a mayor's committee to study the community benefits of youth sports programs, that should be included. Do you serve on the PTA board at your child's school? Leave it off. If you're an elected member of the community's school board, put that in under community involvement. Get the idea? The employer will buy into activities that either lend prestige to the firm or illustrate skills you can transfer to the workplace. The employer doesn't want to read entries in your resume that indicate priorities that will take time and energy away from your career.

Again, omit all personal information. Marital status? *No.* Number of children. *No.* Salary? *Never*—you'll cover that in the interview and in the cover letter if necessary. Reason for leaving a job? *No.* Hobbies? *No.* So you like hunting, boating, and camping—*who cares?* What does that have to do with your ability to do the job? Health? *No.* That one is a real joke. Have you ever seen a resume on which an applicant wrote "Health: Below Average" or "Health: Poor" or "Health: Terminally Ill"? No—everyone writes "Health: Excellent." Therefore, it means nothing. And it doesn't belong on your resume, so keep it off.

WHEN YOU COME TO THE END, STOP

Finally, we come to the traditional closing statement on 98 percent of all resumes: "References available upon request." Remember, we don't want your resume cluttered up with useless information, which is just what this is. It's implied—you don't write it in a resume. There might be one or two human resources managers in the world who don't understand that references are always available upon request. But cluttering up a resume on the remote possibility that somebody might read it is not a smart approach. If the guy reviewing your resume is such a rook that he doesn't comprehend this, you probably don't want to work at that company anyway.

You are now at the end of two pages, which means that your resume is complete. "But," you say, "what about my publications and the training courses I've taken?" Don't panic! For those of you who have additional career information that you feel is relevant to your qualifications as a candidate for a position, place such data on a third page. However, as a supplemental page, it should not be sent out with the resume but should be presented at the interview. Your resume should remain two pages and only two pages. (Exhibit 3.3 is a sample supplemental information page showing the various categories that are pertinent to career advancement.)

EXHIBIT 3.3
Examples of Headings for Supplemental Information

SUPPLEMENTAL INFORMATION

Language Fluency

Fluent in French, working knowledge of Spanish

Additional Education

In-House Technical Courses: Utilities, VMS Concepts, Datatreive, DECWrite, Six Sigma, Customer Satisfaction, DECNET, VAXMAIL, ALL-IN-ONE

Honors

Sigma Theta Tau
Y.W.C.A.—Outstanding Woman 1993 Award
Dean's List—1991–1993, three semesters
College Expenses Earned—Undergraduate: 60% Graduate: 100%

Military

Captain, Medical Service Corps, United States Army, 1990–1996

Professional Affiliations

Member, Natural Gas Association of Houston

Civic Associations

Metropolitan YMCA Board of Managers, Member, 1994–1995

Professional Registrations

Registered Professional Engineer in 2 states: Alabama, California

Professional Licensure

Registered Pharmacist: Michigan (24185), Texas (21702)
Preceptor: Texas (21702)

Publications

"HP 41 CV Simplifies API Leak Resistance Calculations." Published in June, 1994 of *World Oil*.

Seminars Conducted

Emergency Ambulatory Nurse Practitioner Program July 1994—"OB/GYN Emergencies"

Selected Presentations

Quality Assurance Supervisor in a Pediatric Hospital, Kang, Nancy, and Hotaling, William H.; Mid-year Clinical Meeting, ASHP, New Orleans, LA, December 7, 1991.

RESUME TRACKING DATABASES

We've explained the importance of *verbs* in building your accomplishment statements. Now a note about the importance of *nouns!* Many companies utilize computer applicant tracking systems to manage the glut of resumes they receive and to facilitate the initial selection process. These databases search for *key words* to identify candidates with the background and skills required for positions. For this reason, it is important to include the nouns and technical terms that reflect your skills and knowledge. Standard abbreviations can be included, but also spell out their meaning unless they're common buzz words in your field. Using the technical jargon for your industry and function will come naturally, but be sure not to over do their use at the expense of strong accomplishments.

Also keep in mind that scanners "read" differently than humans so follow these tips:

- Use font size of 10 to 11 points.
- Avoid italics, script, and excessive underlining.
- Avoid graphics and shading.
- Use a laser printer.
- Use an original or high quality copy.
- Avoid faxing your resume.
- Do not use staples.
- Use light shaded paper—we prefer white.
- Do not use columns.

THE PERSONAL TOUCH

Now your resume is complete, but your work has just begun. Stay with us while we construct an excellent cover letter to introduce your resume, or else all your work will have been in vain. As good as your two-page resume will be, by its nature it's impersonal. Your cover letter will solve that problem. With a cover letter, your resume is targeted to a specific individual in the company. Always find out the name of the hiring authority. If you're an engineer, address the letter to the engineering manager, by name. If you're in sales, send it to the sales and marketing manager, and so on. No cover letter should carry the salutation "To whom it may concern." It will concern no one if you don't personalize it. The surest way to get the information is to find the name in trade journals or in *The Standard & Poor's Register, The Dun & Bradstreet Directory,* or other directories. Failing all that, call the company and ask for the name of the appropriate person. If you're responding to a blind advertisement, open with "Dear Sir/Madam."

Think of your cover letter in three parts, and keep it short with generally three paragraphs. (Exhibits 3.4 through 3.9 provide examples of cover letters.)

The first paragraph introduces you and gives your purpose for writing. Perhaps you got the company's name from a networking contact or from an ad, or maybe you read an article in a trade journal about the firm's plans for expansion or introduction of a new product. Whatever your reason for sending a resume, this is where you state it.

In the second paragraph, briefly summarize your experience as it relates to this company's needs. In this section, you're attempting to hook the company's interest by answering the question: "What can this person do for us?" Also in this paragraph (or in a short, separate paragraph), you address salary if you're answering an ad that demands salary history. You must not ignore such a request. That might disqualify you from consideration. You don't, of course, pick numbers out of the air. First, research the company and the industry, and learn approximately what the position will pay before you respond. We'll cover how you do that in Chapter 9.

In the final paragraph, close with a proactive statement. This means that you take the initiative for the next contact. Don't leave it to the company. For example, many cover letters close with the statement, "Please contact me if you think my skills would help," and so forth. No—that's the wrong approach. That's reactive. When you're proactive, you write, "I'll contact you the week of July 7 to arrange an interview." Don't ever be passive when you write a cover letter. You'll sit on your hands and wait forever. Be assertive. Be professionally persistent. Go for it. (Two exceptions to this rule are cover letters to a search firm—Exhibit 3.8—and in response to an ad—Exhibit 3.4.)

Spend a few extra bucks and have your cover letter, like your resume, prepared on a word processor. Much is made of the importance of first impressions in job search—all of it valid. Few people stop to realize, however, that the format and style, plus the opening few words of a cover letter, actually constitute the very first impression they'll make on the company.

Your cover letter should be a product of your resume and your networking efforts. We've discussed cover letters in about 300 words while you've read maybe twenty times that much about resume writing in this book. That's not to minimize the role of a cover letter—there's just not that much to say about it. However, the cover letter is of critical importance, and you should strive for excellence in creating it, just as you do with your resume.

EXHIBIT 3.4
Sample Cover Letter
Response to Ad

NAME
Address
City, State Zip Code
Office Phone Number
Home Phone Number

Date

NAME
TITLE
COMPANY
ADDRESS1
ADDRESS2
CITY, STATE ZIP CODE

Dear SALUTATION:

Your advertisement in the *PUBLICATION* on DATE for a POSITION position is very attractive to me and I am interested in learning more about the position. I have enclosed my resume for your review and consideration.

As my resume indicates, I have twenty-five years of business experience with fourteen years in administrative management and eleven years in human resources. I have managed the Engineering Office Services Department of nearly 200 employees and was responsible for the overall management of a $3 million budget. I conferred with management and employee workforce on benefits, salary administration, worker's compensation, performance/disciplinary matters, and the company policies and procedures.

My compensation requirements are in the $75,000 to $85,000 range.

I welcome the opportunity to discuss this position and my qualifications with you in person. If you have any questions or would like to schedule a meeting, please call me at the above listed number.

Sincerely,

Name

enclosure

EXHIBIT 3.5
Sample Cover Letter
Network Referral

NAME
Address
City, State Zip Code
Office Phone Number
Home Phone Number

Date

NAME
TITLE
COMPANY
ADDRESS1
ADDRESS2
CITY, STATE ZIP CODE

Dear SALUTATION:

REFERRAL suggested that I contact you concerning how my skills and abilities might serve the present or future needs of COMPANY, or other organizations and industries of which you are aware. Enclosed is a copy of my resume for your review and consideration.

As my resume indicates, I am results oriented with twenty-six years of professional broad-based worldwide purchasing and materials management experience. My ability to work with people, to find and implement innovative approaches has resulted in millions of dollars of savings during my career. Recent experience includes ISO 9002 registration and development of a formal supplier improvement process.

I will telephone you shortly to discuss our mutual interests and arrange a convenient time for us to meet. If you have questions or need additional information, please do not hesitate to contact me at the phone numbers listed above.

Sincerely,

Name

enclosure

EXHIBIT 3.6
Sample Cover Letter
Telemarketing Follow-Up

NAME
Address
City, State Zip Code
Office Phone Number
Home Phone Number

Date

NAME
TITLE
COMPANY
ADDRESS1
ADDRESS2
CITY, STATE ZIP CODE

Dear SALUTATION:

Thank you for taking time out of your busy schedule to speak with me today and, as you requested I have enclosed a copy of my current resume for your information. While you do not have any openings within your fine organization at this time, I appreciate your willingness to assist me in my job search.

As my resume indicates, I have more than 30 years of experience in the field of Information Systems and Management in several different industries. My background includes design, development, implementation and support of business applications such as financial, banking, administrative, manufacturing and distribution. I have also been functionally responsible for hardware and software evaluation and acquisition, vendor negotiations, short term and long range planning, as well as computer operations and control.

I successfully managed mainframes, mini-computers and micro-computers, as well as their integration with local area, wide area, public and private networks. In addition, I have been directly responsible for developing training curricula and conducting classes, for technical and user personnel.

If you become aware of a position that matches my experience, please share my resume appropriately. I will be calling you periodically to bring you up to date on my progress. Thank you again for your help and consideration. If you have any questions or I can assist in any way, you can reach me at the above telephone numbers.

Sincerely,

Name

enclosure

EXHIBIT 3.7
Sample Cover Letter
Cold Contact

NAME
Address
City, State Zip Code
Office Phone Number
Home Phone Number

Date

NAME
TITLE
COMPANY
ADDRESS1
ADDRESS2
CITY, STATE ZIP CODE

Dear SALUTATION:

My research indicates that your company may provide me the opportunity to utilize my information management skills to make a contribution to your continued success, while achieving personal career growth.

As my enclosed resume indicates, I have over seventeen years of experience in information management relating to financial and administrative functions. In addition to providing application support and training, my background includes the ability to successfully work and communicate with all levels of an organization. Some of the highlights of my career include:

- Field tested an order processing software, which became the first fully successful field test of this application. Implementation enabled Digital to shut down outdated systems country wide with an estimated savings of $100,000+.

- Assisted in the implementation of four US Expertise Centers which resulted in more effective support of in-house information systems.

- Managed software installations and upgrades by conducting project review meetings.

- Installed a procedure manual for the data center to use during evening work, which reduced the number of calls to analyst for assistance by at least 25%.

I am confident that I can achieve similar accomplishments to contribute to your organization, and would appreciate the opportunity to meet with you personally. I will contact you soon to set an appointment at your convenience. Thank you for your consideration.

Sincerely,

Name

enclosure

EXHIBIT 3.8
Sample Cover Letter
Search Firm

NAME
Address
City, State Zip Code
Office Phone Number
Home Phone Number

Date

NAME
TITLE
COMPANY
ADDRESS1
ADDRESS2
CITY, STATE ZIP CODE

Dear SALUTATION:

I am currently seeking opportunities as an Environmental Engineer. I have enclosed a copy of my confidential resume for your review and consideration.

With over six years of experience in detail engineering design and in the regulatory and compliance field in the refining and chemical industries, I am looking for new and challenging responsibilities in order to continue my career path. As my resume indicates, I have a strong background in detail engineering design and procurement, with excellent working knowledge of Federal and State codes in the regulatory and compliance field. In addition, I have demonstrated capabilities in quality engineering, team work, interpersonal skills, client satisfaction, and problem solving techniques. My compensation requirements are in the range of $55,000 to $65,000, and I prefer to remain in the Houston area.

If you have a client assignment matching my background, or would like to set up an appointment, please contact me at the above phone number.

Sincerely,

Name

enclosure

EXHIBIT 3.9
Sample Cover Letter
Association Letter

NAME
Address
City, State Zip Code
Office Phone Number
Home Phone Number

Date

NAME
TITLE
COMPANY
ADDRESS1
ADDRESS2
CITY, STATE ZIP CODE

Dear SALUTATION:

You may be aware that I am currently involved in a job search. Through the years my friends and associates have been my strongest supporters and greatest asset. It is in that vein that I enclose my professional resume.

In my last position I took a diverse, discouraged, multi-cultural employee population through a difficult transition period and ownership change. This required strong communications skills at all levels, the ability to develop and lead a team and an understanding of conceptual change and appropriate actions needed to make those changes. I also have a strong background in marketing, public relations, problem-solving, organizational development, consulting and training.

In talking with a wide range of companies in the past few weeks, the most pressing need today seems to be for people who have personal integrity and a professional pride in their work. I offer those qualities to a progressive, quality-oriented organization.

Please feel free to call me at either of the numbers listed above if you should need any additional information. I will be following up with you and thank you in advance for your support.

Sincerely,

Name

enclosure

One note of caution: The cover letter is a business letter, not a personal letter (except when written to very close contacts) or poetic creation or prosaic dissertation. Please do not use flowery language or lengthy and complicated prose. Be direct and brief if you want to get the reader's attention. Remember, busy professionals and executives have stacks of reading that just may take priority over your cover letter. If they can't find the purpose of your letter quickly, it will be quickly ignored!

ACCEPT THE CHALLENGE

Striving for excellence is an imperative for your entire job search (and your life, as well). Follow the standards of excellence that we've set out for you in resume preparation, and adhere to the same conceptual approach in every step of your job campaign, up to and including the acceptance of an offer. Don't be discouraged by the bombardment of negatives you'll be hit with in your search. Certainly, there are thousands of others looking for jobs. Of course the market is tough—maybe tougher than ever before. But don't hide from the competitive nature of job campaigning. Respond to it. Challenge the numbers. Most of all, have confidence—both in yourself and in our principles of searching for a new job. The fundamentals are the same as they were 30 years ago and as they will be 30 years into the future.

Having lived in Texas for many years now, we can safely adopt one of the building blocks of Texan philosophy: "If it ain't broke, don't fix it." So it is with resume preparation. Snake oil artists are loose on the streets trying to sell you other ideas. But the tried-and-true system works. The only problem is that most people don't use it correctly. Strive to do it right. Expect to win. If you can't go into a competitive endeavor (which job search certainly is) expecting to win, don't play. It's the positive expectation of success that fosters success. If you don't expect to get the job offer, that attitude will show in all that you do, including your resume—especially your resume. The principles of positive thinking work every day in our offices. They will work for you, as well. Expect to get a job—not just any job, but the right career position for you.

Stop now and absorb what we've covered. Refer to the sample resumes and cover letters. Take the next two or three days to create a winning resume. Then come back and we'll make that resume work as hard for you as you worked at writing it.

CHAPTER 4

The Art of Preparing References: It's Not Just a List of Names

With deference to American Express, we suggest that you adapt the famous credit card advertising slogan for your job search: *"References—Don't Leave Home Without Them."*

Not surprisingly, our view of gathering references links with every other facet of our job campaigning advice—that is, plan and prepare for each step of the process. Coach your references on what you'll be telling interviewers, and elicit their assistance in supporting those statements. Then carry your detailed preparation work a step further. The critical part in the entire reference-gathering process comes when you write the reference letter about your own professional background. Sounds strange, doesn't it? It's not at all strange, but it is a unique approach.

Most often references are barely mentioned in job search advice, except to verify that they are needed and to suggest that you write at the bottom of your resume: "References Available Upon Request." Having written your resume our way, you already know that statement is for use by amateurs only. In contrast, we rate the gathering of references as an imperative in successful job campaigning. Make no mistake about it, if an employer does nothing else in the way of a background check, they will usually verify your education and check your references. Therefore, you must effectively manage the flow of information from your references to potential employers. That's how you make references work for you rather than for the employer.

This step is tough, complex, and subtle. If your relationship with a former boss ranged somewhere between quiet resentment and open hostility, the process becomes even more difficult. But make it happen—there is no alternative. Even if the resume you've just created jumps off the desk into the employer's hands, and even if the interviewing techniques you'll learn in Chapter 8 convince the company that you're their last hope, the job offer you were riding high on could crash and burn if your former boss indicates that your personal interactive skills more closely resemble Saddam Hussein's rather than Mother Teresa's.

That's why we consider references an art, not just a list of names. Since for most job hunters our reference process is an untapped resource, successfully managing the complete scenario can position you for a huge advantage over the competition in the job market. For example, studies indicate that when job hunters endure a long, unproductive search, poor references are the root of the problem in about 40 percent of the cases.

Knowing that, why leave such a critical step to chance? Commit the extra effort and time to ensure that you get a reference letter, along with oral confirmation of the information, that will serve as a powerful complement to your winning resume and interview responses.

The only foolproof way to accomplish that is to write the reference letter yourself. The sequence is as follows:

- Call your potential reference to request the letter.
- Prepare a draft.
- Send it to your former associate with a cover letter inviting him or her to review and edit the draft and asking that the final draft be signed undated and returned on company letterhead.
- Put the resulting document in your job hunting tool kit, and you're beginning to stack some odds in your favor.

If you have any remaining doubts about the validity of this process, consider the case of one "doubting Thomas":

> Tom had developed an A+ resume, which reflected outstanding accomplishments as a vice president, operations. When we suggested that his next step was to draft his reference letters, he looked at us like we were crazy. After considerable arm twisting, he proceeded to develop over a dozen top notch references. As his offers began to develop, he presented his references to the potential employers. He was astounded at the impression they made. As a result, he was able to negotiate a senior vice president title and a significant increase in compensation. He later used his new-found negotiating leverage to achieve a CEO position with another company.

References not only enhance the marketability of candidates with spotless records, but can salvage the careers of candidates who were terminated under difficult circumstances.

MEND YOUR FENCES, NO MATTER HOW BROKEN
DOWN THEY ARE

Most employer-employee relationships can be patched up. Most bosses will cooperate. Most companies are as anxious for terminated employees to find a new position as the individuals are. When you run into an exception to that, you must bear part of the responsibility. And you'd better accept that responsibility now if you're in that situation, because—like it or not—your next potential employer will certainly assign you guilt. If you do have a bad relationship with your ex-boss—if you parted on difficult terms—this is an area where you must use psychological leverage to your advantage. There's nothing to be gained from maintaining a negative relationship with anyone. Our suggestion is that whenever you have a rift with someone in a job setting, bridge the gap immediately. The best way to bridge that gap is to ask for a letter of reference. Psychologically, this causes you to eat a slice of humble pie—which is good for anyone. Also, it causes your boss to rethink your work experience and, usually, to accept his or her share of the blame for the negative results of your previous relationship. Usually, the conclusion to the process is, "The least I can do now is write Tom a letter of reference."

We concede that there are impossible cases in which the resentment and anger simply can't be neutralized. But you can be sure that such a situation will hurt you in your job search. You'll be admitting that you don't have sufficient interpersonal skills to establish, maintain, or repair a key working relationship, and you'll be judged on that. You'll be in danger of joining that 40 percent of the job hunting population whose search keeps tripping over reference problems.

Never write off your relationship with your ex-boss, however, until you've given your best shot at getting a reference. And note that your best shot doesn't mean one phone call or a perfunctory inquiry through his secretary. It means professional persistence and courteous insistence that you expect nothing less. This is another example of what we call psychological leverage. In today's corporate legal environment, however, the reality is that companies are increasingly leery of providing references for terminated former employees. This is very unfortunate since excellent references are an important link in our job search system and are invaluable to your campaign.

Most of the time, however, the difficulty revolves more around pride and wounded feelings than it does around substantive or irresolvable differences between two people. The following illustrates this most clearly:

Pete Smith, a terminated, angry former vice president of administration, entered our program. He did not have a reference from his former boss. We told Pete that he was making a mistake by not attempting to get one. He replied that he couldn't ask for one and, moreover, that he would never ask "that [expletive deleted]" for anything. Our reasoning fell on deaf ears, and Pete lost three straight potential jobs. When he learned that a poor reference was the cause, he came to us and asked for help in getting a reference from that most recent boss. Resisting the temptation to say "We told you so," we constructed a letter of reference, laid the groundwork with a diplomatic phone call, and forwarded the material to his former boss. Without the slightest delay or protest, the reference letter was routed back to us on the company letterhead. Pete got the next job for which he interviewed.

Almost everyone underestimates the importance of a letter of reference. It can kill a job offer to not have one or to have a negative one. As we have indicated, there are situations in which corporate policy prohibits your former boss from writing in support of your job search. Often, former employers will do nothing except confirm employment, with starting and stopping dates of service. But before you give up and accept that policy, try to work around it—in a professional manner. For example, you might be able to convince your ex-boss to sign a personal letter vouching for your performance record; the letter can be on plain bond paper or on his or her own letterhead, rather than the corporation's. This would not have the impact of a corporate letterhead reference, but it's better than no reference at all. And take heart, even when your former boss cannot or will not violate a corporate regulation, at least you emerge even on the scale. Your lack of a reference is a result of corporate policy. Your new employer will get dates only, with no comments on personality or motivation and no confirmation of your accomplishments. Although this certainly won't help you convince the potential employer that you're the person for the job, neither will it detract from your campaign.

When done correctly, writing your references yourself can be as difficult, or even more difficult, than writing your resume. First of all, you must write from the perspective and in the style of each reference, otherwise, they may all sound alike—a dead giveaway as to who wrote them! Secondly, they must validate your accomplishments. Once again, linkage is at work as you return to your resume. For each accomplishment on your resume, identify which of your references can support and vouch for your achievements. Then include them in the appropriate letters. You may also use performance appraisals or job evaluations written by specific references to help you create each letter. Here is one example:

Karen left her former company under difficult circumstances related to performance issues. Her boss was reticent to discuss performance for this reason. To develop an excellent letter without compromising the reference's need for accuracy, Karen selected positive phrases directly from his performance review of her, leaving questionable areas unaddressed. The reference signed without objection and Karen avoided a potentially dangerous reference check.

Another excellent source of information for reference letters is your assessment. Selecting skills and qualities from your self-assessment or other assessment instruments helps to round out the reference letter on some of the personality and style issues in which companies are interested.

Most of our discussion has centered on a reference from your ex-boss, because that's typically the one that is toughest to get and hardest to control in terms of content. Getting it can be fraught with potential for conflict or at least uncertainty. That's not the only reference you'll need, however. We suggest a minimum of three—your boss, your boss's boss, and a peer. If you go beyond three, we suggest getting a letter from a subordinate next. That's extremely valuable to some employers. Conversely, you might want to go as high up in the company as possible for another reference. The higher the title—the more influence—the better. But remember, this is not just a list of names; your top executive reference must know who you are and what you did. If he or she is called, it's imperative that the responses given to a prospective employer will be consistent with what you said in the interview as well as with what your other references said about you.

Consistency becomes the key word here. It's not so much that the prospective employer will perform a cartwheel every time a positive statement is made about you. Nor will one negative comment hurt you that much. Everyone recognizes that personality conflicts exist in all workplaces. What's critical to the process is that, on balance, the employer expects to hear a common thread emerging when your personality, duties, accomplishments, and skills are discussed. That consistency drives this entire process. And of course it is an integral part of our linkage concept, which touches every element of your job search.

SPECIAL SITUATION REFERENCES

Beyond the traditional references, if you are a new graduate you may seek references from college faculty, staff, and organizational advisors. If you are involved in internships, these also may serve as excellent sources for references. For military personnel transitioning to the civilian workforce, seek references from your commanding officer, other personnel with whom you served but who also have transitioned out of the military, and civilian personnel on base with whom you worked. For the return-to-workforce situation, references may come from volunteer organizations in which you were involved. A paid staffer can be especially helpful, since their credibility in evaluating skills and contributions would be significant.

Professional organizations can also serve as excellent references for regular employment roles, especially when involvement was extensive and resulted in significant contributions to your industry.

Finally, for the entrepreneur or consultant, references from clients and customers can be very valuable in soliciting new business. Do not hesitate to ask for these references to validate your contributions.

HOW MANY?

Six references are usually sufficient—and they all must be professional contacts. They all must be people who are familiar with your work experience. What your minister thinks, or your tennis partner, or your neighbor will have absolutely no impact on a prospective employer. Why should it? When do you suppose was the last time your minister gave someone a poor reference? Personal references are a waste of time and do not belong in your job campaigning tool kit.

Usually, references from your most recent employer are of greatest value. However, there are many situations when going back to earlier employers is important—for instance, when you have been with your latest employer only a short time or are still employed; when you are leaving a company that's in trouble or an industry that's in decline; or when your previous experience is of particular value to the new position you are seeking.

In addition, when you prepare your draft letter of reference, don't get too flowery. Keep the statements job-related. Don't try to convince a reader that you are without fault or that Michener could have chronicled your adventures in the office. Keep it simple, straightforward, professional. Obviously, your former boss is not suicidal simply because you no longer work there, so don't try to make it sound as if the company can't stay in business without you.

Specifically, think of a three-phase approach to reference gathering:

1. Get the letter.
2. Put your resume, a copy of the letter, and a brief worksheet outlining your responses to typical, tough interview questions into the hands of all of your references.
3. Immediately upon completion of an interview that has gone well, notify your references that you believe the company is considering making you

an offer and that reference-checking calls likely are forthcoming. Then highlight what was discussed in the interview and tell your references briefly about the company and the person who interviewed you, what job you're pursuing, and what qualifications from your background you highlighted during the discussions.

THE INTERVIEW WORKSHEET

The brief interview worksheet can be as informal as a piece of ruled yellow pad paper. You simply want to cover some of the key questions to which you'll respond in the interview and determine that your former associate can and will support your statements. Remember, don't try to tell your former boss to do this and do that. The entire process involves negotiation, communication, and flexibility. State that you will be saying that you accomplished this, this, and this and ask if there is any problem with that. If so, discuss it and make your points. Walk step-by-step through your accomplishments at the company, reminding your former boss why you are claiming the accomplishments listed on your resume.

This process links with our earlier discussion of truth in preparing your resume. Many of our clients initially think that we encourage people to play fast and loose with the truth, to say whatever looks good in a resume. But that is absolutely not the case. You state what you accomplished in terms that make you appear as attractive as possible to the prospective employer, but you never go outside the limits of truthfulness. If you do, the negotiation step with your former boss will roadblock you.

On your worksheet, jot down typical interview questions and what your responses will be. (You'll learn later, in our interviewing chapter, that your answers to these questions will be identical from one interview to the next, so it's perfectly logical to commit them to paper.) For example, prep your reference with your responses to these questions:

- How do you know me?
- How long have you known me?
- What specific results or accomplishments have I provided for the company?
- What are my strengths and weaknesses?
- Under what circumstances did I leave?
- Would you rehire me?
- How did I get along with people?
- Did I meet deadlines?

- Do you know of anything that would disqualify me from performing the job in question?
- Is there any other information you can share?
- Is there any other person in the company who can discuss my work performance?

Remember, your references must have your resume, preferably the worksheet, and a copy of the reference letters they have agreed to sign in their possession. Moreover, they should be on the person's desk when the reference checker calls. That's the purpose of your last-minute, postinterview phone conversation with each reference. It gets you fresh in his or her mind, and you can encourage the reference to pull out your file and be ready to confirm the responses to which both of you have already agreed.

Exhibits 4.1 and 4.2 provide examples of the cover letter and the draft of the letter of reference. Notice how the reference letter validates the accomplishments of Paul Lee from Chapter 3.

One more key point—along with your letters, carry a list of references in your job search tool kit everywhere you go. Your four, five, or six names should be listed as shown in Exhibit 4.3.

PREPARATION IS THE KEY

Put all the information in your tool kit, and you're ready to face any job search scenario with a high-impact, impeccably professional stack of assets in your corner—your resume, letters of reference, and a list of references. Be certain that you have multiple copies of each, and present them to each interviewer you meet at a company. Preparation is what job search is all about. Most often, landing a job will require multiple interviews over an extended period of time. On occasion, however, a window of opportunity will open, perhaps only for hours. That's the eventuality for which you always want to be prepared. By arriving for your interview with a tool kit full of information, you're ready for multiple interviews, you're ready for a reference check, and you're ready to entertain a job offer today. Whether or not you accept it depends on other varied factors that we'll address in subsequent chapters. In every case, however, whether it takes two hours or six weeks to draw an offer from the employer, you want to be ready. Have your references coached and prepped, with the appropriate papers on their desks—ready to support your statements and your career future.

See how our professional approach to job search unfolds—each step linked to the one before and the one to come next? You take a proactive

EXHIBIT 4.1
Cover Letter Requesting a Reference

PAUL LEE
Address
City, State Zip Code
Phone Number/Fax Number

August 20, 1995

Mr. Brandon Smith
President
Bayou Development Co., Inc.
PO Box 334
Houston, Texas 77002

Dear Brandon:

I appreciated the opportunity to speak with you last week and would like to thank you for agreeing to write a letter of reference on my behalf. To date, I have initiated a very aggressive job search campaign and am confident that letters of reference will play an important part in obtaining a new and challenging opportunity in a timely manner.

As we discussed, in order to assist you I have enclosed a draft letter for your review and consideration. I would encourage you to make any changes you feel necessary and then ask you to return the final letter to me on company letterhead, undated. Also enclosed is a copy of my resume for your information.

Brandon, I appreciate your assistance very much in this matter. Please let me know if you have any questions or if I can be of assistance to you in any way.

Sincerely,

Paul Lee

PL:ccr
enclosures

EXHIBIT 4.2
Draft of a Letter of Reference

COMPANY LETTERHEAD
(DRAFT)

To Whom It May Concern:

It gives me great pleasure to introduce Paul Lee. For two important assignments at Development E&C-- General Manager, Marine Engineering and Manager of the Mobile Office--I was his direct supervisor.

The Mobile Office was opened to provide design engineering to the local plants of Development E&C's Gulf Coast customer base. Paul started the office and served as the first manager. During the start-up phase, his management duties included site selection, staff development, strategy implementation and business development. Most of the work was obtained by calling at the local level in the engineering and maintenance departments or the purchasing department of the plants and mills in the surrounding area. The ability to become competitive against local competition quickly required a thorough understanding of the local conditions and the overall engineering business, careful planning, cost control and prudent management. The action plan successfully implemented for Mobile is an example of Paul's organized logical approach to solving complex tasks. The office has grown rapidly both in reputation and size of staff. Today it is one of Development E&C's major domestic resource centers. Again, much of the success the office has earned is the result of the efforts of and traditions established by the original management team assembled by Paul and the dynamic leadership he provided.

I was particularly pleased when the $1 million investment to start the office was recovered one year ahead of plan despite very difficult market conditions and a general downturn in the economy. This achievement further demonstrates Paul's unique business skills and ability to impact the bottom line.

As General Manager, Marine Engineering, Paul was responsible for maintaining Development E&C's offshore engineering capabilities in the Houston office. His energy, strong technical background and overall management skills made him ideally suited for this assignment. In a very competitive market his group was able to translate the value of our marine engineering credentials for technical excellence and innovation into awards of more than $19 million of high margin design work from Exxon. Paul's creative approach, leadership and organizational skills were instrumental in our winning acquisition strategies for these projects.

As a final point I would like to comment on Paul's integrity and character. In many challenging assignments, he has always maintained the highest standards of quality. His work ethic and commitment to excellence are outstanding personal traits.

It would be a pleasure to assist Paul in any way that I can. As an executive, he would make an excellent addition to any organization. Please call me if you have questions or desire additional information.

Sincerely,

Tommy E. Carlin
Vice President, International Development

EXHIBIT 4.3
Sample Reference List

PROFESSIONAL REFERENCES FOR PAUL LEE

Mr. Edwin Galworthy
President
Development E&C, Inc.
3204 Temple Avenue
Houston, Texas 77036
(713) 555-1212

Mr. Tommy E. Carlin
Vice President, International Development
Development E&C, Inc.
3204 Temple Avenue
Houston, Texas 77036
(713) 555-1212

Mr. Brandon Smith
President
Bayou Development Co., Inc.
PO Box 334
Houston, Texas 77002
(713) 555-3454

Mr. Perry Winstead III
President & CEO
Melanesia Exploration, Ltd.
61, Old Shell Road 4455
Bangkok, Thailand
011-064-44322-33

---

posture to touch every base, to cover any eventuality. And you anticipate events—you don't react to them. The numbers for an employer's search work like this: Start with 250–750 resumes in response to an opening; screen out 75% on the first reading. Forward the remaining resumes to the hiring authority; screen out all but eight. Interview those eight and invite five back for follow-up sessions. Cut it to two candidates, and finally pick the winner. Except for the first cut, this screening process is seldom cut and dried. In each step of the process, there are small distinctions between winners and losers.

Martha was interviewing for a director-level position for the first time. After considerable negotiation, she accepted the position. Later her new boss shared with her that while she was not initially the number one candidate, her strong references pushed her ahead of her competitor, whose references were poorly prepared and failed to validate his accomplishment/capability claims.

That's what our philosophy of psychological leverage is all about. We want you to be a half-step ahead of the competition, just as Martha was.

That doesn't come easily, however. It's an outgrowth of your time and effort, hard work, consistency, preparation, and discipline. Always, the winners in any endeavor will tell you that there's a direct correlation between hard work and good fortune. And nowhere is that "hard work/good luck" scenario more evident than in a job search. So put linkage into action in gathering your references, and enjoy the fruits of your extra effort as your job search builds momentum.

CHAPTER 5

Build Your Network: Eighty Percent of *Successful* Job Hunters Can't Be Wrong

As you no doubt have already noticed, we are not at all shy about telling you what *won't* work in job search. With the same degree of confidence, when we find a technique that does work—such as a two-page, chronological resume or networking—we'll tell you straightaway. You now know that a two-page, chronological resume should serve as the drive wheel for your job search. But the fuel for your search engine is networking.

We're well aware that networking has fallen into disfavor among so-called "savvy" job hunters. Many self-anointed "experts" now claim that networking is passé, that the American job market has been just about net-worked to death. Well, we dismiss that nonsense out of hand. Successful job hunters are like salmon swimming upstream. The one percent courageous enough to go against the current instinctively struggle to reach the river's source. Although the majority of job searchers looking for an easy placement float downstream, the one percenters who take control of their campaigns know that they must go against the current to get to where the jobs are. The truth is that if you wish to join our *One Percenters Club* of successful job hunters, you must unequivocally accept the concept of networking. Further, you must study it until you're a master. When you can make the telephone sing as though Chopin had scored a networking concerto for it, you will begin to break loose from the masses out there who are failing at job search. In our view, those who bad-mouth networking are selling you a rotten bill of goods—suggesting that networking is nothing more than another transitory fad in our disposable society. This reveals their purely commercial intent: Peddle it, use it, then discard it like an empty plastic soft drink container. Then search for a new fad—another hot-button that will sell a few more books or videotapes, or schedule a few more talk shows.

Job hunters, if you swallow that—if you accept the flawed logic that networking is old and cold—you're practically guaranteeing failure in your campaign. Networking is not and never has been simply a manifestation of pop culture. Rather, it is one of three key strategies to a winning game plan in job search. For strategy A, we created the resume (yours should be complete by now). For strategy C, you will put on an interviewing performance that ensures that the employer will want to put your name in lights, to say nothing of offering you a job (you'll learn all that in Chapter 8). As important as these two strategies are, however, without networking you're trying to skip a step, a very difficult proposition indeed.

When you utilize networking, strategy B is in place. This assures proper use of linkage in your job search, and it practically guarantees that you'll be a step ahead of the rest of the world in locating and accessing job openings. Even beyond specified openings, truly excellent networkers create their own positions by identifying an employer's need, then selling their skills and background as the solution. So take our word for it; we've learned from many long, difficult counseling sessions with clients trying to make the tortuous journey from A to C without networking. Use our A, B, C strategy in your search, and let linkage build your momentum.

This is not meant to minimize the difficulties of networking. The reason this concept has slipped from its favored status among job search "experts" who are always looking for a hot fad is simply because too many people use it unprofessionally. Each time some jerk calls a company executive without a conversational agenda, without direction, and without goals, he wastes everyone's time. As a consequence, the road is that much rougher for everyone who follows. Your task will be that much more challenging.

Don't confuse the issues here, however. Just because networking is misused, abused, and trivialized by amateurs doesn't mean that you must choose an alternative. Quite simply, there are none. U.S. Department of Labor statistics prove that 80 percent of people who find jobs in this country do so by networking. In our view, that figure is probably conservative. So don't listen to the charlatans who are trying to sell books and job search fads simultaneously. Don't buy a ticket on their bandwagon. Effective networking gets jobs. The more you do it and the better you do it, the sooner you'll be selecting the best position from among several offers.

HANDLING THE NO'S IN NETWORKING

So much negativity permeates job search that people despair easily during the journey. *No's* are a major part of the process. We mentioned earlier the juvenile system of working through the no's and rejoicing because each no means that you're getting closer to the ultimate yes. Although this is an attempt to instill positive thinking, it overlooks the more proactive approach. Our promise to you is that when you network effectively, you do more than move toward the final yes. In fact, you modify, or even circumvent, the no's. Rather than receiving a rejection, a good networker can transform an unproductive conversation into a lead at another company, with another person—another potential job opportunity, another potential *yes*.

With effective networking, you take command of your job search. Certainly, there will be no's. Rest assured that you will run into jerks who won't even give you the time of day. But remember, you can make the numbers work for you. When you're making twenty-five, forty, or fifty phone calls a day, it is not so depressing to get a no, even from a 101-proof jerk. The trick is to distill out nonproductive calls after about ten seconds and move along to your next call. You'll learn the fundamentals of using the phone—what to say, what not to say, how to set goals for each day and each phone call—in Chapter 7. Our point here is that you must commit now to the philosophy of building and using a network in job search. If you're swayed by any advice to the contrary, you're only postponing success and complicating your job search.

We've counseled with thousands of clients in our Houston outplacement facilities, and we can attest to the fact that good networkers never sit idle—wallowing in self-pity, drowning in rejections. They stay up, active, and positive. They don't have time to be depressed, because they're so active on the phone. Moreover, results sustain that positive momentum. When you do networking the right way—when you fully commit to it—the constant leads and new information you obtain will guarantee that you won't be defeated by rejection. Although there are many negatives to overcome in job search, they should never dominate your life. The people who sit by the phone, depressed, are typically those who rely on search firms and newspaper ads to do the work for them. We agree that the situation is tough to go through, but at the risk of sounding unsympathetic, those people are getting out of job search just about what they put into it—nothing. That's the nature of job search when you abandon the tried-and-true principles set forth on these pages—when you won't put in the time, effort, and dedication necessary to take charge of your own campaign.

NETWORKING GIVES YOU A MARKET ADVANTAGE

The statistics from the U.S. Labor Department cited earlier—that 80 percent of jobs come from networking—become even more dramatic when you consider the following ironic pattern. Although only 10 to 20 percent of jobs are found through ads and search firms, our informal surveys indicate that about 80 percent of job searchers concentrate their searches there. These are, of course, the simplest ways to look for a job—that's what draws the majority to them. By contrast, only 20 percent of job searchers concentrate full-bore on networking.

Imagine it! If you buy into our theory, you're shopping in an area where 80 percent of the merchandise is located but only 20 percent of the shoppers. If that supply/demand market advantage doesn't convert you to networking, you're just not as serious about your job search as you may think. Our feeling is that many people who fail to buy into the concept of networking misunderstand what it is and what it isn't. The statement "Network your way into the hidden job market" can be intimidating to a novice, even if you're a novice with twenty-five years' experience in health care, in general management, or in any other field. So let's dissect that statement:

• *Networking:* If you can talk, you can do it. Cold-calling on the phone is very difficult initially, but it's a learnable, doable skill. If you think, "I'm an analyst, not a salesman; we don't do that" or "I'm a senior VP and chief counsel; we don't do that at this level" think again. If you want a job, you'll do it. Does networking mean talking to important people who can offer you a position? Yes, it does, but that's only one very limited fraction of the whole equation. In total, networking means talking to everyone—personal and professional acquaintances and friends as well as brand-new contacts—telling them your situation, and asking if they can assist or refer you.

• *The hidden job market:* This one throws a lot of people, and it's probably somewhat misleading. Our view is that too many people think that the hidden job market means a closed market, with all the jobs reserved for insiders or the sons-in-law of the chairman. Without dwelling on family relationships, trust us—many board chairmen would much rather hire you than their sons-in-law. So, in fact, that job isn't hidden, it's just not public knowledge. It will come open and be filled before most people know about the vacancy. Frequently, that includes the corporate human resources department—to say nothing about search firms or readers of newspaper ads. Your challenge is to make a networking contact at the right place and the right time to learn about that "hidden" job.

LUCK HAPPENS WHEN OPPORTUNITY MEETS PREPARATION

Is all this luck? You'd better believe it is. But we guarantee that networkers who place 25 phone calls a day are the ones who always get lucky. We all have a tendency to think of successful and famous people as being lucky. If you're a *one percenter* who makes 25 phone calls a day, you'll have a chance to tap into some of the same kind of luck. That's what we want you to strive toward. Similarly, best defined, the hidden job market is really analogous to an iceberg. More than 90 percent of it is out of sight. But just get below the surface and you'll find out how big it is. That's precisely how the job market operates—not so much hidden as out of sight to the superficial job seeker.

The elements of success in networking center on confidence in what you're doing, coupled with the requirement that you make each networking contact a true exchange of information. People who use a networking contact to get what they want but give nothing in return are the people who are contaminating the networking landscape for the rest of us. For example, we can't stand the phrase, "I'd like to pick your brain." That's an insult to us; we infer from that statement that someone wants for free what it took us years of hard work to build.

As part of your job search, you'll be researching companies and industries, so be prepared to share that information if it's useful to your contact. Also, offer to help him with a problem if you can. And don't forget, for your hottest contacts, *The Number One Rule of Networking: Everyone Likes to Eat.* The corollary to that is *Rule One-A: Everyone Really Likes to Eat when someone else pays for it!*

Our point is that you must be prepared to give back while you receive. And commit to certain fundamentals—such as asking for one minute of the contact's time (generally, that gives you license to take three minutes). Just be certain that you don't waste anyone's time—yours or the contact's. Get in and out quickly. (We'll cover all the do's and don'ts in Chapter 7, under telemarketing.)

If you're like most people, you've probably listed five to ten people that you think can help you find a job. Our network includes over 10,000 names. We're not insisting that yours be that extensive, but five or ten just won't get it done. If you don't have at least 100 names listed, you're not thinking creatively. Consider these sources:

- Family members.
- Colleagues, present and past, and executives for whom you've worked.
- Classmates, teachers, campus placement officials, and alumni.

- Fellow members and alumni of organizations, fraternities or sororities to which you belong.
- Professional acquaintances: lawyers, stockbrokers, accountants, bankers, real estate brokers, insurance agents, elected officials, industry leaders, consultants, doctors, dentists, salespeople, and so forth.
- Community members in clubs or associations to which you belong, neighbors, church members, local merchants, fund raisers, sponsors of performing arts, and wealthy people.
- Officials of professional organizations, whether or not you are a member, as well as speakers at any of their meetings.
- Suppliers, previous customers, even creditors.
- Editors and writers for trade journals.
- The local chamber of commerce.
- Anyone and everyone on your Christmas card list.
- Computer bulletin board contacts.

Finally, don't forget your checkbook as another source. Anyone to whom you've written a check within the past year can be considered a possible network contact.

Remember, build your contact list on the strength of your acquaintanceship or friendship with each person. *Do not*, at this time, attempt to evaluate whether or not these people will be able to help you. That is a time-wasting, subjective process that is inherently self-defeating.

One of the most obvious contacts is one that is frequently overlooked— a former boss. As a result of speaking with just such a contact, one of our clients recently obtained exactly the position he was looking for.

> Henry Little wanted to move from a huge, billion-dollar company to a small, growing organization where he could utilize his entrepreneurial skills. Among the primary contacts he made was Joe Stratton, his former boss. Joe suggested a company that, as a subsidiary of a major U.S. firm, could offer him a ground-floor opportunity in a dynamic entrepreneurial environment—and one with significant financial backing. After four rounds of interviews, Henry got the job he wanted. Had he not contacted his former boss, he never would have discovered this opportunity.

Don't judge your contacts: list them and use them. In a loose-leaf binder, or computerized personal organizer, record on a contact form each name, phone number, title, address, the initial contact and when and how you will follow up, plus that follow-up contact and what happened in the follow-up. Let's stop here for a key point. Job hunters and those who offer advice on the subject wrestle interminably with the question of timing follow-ups to contacts: "How long should I wait?" Stop all that nonsense and think. Communicate. The quickest, simplest, and most direct way to resolve the question is to ask your contact. There is no set formula, no right or wrong answer. Simply ask your contact when he would be agreeable to a re-contact, and note that in your record book. (Exhibit 5.1 provides a form for listing personal/professional contacts.) Chapter 7 discusses record keeping further.

THE NEXT STEP

Now for the critical part of networking—going beyond the initial contacts. Seldom will the 100 people on your list of primary contacts actually provide you with a job lead. What they can do is provide you with another level of contacts. So you must develop techniques for expanding your network. Even the second level of contacts usually doesn't ring the bell. But when you broaden and deepen your network to the third tier—your tertiary network—you will begin to access viable job leads. To that end, part of every networking contact should include questions such as "Do you know who your counterpart is in XYZ company?" Again, we'll cover all the techniques of telemarketing in Chapter 7. But rest assured that you must push each contact to the limit if you're to succeed at networking. Your goal should be to get at least two or three additional names from each contact. Assuming that you start with 100, do you begin to see the impact you're about to make on the job market?

Remember, you must, *without fail,* send a thank-you letter to each productive contact. Obviously, you don't want to waste time on the jerks. But if a person takes the time to try to help, acknowledge that with a thank-you note and resume. Of course, if you arranged a follow-up contact with the same person, confirm that in the letter as well. The thank-you letter should be very brief, but it's essential. It confirms to the network contact that he's dealing with a pro when he's talking to you.

WHAT ABOUT HUMAN RESOURCES?

You're probably wondering why we haven't mentioned human resources as a contact. It's not that we don't like human resources, or that they are unimportant to the hiring process. But when it comes to networking, they are not usually your best starting point. As you network within a company in regard

EXHIBIT 5.1
Personal Marketing Plan: Personal/Professional Contacts

DATE: _____

NAME/AFFILIATION PHONE NUMBER	RESULT OF CALL		
	CALL BACK	WILL RETURN	SEE RECORD

to a specific opening, you will probably make contact with human resources at some point, and they may even conduct your first interview. However, your initial networking target should be the *hiring authority,* who is usually the top person in your functional area or the person to whom this position reports. In addition, your initial networking contact may be someone you already know either within or outside the target company, who has some association with the hiring authority. If you have no "warm" contact to help you get to the hiring authority, then target him/her directly with a "cold" contact. Here's a classic example of why this strategy is necessary:

> Deborah had networked within a company from several directions; leaving no stone unturned, she included human resources, sending them a letter and resume. She also contacted the hiring authority, as well as Linda, a former associate in another department. When she followed up with a phone call to the hiring authority, he indicated that he had received her letter with resume, and had also received Deborah's resume from Linda along with her recommendation. Impressed, he suggested an interview, which led to a series of interviews, an offer, negotiations, and Deborah's acceptance of the final offer. Later Deborah received a post card from human resources thanking her for her resume but indicating that there were currently no openings!

OTHER NETWORKING LEADS

Theoretically, the networking process should never end, but inevitably you'll hit a few days when your contact potentials seem to have dwindled. What then? Do you go into withdrawal and begin to hallucinate that you'll never find a job? Not if you use your head and develop a list of target companies besides those your personal/professional referral network helped turn up. Potentially, this is where cold-calling can really turn frigid. But don't panic—your research on the companies and industries you target will provide you with the knowledge and confidence to warm up your calls and produce new leads.

In our outplacement facility in Houston, we have an extensive library of directories, databases and reference tools available to our corporate clients for developing their target company lists. If you do not have access to a specialized job search and career planning library to help you identify companies as targets for your new position, your public library should have many of the needed directories, databases and other publications. There are five major reference sources for researching target companies and industries:

- Directories and databases.
- Annual reports/10K reports.
- Newspapers and other current periodicals.
- Professional associations.
- People in general.

Exhibit 5.2 provides a listing of suggested resources that are invaluable to your research. If you use them, you will never deplete your list of cold-calling prospects. When you first begin to review the directories and databases, you'll likely be overwhelmed with the sinking feeling that you're about to look for the proverbial needle in the haystack. Obviously, you must narrow down the target area on the basis of your preferences as well as market realities. The following are some of the criteria to consider in targeting companies:

- Type of industry.
- Products/services.
- Growth/decline industry.
- Geography/locality.
- Job availability.
- Company size.
- Corporate culture/management style.
- Employment policies.
- Compensation/benefit policies.

Research as much information as you possibly can about a company and its requirements.

- Read materials about the company.
- Arrange a tour of the company if possible.
- Inquire about the nature of the work.
- Learn about possible job functions.
- Study job requirements.
- Ask about recruitment policies.
- Find out why management hires the people they do.
- Ask about the potential for advancement.
- Learn what you can about compensation, benefits, perks.
- Keep notes on each company you explore.

Exhibits 5.3 and 5.4 provide forms on which to list your target companies by high, medium, or low priority and to record your research notes.

EXHIBIT 5.2
Sources of Company Information

LOCAL DIRECTORIES

The following are examples of Houston and Texas directories. Check with your local library and chamber of commerce for similar directories of businesses in your locality.

Chamber of Commerce Directories
Directory of Texas Manufacturers (Volumes I & II)
Harris County Business Guide
Hi Tech Texas
Houston International Business Directory
Houston 1000
Houston 100
Texas Top 250

NATIONAL/INTERNATIONAL DIRECTORIES

Directory of Corporate Affiliations (National & International; Public & Private)
Dun & Bradstreet Million Dollar Directory
Hoovers Handbook
Standard & Poor's Register
Thomas Register of American Manufacturers

ADDITIONAL SOURCES OF INFORMATION

Almanac of American Employers
Alumni Directories
American Almanac of Jobs and Salaries
Association Directories
Associations Yellow Book
Business Periodicals Index
Business Week: Scoreboard
Company Reports - Annual, 10K, Proxy
Directory of Occupational Titles
F & S Index of Corporations and Industries
Forbes: Annual Report of American Business
Forbes 500
Fortune 500
Inc. 500
Industry Specific Directories
Industry Specific Publications
Moody's Investors Services
National Business Employment Weekly
National Ad Search (weekly)
Newspapers and Business Publications
Special Issues Index
Standard & Poor's Corporation Records
Standard & Poor's Industry Surveys
U.S. Bureau of Labor Statistics: Area Wage Surveys
Valueline
Wall Street Journal Index
100 Best Companies to Work for in America

CD ROM DATABASES

Career Search
Disclosure
Directory of Corporate Affiliations

EXHIBIT 5.3
Personal Marketing Plan: Target Companies

DATE: _____

Circle to indicate priority: A (high)   B (medium)   C (low)

TARGET COMPANY/ DECISION MAKER (Name & Title)	RESULT OF CALL		
	CALL BACK	WILL RETURN	SEE RECORD

EXHIBIT 5.4
Personal Marketing Plan: Target Company Research

Prospective Job Title _____

Hiring Authority _____ Title _____

Other Contact _____ Title _____

Company _____ Telephone _____

Address _____

Research Source (person, directory, etc.) _____

Size (employees, sales, income) _____

Industry _____

Products/Services _____

Growth _____

Organization/Subsidiary of _____

Employment Policies _____

_____

Compensation/Benefit Policies _____

_____

Current Industry Information:

Current Company Information:

COMPUTERIZED DATABASES

Developing target lists of companies is facilitated by the use of computerized databases of companies. There are a number of databases available and the range and ability to manipulate data varies widely, affecting their usefulness. For public companies, access to SEC data including annual, 10K, and quarterly reports is ideal. To target companies in specific geographical areas and industries efficiently, the database must be designed to search by multiple variables including industry segment, product, key words, geographical location, and size. Databases which are particularly useful for identifying target companies include private as well as public companies, and provide access to divisions and subsidiaries of larger companies. Effective databases can reduce research time significantly and expand your list of target companies beyond your personal and professional contacts—a real boost to the networking process. Check with your public and university libraries to enhance your research capabilities.

ON-LINE INFORMATION SERVICES

In our technologically driven marketplace, the on-line information boom has provided new ways of networking. Resume databases, on-line job postings, specialized bulletin-board services, and electronic job and career research resources can be useful tools, but be cautious in their use. Similar to ads and agencies, these "listings," while electronic, can still be dangerous! When it comes to resume databases, ask first who has access to them. If searches are included without your control of your resume, steer clear. With job postings, keep in mind that all other users have access to the same listings—remember the 80-20 odds! Beware too of listings by search agencies—know to whom you are sending your resume. (See Chapter 6 for cautions on the use of search firms.)

Universities and associations are using on-line services to meet student and member needs. These bulletin boards can give you access to a "warm" network of contacts. While the information super highway and these high-tech methods of networking can provide access to vast numbers of contacts, the traditional methods of calling and following up are still essential to getting in front of the hiring authority to get the offer.

FACE-TO-FACE NETWORKING

While research and telemarketing are essential to effective networking, nothing energizes your network more than face-to-face contacts. Getting in front of people, shaking hands, smiling, conversing, and sharing information may sound like socializing, but when it comes to your job search, these encounters are networking at its best. Wherever you meet people, make it an opportunity to network:

- Association meetings—civic and professional.
- Club meetings and activities.
- Church gatherings.
- Luncheons.
- Shopping, banking, appointments of any kind.
- Conventions.

Following are some typical examples:

> Craig went to the club to exercise three times a week. After a particularly hard workout, he decided to take a whirlpool bath. As he chatted with a fellow club member whom he had never met, they started to discuss his job status. The result was a lead which ultimately led to an offer!

> Beth was doing some grocery shopping and as she waited in line, she began conversing with another shopper. She mentioned her job search—one thing led to another until the shopper asked for her resume which Beth just happened to have in her car. She obtained the shopper's name and number to follow up.

> Cliff was on a flight and began a conversation with another passenger, who he learned was an attorney. As they shared information, Cliff realized that the attorney could be a source of clients for his expert witness consultancy. They exchanged business cards. Cliff later followed up with a resume and a phone call which resulted in additional business.

Wherever two or three are gathered together, it is an opportunity to network. If you are an introvert, this is no time to be shy. Take the initiative and practice being an extrovert! To help you develop opportunities for interaction, follow these tips:

- Structure networking opportunities by attending scheduled activities.
- Follow-up your letters by suggesting one-on-one get togethers.
- Offer to assume formal roles in associations or other clubs in which you have a greater chance of developing contacts.
- Offer to help at the registration table for conferences or other formal meetings.

Here are additional tips on how to "work the room" at association meetings and other gatherings:

- Keep a positive attitude and be friendly.
- Read name tags and use names frequently.
- Have business cards available, even if you are currently unemployed; be sure to collect business cards and follow up with those you meet.
- Similar to your two-minute response to the interview question, "tell me about yourself," prepare a self-introduction.
- Prepare several conversation topics that would be of interest to attendees as well as questions to ask.
- Look for loners—they are probably introverts who would just love to be approached!
- Set a goal for number of contacts you would like to make for the meeting.
- Circulate and have fun.
- Follow up with contacts and expand your network and your leads!

THE PROCESS

In summary, think of networking as a five-step process:

1. *Prepare your contact list.* Include not just important decision-makers but everyone who may be able to help you. Also include your list of target companies.
2. *Send a resume and cover letter to each of your primary contacts.* Just because a contact happens to be your brother, you're making a serious mistake if you assume that he knows all there is to know about you and your career.
3. *Use your contacts properly.* Be aware that your network will usually think more in terms of jobs open or not open than in terms of your individual skills and background. Help keep each contact focused on you—on what you've done before and can do in the future as well as on how potential employers might use your skills and experience. Remember to offer your assistance to your contacts in any way possible.
4. *Always ask permission to use the name of your contact.* Then do just that, both in phone conversations and in correspondence. Nothing drives the networking process more quickly and more effectively than a personal reference. That's how you break through into secondary and tertiary contacts. Always open the conversation or letter with a phrase such as "A mutual acquaintance, John Robertson, suggested that I contact

you." The body of the letter (or phone conversation) should very briefly summarize who you are and why you're making contact. Then close with a proactive statement about calling or visiting soon to discuss mutually beneficial ideas.

5. *Follow up.* Again, let your contact set the schedule. Just be certain that you adhere to it and recontact each person within the agreed-upon time. Report back to your contact when a lead pans out. It's not only professional to do this, but it keeps that person aware of and interested in what you're doing and where you're going. Even if a secondary contact doesn't develop into a job lead, when you keep your primary contacts advised, you're inevitably drawing them closer to your corner for future contacts and assistance. This is how psychological leverage works in networking. In your initial contact, you've offered to help them in any way possible. You've been thorough, courteous, and professional in following up each time, and now you're reporting back with a progress update and another thank-you.

Always keep your goals foremost in your mind for each contact. First, you want leads about openings. Failing that, you want the names of other people in the firm or elsewhere with whom you might talk. Keep pushing, deepening and broadening your network. Here's an example:

> Todd Moore, a senior executive with an extensive network, has a base of contacts that requires tremendous organization and persistence to work. Todd was getting a bit discouraged after a few months and was beginning to wonder whether he would ever find the right position. To take a new tack, we suggested approaching a couple of the firms with which he was carrying on discussions about consulting proposals. This would get his foot in the door until a permanent position could be found or created in the organization. The approach worked. Todd's aggressive networking paid off.

The realities of a transitory economy, with so many people displaced, can work to your advantage. Although your unemployed status might once have labeled you as an undesirable or a chronic problem case, unemployed people now are generally viewed as first-rate employees who are victims of the economy. Members of your network usually have been recently unemployed, know they're about to be, or are scared to death that they might be in the immediate future. As a consequence, most people are more willing than ever to help you.

This is another example of how important positive thinking is. Don't dwell on the negatives of a difficult economy. Think of how you can transform the negatives into positives. Make the situation work for you, rather than against you. Very often, this requires nothing more than an attitude change. Never underestimate the critical importance of a positive attitude. Like your resume and interview, your networking contacts will live or die on the strength of your attitude. If you expect a networking contact to be unsuccessful, we can just about guarantee that it will turn out that way. So pump up your mental state, and put your networking skills into action.

One of the hardest things to do in a job search is to continue even though you have a really hot offer in the works. Remember that no job offer is official until you're sitting in your new office on your first day!

> Janice Schultz was made an offer and accepted it. She immediately abandoned her efforts elsewhere, only to discover later that the person who had made the offer did not have clearance to do so. The offer was rescinded, and Janice had a lot of catch-up networking to do.

If you internalize the principles outlined here, coupled with the tele-marketing skills you'll learn in Chapter 7, you will be headed in the right direction—swimming upstream. Remember not to pay any attention to the doom-and-gloom preachers, who are floating downstream with all the search firms and newspaper ads as flotsam and jetsam. Your route will be more difficult in the short term. It will require large measures of courage, confidence, perseverance, and dedication. But your upstream direction will lead to what smart campaigners are looking for—jobs.

CHAPTER 6

Search Firms: How to Distinguish the Pros from the Peddlers

When we say that you, and only you, can get yourself a new job, does that give you a clue to how we feel about search firms? Certainly, that statement does not minimize the importance of the assistance others can give you in some of the key segments of job search, especially networking. Obviously, the essence of networking is help from other people. You draw upon every person with whom you've had contact to help you locate job openings a step ahead of anyone else. But your networking contacts, vital as they are, can only help you. They can alert you to openings, give you leads, or, at best, provide introductions—but they won't get you a job. And regarding search firms, we repeat that statement with emphasis: They won't get you a job.

Do not count on headhunters, search firms, or employment agencies to act in the best interest of your career, your future. Certainly, a high-quality, professional search organization can assist you effectively, but be sure that you don't assign too much faith in, or responsibility to, the search firm. They can assist with leads, help you understand the corporate culture, and prep you about the person with whom you'll be meeting. But never lose sight of the fact that you get a job through a winning resume and excellent references, coupled with a powerful interviewing presentation.

Equally important, you must then negotiate the best deal you can get. Again, you alone can accomplish that. Negotiation is when the money's on the table, when you apply all the skills you'll learn in Chapter 9 to secure the best deal possible without jeopardizing the job offer. Your skill at this scenario will ultimately be reflected on the bottom line, every day you work for

117

that company. This is why your trust is misplaced if you think that search consultants can guide you through the negotiation process. In every case, no matter what they call themselves, the search firm represents the company and its interests, not yours. Inevitably, the bottom line they're protecting is the employer's and their own, not yours.

We are assuming that if you elect to be involved with any search firm, it will be a top-quality, professional organization—a real pro at the business, one that typically works on a retainer arrangement with corporations. We suggest that you don't associate with the lower-echelon agencies that work on a contingency basis. If you must, do so very carefully. As in every phase of your personal and professional life, you will be known by the company you keep, and there's a lot of bad company in the search firm business. Not for a moment are we suggesting that no contingency search agencies are staffed with competent, ethical people. But beware of unemployed jerks who hustle telephone contacts because they couldn't find any other job. Many of them are starving on a straight commission setup.

Do you imagine that a person like that can possibly help you? Not only will most be unable to help you, but they'll tarnish your name just because you've allowed it to be associated with theirs. Admittedly, we get emotional about this point, primarily because we've seen so many people disappointed—losing job opportunities or, worst of all, getting suckered out of huge sums of money when they can least afford to lose it—all because they signed the wrong piece of paper at the wrong time in the wrong place so that some charlatan posing as an executive search consultant can line his pockets a little deeper without doing anything to help the job seeker.

DON'T STACK THE ODDS AGAINST YOURSELF

Emotion aside, however, consider the cold, hard statistics from the U.S. Department of Labor which are consistent with the results of our own client base. How do people find jobs in the United States? About 5 to 10 percent get them through classified advertisements. Another 5 to 10 percent find them through search agencies. But 80 to 90 percent locate them through networking. We've already illustrated, in the chapter on networking, how the numbers work against you when you concentrate on ads and search firms. At best, 10 to 20 percent of the jobs are there, yet that's where 80 to 90 percent of job hunters look. Other statistics on employment agencies and search firms provide an even stronger indictment against their effectiveness for you. One recent survey showed that only 2 to 3 percent of all the clients at search firms actually found positions. The greatest number of people are chasing the smallest percentage of jobs when they operate this way. Those are incredible odds to bet on, yet most job hunters do—day after day, year after year. That's how a lot of incompetents stay in the search business, along with a small cadre of outright thieves.

FINDING THE LEADERS

Briefly, here's how the search business works. At the top of the industry are the best retainer firms. You find these listed in a compilation of leading executive recruiting firms published annually by *Executive Recruiter News.* There you can isolate the biggest, the best, the most reputable search organizations in American business. Associating your name with these reputable firms will not usually tarnish your reputation; in most cases, it will create a positive impression on an employer. An additional source for identifying executive search firms is the *Directory of Executive Recruiters,* an annual publication of *Consultants News.* Typically, a retainer firm operates with candidates who earn higher than an established minimum salary. If you don't earn more than their minimum, they usually won't accept your resume. Their retainer arrangement with companies is typically based on a one-third/one-third/one-third fee structure. They get a third of the fee when they submit a number of resumes of qualified applicants, another third when interviews are conducted, and another third when placement is accomplished.

This fee structure guarantees that they are not just peddling flesh to a potential employer. The retainer firm sends only top-flight, qualified pros on a confidential basis. There is implicit trust between the search firm and the potential employer. Obviously, you benefit from that professional association. To illustrate, a really upper-echelon retainer search firm might spend hours on the phone with a company, performing a needs analysis to discover what the company really requires in an applicant for the available position. Such firms operate with subtlety, discretion, and professionalism. They are paid for their time and professional services, not for sending an army of warm bodies from which a company can enlist employees.

In contrast, many contingency search firms operate quite differently. They are at the other end of the scale. Often, this is where the incompetents gravitate. If you're an engineer, you'll likely be talking to an unemployed engineer. Or if you're a systems analyst, you'll be talking to an unemployed programmer. The search agency hires these people primarily because of their contacts in engineering or DP departments. What drives their business is acquiring new job listings from employers, not servicing you, the job hunter. The company is the customer; you are nothing but a potential peg to fit an empty hole in the search firm's revenue board. How well you fit is of little concern beyond the prospect of a fee.

Typically, when a contingency search firm gets job listings, it will be one of several such agencies with identical marching orders, hustling to get there first with the most—to get the right (or wrong) person hired so that they can snap up a fast commission and survive another thirty days. It's a dash to the finish line, and the first huckster that shows up with a warm body gets the prize. We fully understand how callous, tough, and cynical that makes us sound. And it may be depressing if your income isn't high enough to qualify you for a retainer search firm. So, then, what do you do? Do you use a contingency firm anyway? No—you do it yourself.

If you can't deal with a pro, don't waste your time with a peddler. You can do a better job working in your own interest than any of the contingency peddlers will ever do for you. If you follow our guidelines on networking, time management, positive thinking, and self-discipline, you'll do it better in every case. How does a search firm develop job listings? On the phone—cold-calling. How do you telemarket and network your way into job openings? The very same way. The difference, of course, is that when you get a hot lead, you'll jump on it one step ahead of the rest of the world. But when a contingency search agency generates a lead, they'll send you and anyone else they can scrape out of the resume file whose qualifications are even close to those listed on the job order. So it is that many people complain bitterly that job hunting is a numbers game at which you can't win. It may be—but only if you play it the lazy way, expecting someone else to do your work.

Basically, many contingency firms move bodies; they shop commissions, servicing companies as their clients. They are not primarily interested in your job objectives and career goals. Consider some other claims that many agencies will make to sell their services:

• *Salary information:* They'll tell you that they can help you grasp the dynamics of the marketplace—what your skills are worth under current conditions. Moreover, they'll offer to help you negotiate compensation. Don't buy that for a minute. Again, they are servicing the company, while simultaneously looking for a quick placement. You may bring skills and experience worth $50,000 to the marketplace. But if an agency can manipulate you into accepting a $40,000 offer, they'll do it every time, without regard to your income potential or needs. First, they'll talk you into accepting the $40,000 by bad-mouthing your experience and background. Quite naturally, your $50,000 skills will blow all the $40,000 competition out of the water, and you'll get the offer. The result is that you're saddled with lower compensation than it was necessary for you to take, with a corresponding setback for your future income potential. The agency gets what it wants most, of course—a fast payday.

- *Job leads:* They claim to network into job leads by the hundreds. We've already stated that, in every case, you can do a better job looking out for your own interests, but there's a more ominous overtone as well. Incredibly, once an agency gets your resume (and be alert that when you give any information on the phone, they might be writing down everything you say to compile a brief resume outline), some of these charlatans will even send an unauthorized resume to companies without your knowledge or permission. If they have your complete resume, often they will shotgun it all over the place. If you have networked your way into a job interview, it would not be unusual for your resume to have hit that company from another direction if you're also working through a contingency search firm. Not only is this unprofessional and damaging to your interests, it can lead to an ugly fee dispute. The company may believe that the hire was accomplished directly by you, but the agency may send an invoice on the strength of the resume it had sent. Here is one example:

> Jerry had networked into an organization and was promised an interview upon the return of the hiring authority. When he followed up with the company recruiter, he learned a search firm also had submitted his resume for the position and the company was not willing to pay their fee. Jerry was shocked since he had not given the firm permission to use his resume. The company would not interview Jerry until he got a letter from the agency retracting their fee claim. While it was a time-consuming and frustrating process, Jerry finally got the letter and was interviewed for the position. After that experience, Jerry understood the importance of controlling his own campaign.

This is *not* an unusual occurrence. This scenario constantly plagues corporate human resources departments. If you think a contingency search firm is looking out for your best interests, just get caught in the middle of a fee dispute between such an agency and your new employer. The battle can get nasty—and you are the ultimate loser, no matter how the problem is resolved. The company hired you to solve a problem it was facing. But when you walk in with a fee dispute trailing in your wake, you become a new problem, not a solution. This can ultimately eliminate you from contention for the position.

- *Coordinating your search for more efficiency:* This is another agency tactic that can lead to a fee dispute problem. Without fail, a search counselor will say something like "Keep me posted. We're working together on your search, and we don't want to duplicate our efforts. So if you have a contact working, let me know about it." (Job hunters, if you swallow that kind of verbal effluent, we have a nice piece of land at the bottom of a lake we'd like to sell you.) Although this may sound logical and in your best interests, it most assuredly is not. When you're told, "Keep me posted—let me know where you're interviewing," the search firm is, once again, doing nothing and hoping to profit by it. The agent is fishing for an easy commission, looking to capitalize on your hard work. It's incredible, but it happens every day in the contingency search business. You notify the agency that a contact looks good, and what happens next? The search agent shoots in your resume and calls the company, claiming that he represents you in your search. That gives him the right to invoice the company if you get the job.

Obviously, that can lead to the unfortunate fee dispute scenario we just described. But there are other more immediate problems. Despite the fact that you've done the work, the search agent's claim to represent you means, in effect, that you've just acquired a 30–40 percent price tag on your head. How much does that assist your job search? Not much, we bet. What if, for example, you're one of three very close finalists for a position that pays $60,000 annually. By your call to the search firm to keep them posted, their fee gets added to that; you now carry a first-year price tag of $80,000, while your competition, not represented by a search firm, will come in for $60,000. What do you think of your chances now? Moreover, the worst of it is that the effort was all yours. The contingency firm did nothing for you, only for itself. You threw a possible commission right into their laps, and they likely threw you right out as a prospective employee of that company. That's the type of unethical search practice that sends our blood pressure boiling. We see it every day. It's such a waste—so damaging to your immediate search and, potentially, to your career. To summarize our discussion of search firms, we strongly recommend that unless you're in a position to utilize the services of a top-echelon retainer firm, just don't deal with search agencies.

ON THE OTHER HAND . . .

Having said that, we'll back off our fighting mark a half-step. As critical as we've been about many contingency firms, let us stress, again, that our opposition to them is rooted primarily in our conviction that they just don't do very much for you. They are unable to help you more than you can help yourself. Obviously, there are some benefits in using an agency. Even if the statistics indicate that only 5 percent of people get jobs through agencies, that 5 percent is enough to qualify agencies as a valid source of job information. Many agency people are honest and dedicated, and they can help you get job leads and assist you in preparing for interviews and in critiquing your interviewing style. If you're dealing with a reputable firm and an experienced counselor, you can enjoy some benefits, as long as you're aware of and guard against the downside potential.

TEMPORARY AND CONTRACT AGENCIES

A third category of agencies are the temporary employment and contract agencies. The growing trend in companies to use temporary and contract employees at all levels has caused tremendous growth in these agencies. While once the domain of clerical and secretarial workers, there are now hundreds of agencies who serve companies' needs for technical, professional, and even executive talent. Often referred to as contingency workers, this growing segment of the job market has created many opportunities for part-time and short term assignments. Outsourcing of various company functions has also contributed to this trend.

When considering the use of temporary and contract agencies bear in mind the following positive and negative factors:

Positives	*Negatives*
Provides cash flow while seeking full-time employment.	Detracts from the job search effort.
Provides opportunity to experience what a job or company is like before committing long-term.	Often pays lower compensation and no benefits.
Can lead to full-time employment.	Multiple short-term assignments may limit breadth of your experience and accomplishments.
Meets the needs for a flexible work schedule for students, retirees or young mothers.	Limits involvement and commitment both to and from the organization—you may feel like a second class citizen.

Whether you obtain the contract or temporary assignment through an agency or your own networking efforts, these pluses and minuses can apply. If you prefer contingency work, however, we encourage you to first seek to market yourself rather than going through an agency. Why? Rather than the agency skimming their percentage off your rate, you will gain the entire fee, in which case, the chances of experiencing the negative side of contingency work are reduced. In some cases, you may actually be able to make more money by marketing yourself for temporary or contract work than you could make in a full time position. Similar to the consultant role discussed in Chapter 2, you may discover that the independence of contract work is right for you.

SOME GUIDELINES

The most important guideline in using search agencies is to adapt the way you allocate your time to the statistics we mentioned earlier. If you use search organizations, devote no more than 5 to 10 percent of your time to them. That's effective time management in your job search. This means that if you work a fifty-hour week on job search—which we classify as the minimum—you will spend no more than two to five hours a week on agency contacts. When you are with a company and looking for a job, it is especially tempting to rely strictly on search firms to conduct your search. Although the time to spend on your search is obviously limited, our cautions about allowing the search firm to control your search still apply. Use evening hours for researching target companies and early, late, and lunch hours for networking. Conducting a job campaign while you're still working requires expert time management, but it can be done.

If you elect to use agencies, be certain that you control the relationship. Be assertive. Watch out for your own interests, because its likely that no one else will. Here's an illustration:

> For personal reasons, Joe Smith, a former client of ours, was anxious to relocate from his home in Houston to Chicago. Before he came into our program, Joe's first instinct was to go to a search firm. Then he thought, "If only one search firm is trying to find a spot for me, wouldn't I have more of a chance if 50 firms were?" So he prepared a letter of introduction and was planning to send them to fifty different firms. Then his former company enrolled him in our outplacement program. In our first meeting with Joe, we learned of Joe's intentions and pointed out to him the folly of that move. "Your resume will be coming to potential employers from every direction," we explained. "They aren't going to know which search firm is entitled to the fee, and as a consequence, not one of them will consider you." Joe was shocked by the risk his seemingly logical plan involved. He took our advice and ultimately found a position with an excellent firm in Chicago through his own networking efforts, never using a search firm.

Exhibit 6.1 provides a form to list your search firm contacts. Follow these additional guidelines: Remember that the consultant, not the agency, will be responsible for your satisfaction in dealing with that firm, as well as for your success in accessing job leads through the firm. With that in mind, go to the agency (once again, be careful what you tell them on the phone) and determine who the best counselors are in your functional area. Interview the counselor, and make certain that he is professional, competent, and knowledgeable about your function. Then find out how long he's been with the company and in the industry. Learn what companies the agency represents, so that you can strategically select an agency that will best help you cover the market and best complement your search. In other words, you're taking charge of the situation. You're making sure that the agency doesn't duplicate your efforts, and you're also blocking them out of any easy fee collection. In addition, request that they never send your resume anywhere without first getting your permission. Finally, never sign any agreement with a search firm unless you absolutely and fully understand what the agreement obligates you to do. Substantial amounts of money are involved in recruitment of employees through search firms, and the contracts are usually designed to protect the agency's right to collect a fee, even if this means that you will ultimately be responsible under a specified set of circumstances. To be safe, do not use an agency that requires you to sign an agreement.

THE PITS

Don't for a moment confuse the different segments of the industry, however. At the top are the retainer firms; on the bottom are the low-level contingency agencies. And somewhere so low that they can't be measured or categorized are the up-front fee operators. These are the slumlords of the industry. They may call themselves "executive job search consulting services" or "retail outplacement consultants." It's easier to identify them by their method of collecting money. In short, if someone wants your money up front, get out while the getting is good!

We don't have any problem with people getting paid for providing excellent services. That's how we run our business—our clients are, without exception, corporate-funded. But legitimate companies may also bill an individual job hunter for finding that person a job or even for writing a resume. We might question the practice, but there's no question about its morality or ethics. It's simply a judgment call. But the up-front fee collectors who take your money and give you nothing in return are a plague on the American job marketplace. Job hunters who are emotionally vulnerable will pay upward of

EXHIBIT 6.1
Personal Marketing Plan: Search Firms

SEARCH COMPANY/ CONTACT (Name & Title) Phone Number	RESULT OF CALL		
	CALL BACK	WILL RETURN	SEE RECORD

$5,000, $10,000, or $12,000 and get nothing but a resume and a list of target companies that hasn't been updated since your grandfather looked for a job. Nothing. The best advice we can give you is, if someone wants your money for providing excellent services, that's fine—that's free enterprise. But if some low-life sponge tries to get your money in return for nothing but a lot of fast talk, fancy acronyms, and stacks of computer printouts, get out of there as quickly as you can. Then write to anyone and everyone you can think of— the Better Business Bureau, your representatives in Congress, your mayor, your district attorney, your state legislator. And write to us. Before our business careers end, we'd consider it the greatest professional accomplishment if we could eradicate this kind of scum from our industry.

In short, keep your money in your pocket, and don't think that anyone else can do your work for you—even a reputable search organization. Even if you conduct your job search in accordance with every one of our tough rules, you still must understand that rejection is part of the process. We know from experience that's one psychological motivation that drives people to rely on search firms. They think that someone else will bite the bullet, make that tough cold call, soften the ground to make the interview less stressful, and exercise that delicate, subtle pressure to negotiate the best deal possible. Meanwhile, they sit on the sidelines, hoping to enjoy the fruit of someone else's labor. And we believe it's not necessarily because of slothfulness, but rather because of fear of rejection. Whatever the motivation, such expectations are nothing but wishful thinking.

Yes, a search firm may be able to place you—not primarily to your advantage, however, but to a company's advantage. Moreover, a search firm can never do it as well as you can if you continue reading, learning, and putting our advice into action for your job search today and your career tomorrow.

CHAPTER 7

Telemarketing Yourself: The Technology of Networking

Whether they are used to earning minimum wage sweeping floors or six-figure megabucks charting the course of an international corporation, jobless people invariably ask the same questions: "Who's hiring?"

The question can be stated in several ways, but whatever sophisticated terminology the corporate quarterbacks may use to ask it, like all job hunters they gravitate toward any source of job leads. Many imagine that those leads are grouped on some master list of companies that are hiring in their particular discipline. It's amazing to us, but even senior-level human resource executives, who should know better, think that new positions will materialize on a list, like manna from heaven. Well, if you're on a first-name basis with Moses, that might happen. But if you're like the rest of us, forget it. And get to work.

Not only is the "master list" concept unrealistic, but—more important—it runs counter to our basic premise of job search. If anyone gives you a list of companies that are hiring, you immediately place yourself on the wrong side of the job search equation. About nine out of ten job hunters concentrate their search efforts in the minority slice of available jobs, diluting their possibilities for success with such lists.

From word one in this book, we've stressed that there's no revolutionary innovation, no easy path to finding a new position. The traditional methods work if you labor hard enough at implementing them. Nowhere is that more true than when you're contacting companies, and generating job leads.

Is there a secret, fail-safe path to success? You bet. But it's only a secret because it's been pushed back into a dusty corner in the world of job search advice, outdated by more glamorous, high-tech instruction. It's dated, but not obsolete. Our secret, it shouldn't surprise you to learn, is work, then more work—coupled with dedication, preparation, discipline, planning, learning, and positive thinking. These will drive your job search, and they will ensure success. And there's not a single shortcut in this recipe. In our view, working hard means an absolute minimum of ten hours a day—If you ask successful people what makes them successful, invariably they will say, hard work! Be prepared to put similar time and effort into your job search if you expect to succeed.

HOW DO YOU FIND THE JOBS?

You pick up the phone and call each company, each department manager, and ask if they're hiring. So who's hiring? A select few, if you follow the herd mentality. Everyone, if you learn networking and cold-calling skills. The telephone and the business letter are your communication tools in this stage of job search. We'll discuss networking and talking to employers in the context of telephone work. Incredibly, we still come across advice that it's fine for job searchers to visit employers to fill out applications if they're uncomfortable or inexperienced on the phone. This suggestion is so absurd that it belongs in the *Guinness Book of Records* as the world's worst advice. Stay out of your car until you begin to arrange interviews—or at least until you've cultivated a contact to the point that a lunch or breakfast meeting might be productive. But if you spend your day driving around filling out applications, you're not looking for a job—you're wasting time, avoiding your spouse and kids, or just plain cruising. We call it the *windshield mentality*. Pure and simple, if you do it, you'll still be looking for work the day the sun rises in the west.

So we're agreed, right? You'll work the telephone to find job leads. If you're a novice on the phone, before you start, go ahead and draw a sketch of a monster face and tape it to the phone. We know that's how bad it is for most people who are new to the process. That little mechanical instrument becomes the enemy. But that enemy's weapon is fear, and fear grows from a lack of confidence. Accept that. It's normal to start out a little shaky, with a degree of uncertainty, on your initial calls. That's the primary reason we suggested (in Chapter 5) that you don't call your best contacts, your closest professional friends, first. Call the strangers first; learn while you're working the coldest contacts on your list. After the first 20 or 30 phone calls, your technique will begin to develop, and you'll be ready to approach and solidify some of your hotter contacts.

Like any endeavor, however, your technique won't improve if you keep repeating mistakes. You can't slop your way through twenty phone calls, learn nothing, change nothing, and expect the next call to part the sea. As you tele-market, analyze what you say and what the reply is—what works and what doesn't work. Above all, listen. Telemarketing is a communication technique. Whenever we use an unfamiliar technique, we tend to become preoccupied with what we're saying. It's fine to script a conversation but don't fail to listen and react to the other person's comments.

Think of your evaluation process in two tiers. First, analyze your style—how you communicate your message and how smoothly you break from your preplanned script into a free-flowing conversation with your contact. Then evaluate what you say. As an illustration, suppose that you consider as the highlight of your professional career the redesign of a tool that eliminated a $23 zerk fitting. But if each time you mention your accomplishment to cold-calling contacts it generates nothing but silence on the other end of the line, that's a good indication that elimination of zerk fittings doesn't pull a lot of weight in this year's market. Change your presentation. Be flexible, attentive, and persistent. Don't stumble through your calls. Improve.

The guideposts to a fruitful, ever-improving telemarketing campaign are discipline, dedication, and goal setting. Your goal is an established number of cold calls each day. We suggest 25, but set a goal that you can attain with discipline and dedication. If you want to start at 10 or 15, fine. But commit now toward reaching that number and *improving* with each call. Never lose sight of your short-range goal with each call—an interview. Your fall-back goal is to get the names of three, four, or five other people you can call.

Your command of goals and time makes this process of contacting companies work. (Exhibits 7.1 and 7.2 provide forms to help you organize your time—a daily action plan for which a daily calendar may substitute and a weekly activity summary.) Surely we don't need to justify the importance of setting goals; you undoubtedly have utilized the technique in your professional career. Just be certain that you don't abandon goal setting now that you're navigating in unfamiliar territory. You need goals now more than ever. Our favorite truism about goal setting is an often-quoted statement: "Those who do not set goals are forever doomed to work for those who do." Adapting that for job search, we can say: "Those who do not set goals are doomed to finding new positions much later than those who do."

WORK THE PHONE AND IT WILL WORK FOR YOU

This all leads to a radical departure from the ritualistic advice most job searchers revere. Everyone ventures out, forewarned and forearmed, to

EXHIBIT 7.1
Personal Marketing Plan: Daily Action Plan

DATE _____

My Goals for Today Are: _____

_____

My Activities to Accomplish These Goals Are:

7:00 _____

7:30 _____

8:00 _____

8:30 _____

9:00 _____

9:30 _____

10:00 _____

10:30 _____

11:00 _____

11:30 _____

12:00 _____

12:30 _____

1:00 _____

1:30 _____

2:00 _____

2:30 _____

3:00 _____

3:30 _____

4:00 _____

4:30 _____

Remember—Looking for a job is a full-time job!
(Record daily accomplishments on Weekly Activity Summary.)

EXHIBIT 7.2
Personal Marketing Plan: Weekly Activity Summary

WEEK BEGINNING: _____

				RESULTS			
ACTIVITY		M	T	W	TH	F	TOTAL
Networking							
Personal/professional contacts	1.						
Target companies	2.						
Search firms	3.						
Letters							
First contact/cover	4.						
Ad response	5.						
Follow-up/thank-you	6.						
Interview Preparation	7.						
(research and practice sessions)							
Interviews							
Informational interviews	8.						
Job interviews from networking	9.						
Job Offers	10.						

resist depression and to shake off rejection. But succumbing to rejection just doesn't happen to our clients in Houston if they follow our principles. Time after time, across the board of professional disciplines, they find new jobs faster than they had dreamed—and not just a job, but a better position, for more money, with a better company.

Many people are telling job hunters that cold-calling is so tough that it's all right to avoid it as a job search technique. That advice might make you feel better, but it won't help your job search. In fact, its dangerous to your career, because you will miss out on many potential opportunities.

Your job search is not governed by the economy, any more than a salmon swimming upstream is driven by the river's current. It is a fact of American business that companies hire people every day. Companies in bankruptcy proceedings do it; companies with absolute, worldwide hiring freezes do it. By networking, telemarketing, and cold-calling, you can access those job leads better than your competition.

When you do, you won't have to worry about lists of jobs or lists of companies that are hiring. In fact, you won't even have time to wish for their existence. Your positive momentum will build; you'll be busy and confident. Our point is that when you work the phones properly and get a rejection in spite of your improving technique, it's only one of 25 calls. Part of your technique is to get off the line quickly—don't beat on a dead contact. You don't have time to waste. You'll hang up believing that the company lost its chance at you, and you'll move along to the next contact.

Of course, there's a fine line between confidence and arrogance. Don't be so confident that you're rude and just blow people off the phone. But believe that you have skills and background to help that company. If it's not a good match, try the next company. Always be a pro.

There's one final point to be made as we try to short-circuit every possible argument anyone can mount about why they shouldn't telemarket. Frequently, we talk with senior executives or people in traditional professions—medicine, law, accounting—who respond, "We don't do that. It's considered beneath a lawyer's standing to get on the phone and ask for help" or "That doesn't work at my level. Companies only hire through search firms at the senior levels." All we can say is, if you think cold-calling another lawyer for help is more demeaning than going for a year without a job, then there's not much we can do to help you. Even if a position is contracted to a search firm, how do you expect to find out about it? When looking for a job, *no one* is too good or too important to utilize proven techniques to get that job. So we dismiss any protest about telemarketing. It's the most important technique you can use to find job leads. And it works for everyone, not just sales or marketing people who are pros on the phone. People who say that they cannot or will not telemarket are blocking themselves from their own potential. It works for everyone. And the skills are learnable.

> Pete was a Ph.D. chemical engineer who had been laid off. In addition to being an introvert and technically oriented professional, Pete was Asian and English was his second language. For the first couple of weeks that he was in our outplacement program, Pete walked around the facility like a "zombie." We kept prodding, encouraging, and reinforcing the importance of networking and telemarketing, but Pete just didn't seem to get it. Then one day he had a big smile and was all excited. Pete explained that he had made a cold contact that resulted in an interview opportunity. We asked what made the difference for him and he said, "I tried it!"

Yes, you do have to try it for telemarketing to work. By the way, as a result of Pete's success, he became one of our model clients, encouraging others and setting the example. Not only did he succeed in placing in a better job, for better pay, but he discovered a new talent that led to a business development position. He continued to apply the marketing techniques he had learned in *The Total System* to succeed in his new job.

TIME TO START

With that in mind, let's get started on just what you say and how you say it. We mean, literally, *get started*. This is the phase of job search when procrastination is more prevalent and most destructive. To be sure, generating momentum on the phone can be difficult. We are all prone to make three or four calls, then fiddle around with paperwork or research or some other "non-prime-time" pursuit. Soon, you'll have mused away the morning. Come noon, you can say with conviction, "This telemarketing is tough. I'm exhausted." It's easy to get caught in that trap, so set your mind now to avoid it. Set your goals and meet them. If you don't meet your goals, work on your efficiency, or shorten your horizon slightly. But your goals and time management are the benchmarks for success. Don't fail yourself.

Let's look more closely at our daily telemarketing goal of 25 calls. We're actually understating our own pace—we could place 25 calls in half a day. Initially, many calls are one-minute placement calls and the contact "will return the call." You may have to call these contacts again and again to get through. We feel that we're expert in nurturing the good calls within a couple of minutes and decapitating the bad ones in seconds. Our point is that you should set a goal you can reach, then build upon it. Both the numbers and the quality of your cold-calling should increase. As we touched upon earlier, telephoning and interviewing are your "prime-time" events in job search. They must be done during business hours. Researching, reading, responding to ads, and writing letters should be done in the evening or on weekends. This is linkage in action again. Remember our equation for where the jobs are. Networking generates about 80 percent, ads and search firms only 20 percent. That is precisely how we suggest your allocate your time. Most of job search is phone work—networking and cold-calling.

A SCENARIO FOR COLD-CALLING

To prepare for your cold-calling, we suggest that you create a written script. We have used scripts for years in developing our company's business, and the same principles apply to your job search. There are certain fundamentals of selling that every cold call should contain. Remember that job search is a selling situation. In compiling your cold-calling script, include the following elements:

- The full name of the person you're calling: We suggest that you use the first and last names in your initial contact with a secretary. If you use Mr. or Ms., it can give the impression that you're operating out of your league. And if you use the first name only, that's too familiar and inappropriate for any initial business contact.
- The name of the person who referred you (or the publication from which you got the company's name).
- Why you are calling: First, you want a job; second, you want more names.
- Why your qualifications match the needs of the company.
- What your specific occupational skills are.
- Why a personal meeting can be helpful to both you and the company: The incentive for the contact meeting may be an interest in your background, your industry or product knowledge, the people you know, or ideas you can share.
- A time limit: Frequently, you'll be cautioned that you should not waste the employer's time; that you should hurry and get off the phone; that two minutes is plenty, and the employer's been gracious to give you that much. All these points are valid, but the motivation's all wrong. Certainly, get off the phone quickly, and don't waste time. But it's *your* time that must not be wasted as well as the employer's time. When you accept that precept, you will have taken a major step toward understanding and implementing a telemarketing program.
- The three R's: Read, Reread, then Role-play your script with another person. That's the only way to make it work when you go on wire with the hiring authority.

Keeping accurate records of your telemarketing is as important as having a script. You may have had secretaries or clerical staffs to handle all your grunt work in the past. Well, welcome to life in job search (or in an entrepreneurial organization, for that matter). There are no overlapping layers of staff. The grunt work is now your responsibility. Be sure that you maintain a simple but effective record of company, person, secretary, what was said, and what is to happen next. (Exhibit 7.3 provides a form for keeping a record of a telephone conversation. We recommend organizing these alphabetically by company name in a notebook for easy access as your network grows.)

Look over the following sample script. Adapt the responses with which you're comfortable, but remember that they are only script suggestions.

EXHIBIT 7.3
Personal Marketing Plan: Record of Telephone Conversation

Name _____ Telephone _____

Title _____

Company _____

Address _____

_____

Secretary _____ Other Names _____

Subject _____

Date	Conversation Notes/Referrals:

Develop your own style, and alter that style to mesh with the personality of the person on the other end of the line.

You: Good morning, Mr. Hardsell, this is [your name] calling. Fred Goodguy at TestTube Corporation suggested that I call. Could I have a few minutes of your time?

Mr. Jack Hardsell: I'm very busy; I have only a minute. [That gives you license to take three minutes.]

You: As a result of a recent corporate reorganization at [former company], I am currently exploring opportunities for new career directions. Fred suggested that your data processing unit would double its staff this year [or that he had an extremely strong base of contacts in data processing]. [Or you read about his company's expansion plans, new product merger, or the like, in the *Wall Street Journal*.] I wonder if we might meet to discuss your expansion [or if he'd share some of his contacts].

Give him a chance to respond, then proceed on the basis of his comments.

You: To give you a better idea of my background . . . [briefly tell him those parts that will have the most impact]. Is there a need in your [company, division, department, etc.] for someone with my skills?

Asking a question helps ensure a dialogue in which you can gain as much information as possible from your contact. Again, give him a chance to respond and assist you.

Close with an invitation to lunch or with an attempt to set up an appointment. As a minimum, get a few referral names:

You: I really appreciate your taking time to speak with me. I understand that there are no immediate needs in your division, but can you suggest others with whom I may speak?

Even in this brief sample, some of the myriad options become evident. Our point is, don't script so closely that you fail to carry on a logical conversation. You want to preplan everything you say, but you don't want to memorize it. Every company, every call, every person will be different. You must react spontaneously, and you do that by practicing.

Count on the fact that some of the Mr. Hardsells on the other end of the phone line will be jerks. But also anticipate that a Mr. Easysell may jump at the chance to interview you and may need a new employee that day. Most people will respond somewhere between those extremes. Remember that you have immunity from the jerks; they can't hurt you. Learn to cut down their phone time to ten or fifteen seconds and move along to the next call. More likely, however, you'll find people cooperative and anxious to help. Unlike many years ago, it's not a disgrace to be unemployed in today's economy of downsizing, mergers, and acquisitions. Generally, it's an experience most of the people you'll be talking to have encountered. If they haven't personally, they probably know someone close who has, or they may even expect to be unemployed soon themselves! So don't feel that you're a deadbeat or that people will treat you like a degenerate because you're conducting a job search. If they try to do so, cut them off.

GETTING TO MR. HARDSELL

Back to Mr. Hardsell—if he's important enough to have valuable contacts, in all likelihood he's important enough to have a secretary. To get to him, you must first get past her, and it's her job to see that that doesn't happen. You've probably heard advice for the best way to dodge the secretary—calling before or after business hours, during lunch, and so forth. The hope is that your contact will pick up the call in person.

Those are valid tactical moves, but only as fallback positions. We always suggest that your first step should be straightforward. Although the secretary's job is to protect her boss, why not consider it your job to win her as a convert to your needs? If you're really skilled on the phone and deal with her honestly, very frequently she'll feed information that will help you catch Mr. Hardsell. Don't ever dismiss that possibility without a try. For example:

You: Good morning. Is Jack Hardsell in? This is [your name] calling.
Secretary: He's in a meeting. May I tell him the nature of the call?
You: Yes. Fred Goodguy at TestTube is a mutual acquaintance. He suggested that Jack might have some information to assist me in my job search.

We like this approach because you're limiting the information you're giving out, but you're never making a false or misleading statement. Don't try to blow smoke at the secretary—inevitably, it will smother you later. At this point, she may take your name and number for a callback (don't get discouraged if you don't punch through on the first call). If you don't hear from Mr. Hardsell that day, at least you've established the rudiments of a working relationship with his secretary. The next day, it's proper to call back and place the message again. Such callbacks are the times when your professionalism can really pay off. Each time, be courteous, supportive of her schedule and Mr. Hardsell's, and understanding of the delay in returning your call.

Simultaneously, however, be persistent. You won't be rude, but you won't be put off, either. That's how you can subtly enlist a secretary's aid.

Another possibility is that the secretary will immediately instruct you to contact the human resources department. Again, don't argue the point. Do as she asks. The call to human resources will likely be unproductive. At that point, call back Mr. Hardsell's office and ask to speak with him. When the secretary states that human resources handles this type of call, you can truthfully state that you're not asking him for a job—you want information, and you only want a few minutes of his time.

Notice that at no time do we recommend that you ask for an information interview (sometimes called a referral interview). First, this country has been "information-interviewed" to death. It's a buzzword with no buzz left. More important, it smacks of a technique that an amateur would use. You want to communicate implicitly to Mr. Hardsell that you're a pro—that you need help now, but that you're the type of person who can be beneficial to him in the future. The term *information interview* does none of that. Don't give the impression that you're stepping up in class. That's a false imagery that is especially harmful to you in job search.

The concept and content of information interviewing is fine; in fact, it's just what we're suggesting that you do. It's the terminology that drags you down with excess baggage. Stay away from it. But do get the information— and the new referrals.

Throughout this process, remember our rules of engagement in telemarketing. When you're talking to Mr. Hardsell's secretary, she may resist all efforts at charm and professionalism, proving her a formidable blocker. Or Mr. Hardsell might be predisposed to be unavailable. Or the human resources department might tell you that your name has been programmed into the computer to self-destruct if your resume comes within a mile of their building.

If that happens, fine. Your fail-safe position protects you. Each of those calls will take only seconds, and you will move along on your contact list. Again, you can't get depressed—you don't have time. Also, don't lose sight of the fact that in a large company, even if Mr. Hardsell and his formidable accomplice won't help you, they are only one of perhaps a dozen destinations for your cold call. If the company is one into which you are determined to network, cut off this contact and develop another within the same organization. And do it all within minutes of telephone time. The following situation will give you an idea how this can work:

> John Powell had targeted a major company as having excellent opportunities to fit his background and skills. When his letter of introduction and cold calls to the vice president of operations produced no direct response, John decided to call one of the directors who reported to the

vice president. To his surprise, the director already had his resume in hand, routed from the vice president. Using the referral from the vice president to his advantage, John had no trouble setting up a preliminary interview with the director. Had John given up on the vice president and not placed the call to the director, he might never have networked into that target company.

With the popularity of voice mail, you may not even get through to a secretary, let alone your contact. While voice mail can be the ultimate "screening device," it can also be your ally. After all, you can leave a very professional and polished message that is designed to peak your contact's interest. This can often be more effective than a handwritten message by a secretary or assistant who may or may not get the message correct. Voice mail is private and usually permits detailed messages. Use it to your advantage. And if you do not get a return phone call, you can usually get through to the secretary by entering zero in voice mail.

To cold-call hiring authorities, you first must have a company to call. Your goal is to network into a department decision maker before he lists a job opening with a search firm or in a newspaper ad. To that end, you must work through your list of personal and professional contacts. We discussed in Chapter 5 what your network is and who should be on the list. You should have built a network of more than 100 names by now. Call each one, tell them your story, and ask if they can help. Most important, get three, four, or five names from each. Your contacts with search firms should also be handled as part of your networking effort. Get names of people and companies from your executive search consultant. If he's a real pro, he'll assist your networking even though there's not an immediate fee in sight. Even when you read the newspaper ads, if you don't get a job offer from a company, try to generate additional contacts from your interaction.

THE CLOSE

Telemarketing is, of course, a selling process. If you've ever been in sales, you know that the most important part of the sale is the *close*. Knowing how to close the telemarketing call can make the difference between another "NO" and a positive, productive call. Following are some of the many closes that can make your job search telemarketing more effective:

1. *Interview/meeting:* "Can we get together Monday or Tuesday to explore how I may contribute to the success of *(division)?*" *(Note:* Always suggest two alternative times to give your contact a choice.)

2. *Drop by with resume:* "I know you're busy, Bob, but rather than mailing my resume, I'd like to drop by with it. I'll only take a few minutes of your time to brief you on my background. Would tomorrow morning or afternoon be best for you?" *(Note:* Try to get in front of the contact rather than sending a resume. Ask several times in different ways to visit them— you'll get far more referrals in person.)

3. *Names of other individuals:* "I really appreciated speaking with you, Bob; I won't take any more of your time, but I wonder if there are others with whom you suggest I speak?" *(Note:* Pick up on any comments the contact may have made to help draw out names.)

4. *Identification of growth companies:* "Are there other growth companies in your particular specialty which you recommend I contact?" *(Note:* Once you get the contact thinking of companies, check whom he or she knows in them.)

5. *Do you know "so & so" in industry:* "Bob, I have a couple of names in your industry that I wondered if you might know. Jim Hart with XZY Company," *(Note:* This is a technique to get specific referrals in target companies you've selected and to get the contact thinking in terms of names he or she can give you.)

6. *Ask for advice:* "Bob, you obviously have been very successful in *(company or industry)*. I'd really appreciate your advice on how to maximize my next career move. Can we get together briefly today or tomorrow?" *(Note:* People are flattered to be asked for advice and like to give it. Ask for advice and you will have an opportunity to get referrals as well.)

7. *Luncheon invitation:* "Bob, I'll be downtown on Tuesday and would like to take you to lunch. That will give us an opportunity to get to know each other without taking time out of your busy schedule. Would that time be good for you?"

8. *Members of association or club:* "Bob, if you're planning to go to our association's next meeting, why don't we plan to get together briefly then? I'll bring my resume and we can spend a few minutes getting acquainted. When will you be there?"

NEWSPAPER ADS AND ON-LINE LISTINGS

When you're reading newspapers, or surfing the Internet, don't stop at the ads or job listings. Other parts of the paper and on-line information sources can be far more valuable for generating job leads. Any news report about growth, expansion, sales records, new territories, new products, or mergers and acquisitions is reason enough for a telemarketing or networking call.

In fact, to make ad or job listing responses pay off, you should always *integrate* them into your networking process. To do that, research the company and position. Find out who the hiring authority is by looking in directories, annual reports, or by calling the company and asking who heads up the particular department to which the position reports. Don't forget to check with your personal contacts to see if they may know with whom you need to speak.

Once you've sent out resumes in response to the ad, not only to human resources, but to the hiring authority, follow up. Even if the ad states "No Phone Calls," do you always do what you're told? Just because some human resources recruiter doesn't want to be bothered, are you prepared to sit and wait for something to happen? Pick up the phone and call the hiring authority. If you get routed to human resources, you can honestly say that they asked you to call! Here are three examples:

Barbara saw an ad for an executive assistant to the president. After responding to the ad through human resources and getting nowhere, she called the president. Her telephone introduction was so bold and professional that he asked her to set up an interview through human resources. Once she convinced human resources that the president really requested the interview (even though they had sent a rejection letter), Barbara successfully interviewed and was hired.

Mike saw a tiny ad for vice president, business development for a manufacturing company in the midwest. He had never heard of the company, so he researched it and discovered that it was partly owned by a larger company with which he was familiar. He knew the chairman of the larger company, so he called him about the position. Needless to say, as the result of his telephone contact, he was subsequently interviewed for the position. Had he responded "cold" to the ad, his chances for being flown in for an interview were far less.

Bill utilized his college's on-line bulletin board to identify companies that were interested in new college graduates. He developed a list of companies in industries and locations of interest to him. Bill then followed the steps of professional networking by researching the companies, contacting them with cover letter and resume, and following up. He so impressed the companies he contacted, that several were receptive to interviews. He received three offers from companies with which he ultimately negotiated and accepted an excellent entry-level training position.

By linking ad and job listing responses to your networking process, your success ratio will rise dramatically.

The fact is that responding to listings without follow-up is a very low payoff proposition. Certainly, include ads and listings in your job search, but don't build your search on them. Like search firms, they are easier to use than networking and cold-calling, but they just don't work as effectively.

If you do respond to ads, foremost among the rules is that you conform to whatever imperatives you find in the ad copy. If they want a resume, don't send some hybrid mutation—send them your chronological resume. If they want a salary history, put it in your cover letter (as we discussed in Chapter 3). You'll hear a lot of advice about answering any ad with your resume, just on the theory that if a company is hiring chemists, it may need technicians or systems analysts as well. That's fine if you have the time. But don't expect too much. Remember that, at best, classified ads are a long shot, and this lengthens the betting odds against you. Blind ads are another source of controversy. (They have only a post office box number, no company name.) Don't assume that it's a second-rate company just because it placed a blind ad. It may be a small firm without the resources to process large volumes of responses. So we're not opposed to your responding to blind ads. Our only warning is, don't answer a blind ad when you are employed. You may be asking your present employer for a job—that blind box number may be down the hall in the next department.

There's always a question about when to respond to an ad. Should you respond quickly, ahead of the rush, or late, after the crush of resumes has hit the human resources department? Our suggestion is to wait a couple of days until the crush should be over, and mail in a resume and cover letter. In this way, there is a better chance your resume will end up closer to the top of the stack of resumes received. If it is not a blind ad, be sure to follow-up with a phone call.

Remember, like search firms, ads and listings are only one source of job leads—and one that does not have a high degree of return. So don't waste a lot of time reading and thinking about how and when to use them. It's foolish to spend time weighing alternative courses carefully when none of the alternatives weighs much in the job search process. Spend the majority of your time with networking and cold-calling.

GREAT SMALL COMPANIES OFFER GREAT POSSIBILITIES

Keep your eyes and ears open for small, closely held, or private companies in your networking. Specifically, entrepreneurial organizations constitute fertile ground for job campaigning. We've thoroughly refuted the notion that you can find a list of jobs and companies, but now we'll retrench a fraction of an inch. To the question "Who's hiring?" we can safely answer: "Small companies." It's estimated that over 80 percent or more of all jobs in the next decade will be created by companies with fewer than twenty employees. Although the percentage of total civilian employment for the Fortune 500 companies has decreased from 17 percent to 10 percent as a result of the corporate downsizing trend, that's no cause to be discouraged. While the multinational corporations struggle through a transitioning world economy, remember that there's more to the job market than corporate monoliths. In fact, small entrepreneurial organizations represent the future of the American job market.

That's the up side—that small companies have the jobs. The down side is that small firms are more difficult to research for a cold contact. Most are private and aren't required to produce public records for the SEC. Once again, we don't have any magic formula to simplify your task, except to stress that the reward justifies the extra effort. You must dig, read, research, think, retrench, and keep sifting through layers of information. Start in the library. Read professional journals, all business periodicals, chamber of commerce publications, as well as municipal, county, and state compilations or guides to businesses registered for operation in your area. Always remember that at this point you're not only working to uncover job leads. You want to find out about the corporate culture, the environment, and the principals of these small organizations. Especially when you're dealing with newer, smaller companies, you must work smart and hard to develop your own information base before you even think about networking and cultivating job leads. To reiterate, once you hook one entrepreneur on the phone, even if you can't create a match, push your contact to the wall—max it out. Get five additional names. Remember, these are usually people who are successful refugees from corporate workstyles. And it's safe to generalize that they'll be more sympathetic and helpful to your networking quest.

NETWORKING/TELEMARKETING ORGANIZATION SUMMARY

To maximize your networking/telemarketing efforts, follow these recommendations:

1. Utilize the *Daily Action Plan* (Exhibit 7.1) or a daily calendar to list your calls. List the name of the company so you can easily recall each person. Check off the name when you have spoken with him or her. As you progress in your calling, you can look back in your calendar to identify those from whom you have not heard and follow up. You can flip forward in your calendar to list contacts you need to call at a later date to follow up.

2. Utilize the *Record of Telephone Conversation* (Exhibit 7.3) to record each contact. Note each call placed, what was said, and referrals.

3. Maintain a *master list of contacts* alphabetically in a notebook or computerized personal organizer (folders are too easy to get disorganized and are not as portable; index cards are too limited in size). For each contact keep together your *Record of Telephone Conversation* along with a copy of the cover letter and *Target Company Research* form (Exhibit 5.4), if used. When calls come in, you can readily access all information on a given company contact.

4. Utilize the *Getting Started* form (Exhibit 1.1) to set your networking goals. A minimum recommended telecommunication goal is 20 to 25 calls per day, including 10 new contacts per day. This is an aggressive, but manageable goal if you use the above outlined system. Without organization, you will quickly bog down as you try to remember who you called, what was said, and when to follow up.

5. *Other forms* presented in the system are very useful and can be added to this basic organization depending on personal need for additional structure.

6. Remember to *follow up* every contact, including ad and listing responses (unless blind). *Research ad responses* for top human resources representatives and the appropriate functional decision maker for the position before responding. This extra effort will increase your chances of being interviewed and enable you to follow up.

7. Be *persistent,* but *professional.* Although your contacts have other priorities, they are more likely to get back to you if you are persistent and have professionally represented yourself by phone, in your letter, and in your resume.

8. Be sure to maximize use of *association directories* in your field, particularly if you are a member. Remember to use *alumni directories* as well. And don't forget your *church membership.* Use other directories and databases to expand your target companies.

9. Seek *face-to-face meetings* whenever possible. The close, "I'd like to drop by with my resume" is one informal, but effective, technique. Also go to association and convention meetings for face-to-face networking opportunities.

10. Read and re-read your materials on networking and telemarketing. In particular, study the closes in this chapter. Remember, *practice makes perfect!* Try it and you will discover that people want to help you, but they can only do so if they know about you and you tell them how they can help.

THIS PROCESS WORKS

Networking is close to our hearts because we built our business from ground zero, to an extremely successful firm, living and working these same principles. Are you beginning to understand how this process eliminates the rejection syndrome that most job search consultants try to sell wholesale? Can you sense that this is a reality-based approach to creating momentum in your job campaign? We think the following chart of positive versus negative approaches to job search illustrates our point perfectly:

Approach	Attitude	Decision	Action	Emotions	Result
+	Learning experience	Try again	Keep improving	Enthusiasm	Success
−	Personal rejection	Withdraw	Quit	Fear	Failure

The chart's message is that when you get a no, it's not failure. It is an opportunity to analyze and improve your technique, an opportunity to isolate weaknesses in your presentation, and an opportunity to put your self-discipline to the test. In reality a no is more productive than a maybe in job search. "Maybe" means that you must maintain your records, follow-up on schedule, and continue to pursue what is, at best, a marginal possibility. "No" means that you can scrub the company and move along to more productive contacts.

We tell our outplacement clients that depression and failure are internally produced and, therefore, controllable. They cannot be forced upon you by the economy or the price of oil or the heartless corporation that terminated you two days before Christmas. It is your choice to be positive or negative, your decision to succeed or fail at job search. If you can buy into that philosophy, you're a candidate for our One Percenters Club.

As our last words on telemarketing, some "if . . . then" reminders:

If	*Then*
You are afraid to cold-call . . .	Get realistic. This is your career, your life. Pick up the phone and talk; each call gets easier.
You have a title . . .	Use it.
You have a company affiliation . . .	Use it.
You got the referral from a news story or report . . .	Verify the position and the name of your contact with the company switchboard first.

If	*Then*
You can't get an interview or job lead . . .	Get three to five additional names you can contact.
You ask a question . . .	Be quiet and listen; don't be so preoccupied with your script that you fail to get the answer.
You leave a callback, or voice mail message . . .	Suggest the best time for a callback. Invest in an answering service or a phone recorder. Never wait by the phone.
You can't get past the secretary . . .	Try again. Then try calling before 8:00 or after 5:00.
You can't make any progress after repeated calls . . .	Ask your original contact to help you if this company is critically important in your search. Otherwise, move along to your next cold call, with your spirits up.

CHAPTER 8

Interviewing: It's a Psychological Tennis Match, So Hold Your Serve

First, let's do a six-question pop quiz on interviewing for a job. Answer yes or no to each question:

1. In an interview, you primarily exchange information. Right?
2. It's a chance for you to learn all about the company—products, services, philosophy, and corporate culture. Agreed?
3. Simultaneously, of course, the company will learn all about you—your strengths, weaknesses, hopes for the future, work style, and personal value system. Correct?
4. You'll be carefully evaluating the company and the interviewer during the process to determine whether you want to work at this place. Right?
5. You'll be prepared to discuss frankly the facts on your resume, paying special attention to a candid assessment of your reasons for leaving previous jobs. Agreed?
6. You'll tell the truth, the whole truth, and nothing but the truth. Correct?

That's the quiz. Before you score it, however, it might give you a clue to the answers if we tell you that those six statements incorporate much of the bromide that is peddled as advice on preparation for the job interview. Indeed, most job hunters (career counselors, too, for that matter) would answer yes to each question. Did you? If so, you're 0 for 6. More important, someone else has the job.

People think that they are preparing for the interview by merely laboring over a list of tough questions that they know they'll be asked. They struggle with the answers. They fret over how badly they'll be hurt by discussions about weaknesses or difficult situations in their work history. They expect to provide candid information about themselves and, in turn, get the same from the employer—a true exchange of information to benefit both parties in the decision-making process. Don't think us cynical, and don't assume that we're suggesting that you be deceptive—but nothing could be further from the truth.

An interview is not primarily an exchange of information. It is a contest in which you are a contender—a psychological tennis match. Your resume has captured the company's interest, proving that you have the technical skills and background to do the job. Now, in the interview, the hiring decision will be made. This is standard job search advice, and we certainly don't take exception to it. We do, however, want you to know how you can best extract the offer. To that end, you must understand that interviewing is an art form, a performance. Your task is to hold your serve by controlling—very subtly—the direction of the interview.

We don't trivialize the interview; we simply snap it into proper focus when we teach our clients that they must approach it as though they are contestants in a beauty pageant or a dog and pony show. In business terminology, visualize it as a sales call. But understand what the process is and what it isn't. We get occasional resistance on this point from individuals who protest, "That's a game. I don't play games." A game is exactly what it is. You can't change that fact; you can only succeed or fail according to your ability to grasp the reality of the scenario and turn it to your advantage.

The interaction isn't created to hurt or deceive anyone. This is a classic win-win situation. You want the job offer; and if you get it, both you and the company will profit. You're not there just to play a game—you're there to win the game. The payoff, of course, is that both you and the employer can win at the same game.

To accomplish that, you prepare. You do your homework. In fact, that is *The First Great Commandment of Interviewing: Plan Every Word.*

Don't say any word that won't help you get the job offer. This is not a time for reflective, introspective responses. This is a time to *sell*, to *market*. You must tell the company what it wants to hear—assuring the employer that you are confident, poised, in control of yourself and your surroundings, and with a personality that contributes to team unity and productivity. In this scenario, there really are no difficult questions, at least not for our clients. That's not an empty promise. You probably know what a devastating experience a tough interview can be, so no doubt you can appreciate what our clients typcially tell us when they complete an interview. Not one or two but an overwhelming majority of our clients say with a grin, "I kept waiting for the tough questions. I was so confident of my responses that I was actually hoping for a chance to answer the objections. When I left, I thought it was nothing compared to the practice sessions the Dawsons put me through." Yes, we admit we're tough. But those conditions are dictated by the Darwinian job market. And our clients—provided that they buy into our principles—are ready for survival in any environment.

You see, each tough question is answered with a preplanned statement, and it's the same for every interview. You don't pause, reflect, stammer, then wade through an emotional response, fighting to control yourself. For each question, you've rehearsed the answer time and again, in advance. Most important, with each answer, you talk about yourself, but you do it in terms of what the employer wants to hear.

Plan and script your answers thoroughly and completely. Memorizing is a word fraught with danger in a situation like this, but we're suggesting that that's very nearly what you must do. Nevertheless, you must interact with the interviewer and respond to the changing dynamics of the discussion. For each tough question, develop an answer that meshes with your background, and ride that horse until you get a job offer. Unwavering consistency is critical. And when we say every word should be planned in advance, we mean every word. That ties in with *The Second Great Commandment of Interviewing: Positioning.*

With regard to individual questions within the interview, think of shooting a game of pool. Every pool shark in the world—and nearly every amateur—knows that the secret of success at pool is not just the shot you're attempting but the shooting position you set up for your next attempt. Ladies and gentlemen, that's also the key to unlocking the puzzle of interviewing success. With each answer, you position yourself for succeeding questions. This is how the interview becomes an exercise in control rather than a draining emotional nightmare. You allow the interviewer to rack the balls. But you make the break to control the interview. Your goal is no surprises—no questions too tough to "play."

You want to convey an image of professionalism and confident persistence. Just be careful not to be too dominant, aggressive, or rude in striving for that control. Actually, the real trick is to allow the interviewer to feel in control even through *you're* the one making the shots.

The building blocks for interviewing success are consistent with all our principles of job search—preparation, practice, research, confidence. But one imperative overrides all others in the interview—concentration. You'll probably have to develop your powers of concentration and extend the time you sustain it to a degree you've never before reached. What powers of concentration must a neurosurgeon command when he's working inside a patient's brain for eight hours? We'll never know, but it's an appropriate frame of reference. In your psychological tennis match, you must anticipate and react to every nuance of the interviewer's mental play with the same degree of intensity. Is this difficult? Without question.

IT'S NOT EASY, BUT IT CAN BE DONE

You thought cold-calling was tough! By now, you should recognize that talking into the phone is really quite simple compared to going one-on-one with the interviewer—nose-to-nose and toes-to-toes. In fact, we rank this process—especially the mandate that you concentrate, totally, completely, incessantly—as number two in degree of difficulty in the entire scope of job campaigning. In our view, only negotiating your compensation package is more subtle, complex, and difficult (and you'll learn that next, in Chapter 9).

That's the bad news. But, as always, we have good news coming along close behind. The good news is that this is the point in job search when our concept of linkage most clearly evolves from theory to reality. When you link your resume and references to your interview, you've hurdled the biggest obstacle in your path to a job offer. As we discussed in the chapter on resume writing, whenever you feel yourself getting into trouble, use your resume as an escape hatch. Moreover, you can build most of your interview answers from the contents of your resume.

For example, the single most difficult (and inevitable) question you'll deal with in an interview is

Q1: "Tell me about yourself."

A: It's in response to this open-ended inquiry that many people talk themselves out of a job offer. But if you structure your answer as we've suggested earlier—starting at the bottom of page two on the resume and moving up to the top of page one with a two-minute biographical sketch of who you are, where you've been, and where you're going—you'll succeed.

1. Start with your *early history*—where you were born, where you grew up. If you served in the armed forces, mention that here.
2. Part two is your *education*. Tell where you went to school and what degree you received.

3. Part three is *professional experience*—a brief description of your jobs since leaving school, explaining the transitions between jobs. Then quickly move to your most recent (or current) position, *explaining how your skills, accomplishments,* and *experience* relate to the opening.
4. Finally, part four is a career plan—a brief explanation of why you and this company would be a *good match,* reflecting facts you learned in your advance research on the firm. In closing, mention what a *first-rate company* this is and that you are *pleased to be interviewed* for a position in the firm.

Quite simply, when you follow these four steps, you've transformed a major roadblock into a positive image of yourself in the employer's eyes. And you're a giant step closer to a job offer.

YOUR TOOL KIT

Every time you go out on an interview, you will take your tool kit with you. The tool kit consists of:

- Your resume.
- References.
- Samples of projects.
- Performance appraisals.
- Background information.
- Documentation of accomplishments.

Your resume and references are essential. However, the latter four items are optional depending on your situation and their usefulness in documenting your accomplishments and their professionalism. Anything that is less than excellent, or that does not present you in a favorable light, or does not "score you points" should *not* be used!

These are not used to cover the interviewer with paper, but if you are asked for specific items or examples of your accomplishments, you have them in your tool kit to reinforce the points you need to make.

A very professional touch is to organize your tool kit in a presentation format using a three-ring binder and plastic protectors. Your original resume, reference letters, and work samples or proposals can be included.

Have a separate copy of your resume, references, and other supplemental data in a simpler cover to leave with the interviewer. During the interview, you can flip through the presentation binder at the appropriate time much as a salesman presents sales brochures.

WHAT IS THE GOAL OF AN INTERVIEW?

Let's pause here to clarify our position. Notice that we're not suggesting that you're after a job in the interview, only an offer. That's a critical distinction, and it's central to our approach to planning and implementing your campaign. We want you to get the best job you can locate, but if you take only one company to the point of an offer, if you have only one offer from which to choose, how can you possibly know which job is best for your present and future? To determine the best possible combination of duties and corporate culture, you must get multiple offers—at least three, preferably simultaneous—then weigh them and choose the best.

Before we move along toward helping you structure a win-win interviewing style that will generate multiple offers, let's deal with the six statements at the opening of this chapter. When we explain why each statement was inaccurate, we're confident that you'll share our viewpoint.

1. In an interview, you primarily exchange information.

   No. Interviewing is a performance by you—nothing more, nothing less. It will require six to nine months for the company to determine whether or not you're suited for the corporate culture and the position. To suppose that anyone could identify a match, for better or worse, on the basis of one or even several conversations is preposterous.

2. It's an opportunity for you to learn all about the company.

   No. You'll already know everything about the company in advance of the interview, based on the information you learned from researching, networking, and cold-calling. Before you walk in, you'll understand what they do and how they do it. That's just another function of your networking. With your cold-calling skills, you learn about the company's products, services, reputation, plans for the future, and workstyle or corporate culture in advance of the interview.

3. The company will learn all about you.

   No. Get serious. Of course that won't happen. Think for a moment about the significant other person in your life—spouse or whomever—and recall what you learned about that person during the first date of your embryonic relationship. It's a good bet that you can't even remember. Again, the employer will learn about you—your skills, abilities, ambition, personality, workstyle—gradually over the next six to nine months. If you try to tell the company all that during the interview, you're conducting job search death-wish style. If you get too deep into your personal business, we guarantee that you'll leave the interview feeling that it was a cathartic experience. We also guarantee that you won't get the offer.

4. You'll be evaluating the company and the interviewer.

No. Not on your life—at least, not on your career. Remember, you're not there to make a decision; you're attempting to get an offer. You'll evaluate later and compare. If you don't have multiple offers before accepting one offer, you're selling yourself, and us, short.

5. You'll discuss your work history frankly.

No. Never. Everyone's work history includes periods of difficulty, failure, or conflict, in varying degrees. But believe us, that is no one's business but your own. Tell the company what it wants to hear and score points in the process. You admired and respected every boss for whom you've ever worked because you learned something from each of them, everyone got along well, the company was fine, and you learned more about your profession than you could have hoped for. You're ever so thankful for all those opportunities to grow and learn. We acknowledge that this answer is full of a substance generally found in fields and collected by shovel, but we're perfectly comfortable with that (the imagery, not the actual substance). You want the job offer. So long as your resume is factual with regard to your work history and accomplishments, the employer knows what he's getting. Once again, the interview discussion is only to confirm that you're confident, capable, positive, and a potential asset to the company.

6. You'll tell the whole truth.

No. Talk about death wishes! Tell the truth—under no circumstance should you lie to get a job. However, although telling the truth connotes honor to us, telling the *whole truth* represents stupidity. To reiterate, please don't think that we're suggesting that you play fast and loose with ethics. Never lie. Answer the questions truthfully, but do so in a manner that won't hurt you. And then stop. Don't crucify yourself with too much information. Every time, tell the truth, but stop short of telling the whole truth—spilling your insides all over the desk. An illustration:

> Dick Ryan was interviewing for a position as division marketing manager in a major corporation. When asked about the extent of travel in a previous position, Dick proceeded to explain: "The travel was very extensive, about 90 percent of the time, which was

very demanding and more than I really cared for." Although the job he was interviewing for required only 50 percent travel, Dick had raised enough doubt in the interviewer's mind about his willingness to travel that he lost his chance. Besides breaking the interviewing cardinal rule of never saying anything negative about one's former position, boss, or company, Dick offered more information than was necessary to answer the question. A better response would have been: "My last position required 90 percent travel. How much travel do you anticipate for the division manager's position?"

If you're asked, tell the truth—but respond only to what you're asked. People wander off mentally, say too much, realize they're in trouble, and then panic. They'll typically say something totally stupid because they're desperate and confused. If that happens in your interview, you're history. So the simple, fail-safe solution is, just don't say too much—just say the right things and keep it simple and to the point. Don't go out on a limb. Don't get into trouble.

To further illustrate the point in terms of business PR strategy, suppose that a company is about to introduce a new product that will gain a dramatically strong market share. Also suppose that there are three lawsuits pending against the company and a projected cash flow shortage for the next quarter. What do you suppose the company will announce in their news release? This country's ingrained values about motherhood and apple pie compel us to tell the truth. Fine—just don't volunteer information that isn't requested. Leaving some information out of your answer doesn't mean that you're a liar; you're just a smart interviewee.

GREAT ANSWERS TO TOUGH QUESTIONS

We've dealt with "Tell me about yourself." Now let's inject a little truth serum into another classic tough question:

Q2:   "Tell me about your weaknesses."

A: You reply: "I have trouble getting along with people" or "I have trouble meeting deadlines" or "My spouse can't stand it if I work on weekends, and I don't like having to deal with that." Fine, you told the truth. What the employer will tell you now is good-bye. He may not speak it for another few minutes, but we guarantee that that response just clicked on in his mind. You're history.

Keeping those three weaknesses for our mythical job hunter, let's alter the responses 180 degrees without really changing the basis of the answers.

Weakness	*Why Not Respond . . .*
Trouble getting along with people?	"I do tend to get impatient with people who are deliberately unproductive."
Trouble meeting deadlines?	"I am a workaholic. I'm willing to put in however many hours it takes to get the work done."
Angry spouse?	"Sometimes I have to be careful—I get so wrapped up in my work that I don't give my family the time they need."

All we're suggesting is that you insist in your mind that you'll take a positive approach to every interviewing question. Work on it, practice, role-play, and conduct postinterview self-critiques (see Exhibit 8.1). For the process of self-evaluation, use the technique we call the interviewing continuum to facilitate an ongoing analysis. Both during and after the interview, think of the discussion as generating positive, neutral, or negative responses. On the interviewing continuum, left is positive, the middle is neutral, the right is negative. You can afford negative points on no questions if you plan to get the offer you really want. You can get by with a few neutral responses. But the great majority must be positive. They must weigh the interviewing continuum to the left if you are to leave the impression necessary to receive an excellent offer.

SOME TOUGH QUESTIONS

Now let's look at some typical tough questions you'll get in an interview. But before you read on, let us caution that these questions are not included for you to merely skim over. The planning and preparation of answers to them is essential to maximizing your interviewing prowess. The only way to succeed is to match your background to a positive, upbeat, convincing answer for each of these questions. Start with your resume. Know every word on it. Another key part of your preparation is company research. You should

EXHIBIT 8.1
Post-Interview Self-Evaluation Form

Company _____ Interview Date _____

Name & Title of Interviewer _____

Position Interviewed for _____

Check if you felt "OK" or "very good" about certain aspects of the interview or if you felt you could have done better and "need to improve" for future interviews.

	Need to Improve	OK	Very Good
1. Personal appearance?	___	___	___
2. Professional first impression?	___	___	___
3. Firm handshake at start and end of interview?	___	___	___
4. Maintained good eye contact?	___	___	___
5. Expressed myself well by talking clearly and correctly?	___	___	___
6. Self-confident, not ill at ease?	___	___	___
7. Expressed interest in the job and career?	___	___	___
8. Willingness to start at entry level or lower level and work up?	___	___	___
9. Minimized employment barriers by presenting them in a positive light?	___	___	___
10. Positive about my previous employer(s.?	___	___	___
11. Demonstrated knowledge of the company and the industry?	___	___	___
12. Described qualifications in a positive manner?	___	___	___
13. Asked pertinent questions about the job?	___	___	___
14. Presented abilities and qualifications in erms of the requirements for this job?	___	___	___
15. Thanked the interviewer and arranged for follow-up?	___	___	___

Areas needing improvement for future interviews:

---

know as much about the company as you possibly can before you arrive for the interview.

Now, here are the tough questions. We'll give some sample answers, but your responsibility is to construct similar positive responses that coincide with your background:

Q3:   Would you rejoin your former company?

A: Most people would say yes, but this question has a hidden agenda. The interviewer wants to be sure that you'll stay on if you're hired, so your response should be something like, "I really enjoyed the opportunity to work there—it's a fine company, and they treated me very well, But it's time to move my career along to the next level. That's why I'm so interested in your firm. I'm considering opportunities at a number of excellent companies, but yours is at the top of my list."

Q4:   What makes you mad?

A: Look out for this one. You might say, "I really think it's my responsibility to avoid getting mad in the workplace. That drains too much productive time. But if there's one thing, it would be people who don't pull their weight, who won't strive for excellence. That may sound like I'm intolerant, but I'm not. I try to give people every benefit of the doubt, and I communicate my concerns to them before I ever get mad." Carefully note this answer. Not only does it defuse a potentially dangerous area of questioning, but it also illustrates our positioning theory. Tolerance might be a concern of the interviewer, and if it is not addressed, it might grow into a large-scale problem. But by linking it to the answer, you've controlled the interview in a professional manner while simultaneously heading off a potential problem.

Q5:   Would you relocate (or travel)?

A: This is an easy one. Your answer is, "Certainly, for the right opportunity." There may be only one set of circumstances for which you would relocate—Cancun for $500,000 annually—but your answer stands as accurate. If the company makes the right offer—the right opportunity—you'll relocate. It's truthful, but it keeps control of the interview in your court. Be aware, also, of the motivation for companies to ask questions about relocation and travel. The information may have nothing to do with the position for which you're interviewing, but frequently such queries originate from a list of prescribed questions to which every new employee must respond. How sad it would be if you lost a job offer because of a careless remark about not being willing to relocate, when in fact the job in question wouldn't require a move.

Q6:   Were you fired?

A: No matter what your circumstance, you were never fired. Rather, you were "part of a downsizing and reorganization." Always blame your condition on the economy or on organizational restructuring, not on the company or on your former boss. Similarly, you were never laid off or cut loose, nor did you "hit the bricks."

Q7:   Why are you leaving your current job?

A: Remember, *no negatives.* Everything about your past job and your past boss are all positive. Was there a *reorganization, acquisition,* or *merger* that caused you to leave your job? Did you quit—was it your choice to leave your job, and if so, how do you explain that? Was your job eliminated? Was there a new innovative technique that came in and caused your job to be obsolete? Was it a *personal choice* because the company no longer offered *growth* and *challenge?* Did you transfer to another company or another department?

The best four-part answer is:

1. A *reorganization* in the company affected my position.
2. Reorganization had *nothing to do with my performance.*
3. I have *references* that support my excellent track record.
4. My extensive research on your company suggests that you can benefit from my experience.

This answer can also be combined with "tell me about yourself" creating psychological leverage as you anticipate this inevitable question at the very start of an interview.

Q8:   What does cooperation mean?

A: "Cooperation means working with subordinates, superiors, and peers to establish an environment of excellence as a member of the team in order to meet organizational goals."

Q9:   What did you think of your boss?

A: "He was an excellent manager. I learned a lot from him, and we had an ideal working relationship. In fact, one of my letters of reference is from him, and I'd be glad to share it with you if you'd like." (By now, you recognize linkage—and there it is again.)

Q10: What books have you read recently?

A: Always keep your responses business-oriented by naming business books that are current and popular. Be sure that you've read the books you name in case the interviewer has also read them and asks more specific follow-up questions about them!

Q11: What are your strengths?

A: Your answer should address the specific agendas of the interviewer. Focus on (a) your interpersonal, supervisory or managerial characteristics, not on technical skills: "I am an excellent leader, decision maker, communicator, motivator. I work well with people. I'm a team player," (b) your willingness to work hard: "I do my homework. I'm willing to do whatever is necessary to meet the company's goals. I value my home life, and I'm willing to blend the needs of my family with the needs of the company," (c) your desire to do what's in the best interest of company: "I'm willing to travel, to relocate, to do whatever enhances the company's bottom line."

WATCH OUT FOR . . .

In part, an abiding self-confidence is a by-product of a thorough understanding and appreciation of the following interview cautions and questions.

Illegal Questions

How old are you? Are you married? Are you divorced? Do you plan to have more children? There's no doubt that these are illegal questions in the sense that companies can not base their selection on these factors, but don't spend time thinking about what is legal and what's not. Even if a question is inappropriate, we suggest that you not dodge it. Respond briefly; then execute a linkage maneuver, pivoting on your resume, to maintain your offensive position. You might say, following a ten-second response to a poor question: "And Mr. Johnson, what's more important to us all is how my experience in a new territory, highlighted at the bottom of page one of my resume, gives me ideal experience to assume a key role in your expansion plans." A final point: Don't assume that any question is illegal.

In reality, there are few illegal questions. Federal laws, however, do make it illegal to discriminate against candidates by eliminating them from consideration because of certain characteristics or experiences. To avoid the appearance of discrimination, therefore many companies avoid asking questions about age, race, or nationality, and so on. To prove discrimination in the hiring process is very difficult and is counterproductive to your campaign. If a company is backward or archaic in its hiring process, imagine what it would be like to work for the company! Rather than worrying about whether a question is appropriate or not, score points by responding in a positive and general way.

Q12: Are you pregnant?

A: "No, and I'm currently on a weight reduction program." (If yes) "Yes, but I intend to return to work quickly. May I ask what your leave policy is?"

Q13: Who will take care of your children while you work?

A: "I have arranged professional child care and my husband is also very supportive in assisting the children. I am very career-oriented and have always managed my job and family responsibilities so they do not conflict."

Q14: Would you have a problem being supervised by anyone younger?

A: "Age is not a factor in my working relationships. I respect people for their position, knowledge and skill. I believe my responsibility to a company is to do my best regardless of characteristics of others with whom I work."

Q15: How old are you?

A: Reveal your age and then go on to say, "As my resume reflects, I have many years of experience which I am confident qualifies me for this position. I know you would not use my age to disqualify me. In fact, I feel my years of experience and maturity are an advantage to *(Company)*."

If it is an area you absolutely want to avoid, respond, "That is an area which does not affect my ability to perform on the job, and I would not allow it to reduce my contribution to the company in any way" or "I keep my business and personal life separate and give 100 percent to the company when at work." Then take control and turn the interview back on course. That's the best message of all—you can handle adversity, and you know the law. The employer isn't dealing with a rookie.

The Federal Disabilities Act has made medical questions prior to an offer illegal. Under this law medical questions can only be asked after an offer is made. If the applicant can't do the primary parts of the job because of a medical condition and it would impose an undue hardship for the employer to make accommodations, the employer can withdraw the offer. However, because these rules are fairly recent, some companies may not have implemented the federal guidelines in their hiring process and on applications. If you are asked a medical question such as:

Q16: "Do you have AIDS?"

Q17: "Do you take any medication?"

Q18: "Have you ever been hospitalized?"

Q19: "Have you ever filed for worker's compensation?"

A: If you do not wish to answer, say, "I believe that is an area more appropriately addressed at the offer. I would be glad to answer all your medical questions at that time and I am confident you will be satisfied with my ability to perform this job at the highest level."

Two-Part Questions

Be especially alert to two-part questions. In the interview, what you say isn't the only factor of importance. The employer is also testing your retention and confidence. He wants to see if you can answer a two-part question without stopping to ask for a repeat of the second part. This is a very basic interviewing tactic, yet many people trip over it.

Either/Or Questions

Q20: Which is more important to you—money or position?

A: The important thing in an *either/or question* is to respond to both. If you say money, the interviewer will say, "Why not position?" If you say position, the interviewer will say "Why not money?" If you say money is not important, they will offer you less than what you're asking. If you say position is more important, the boss feels that you are threatening him or her. To create leverage say, "Both are important." Continue your response in a way such that you score points across the board.

Here are other examples of either/or questions:

Q21: Do you prefer sales or operations?

Q22: Do you prefer computer work or dealing with customers?

Q23: Do you prefer staff or line work?

Q24: Would you be happy in a smaller or larger company or environment?

Hidden Agendas

Most people will face recurring objections about parts of their background. You must custom-design your response in such cases; but in so doing, you must understand that what the interviewer asks isn't necessarily the issue to which he wants an answer.

Q25: Aren't you over (under) experienced?

A: For example, take the 61-year-old former vice president we described earlier. He kept getting objections about too much experience. That meant that he was too old. He defused the objection with this frontal assault: "I have 35 years of experience, and if you want an executive with 35 years in the field, you're going to have to hire an older person."

Be careful that you don't threaten the interviewer—especially if he is your new boss. He may be asking, in effect, "Do you have so much experience that *you will overpower me?* Show how you can use your years of experience to make your boss look good.

Another strategy is to acknowledge that in seeking a lesser position, there may be *trade offs:* it may be more important to you to stay in Phoenix than to seek a higher salary or position. Emphasize to your potential employer that you *fully understand that trade off and have committed to it.*

Conversely, as a new college graduate or return-to-work candidate you may hear the objection, "You're not experienced enough for this position." The hidden agenda may be any number of issues—too young or too old depending on your age, or the perception that training may be required.

For example, a recent graduate, Pete, applied for a computer position requiring expertise in a specific computer language. Pete had taken a course on the language in college but had not used it on a job as yet. When the employer voiced his "too inexperienced" objection, Peter replied, "Sir, having just completed college, I'm used to learning things fast. I'll take extra time on my own to learn your specific applications, to speed the learning curve, and to contribute to your objectives more quickly."

Another example is a businessman who had closed down his entrepreneurial enterprise to reenter the corporate world. Repeatedly, he'd get questions about the nature of running a small business and his successes. Each time, he'd respond about the opportunities and challenges. Each time, he'd fail to get an offer. Finally, he realized that companies were reluctant to make an offer for fear that he'd leave to start another independent business at his first opportunity. So he altered his response to this: "I learned a great deal and treasure the experience but do not plan to return to it. The most important lesson I can bring to your company is the lesson in time management. When you're on someone else's payroll, time management is an abstract goal. But when every minute of your day either adds to or subtracts from the bottom line, you learn time management as a business imperative, not an abstract goal." On his next interview, he got an offer.

Following are examples of other hidden agendas:

Q26: What movie have you seen recently?

A: The *hidden agenda* here is *what do you do in your spare time?* Are you reading, studying, spending time in the library researching the industry and the company, or are you out fooling around? Was the last movie you saw an intelligent movie or an idiot movie? Did you go there to escape from reality, or to improve yourself? Create a response that is job-related.

Q27: Describe how your work has been criticized.

A: A hidden agenda to this question is *are you overly sensitive to criticism?* Are you going to be destroyed when the boss points out there are some things you need to improve? *Never cite criticism that might reveal actual weaknesses.* Instead, give neutral, positive responses that score you points instead of losing you points. For example, "One of the areas I would like to improve—and I have taken it upon myself to do so—is to learn more about the computer field. I believe it is important to improving my performance, and I would like to have the opportunity to learn more about it." You can construct a similar answer in engineering, human resources, or any other field related to your work experience as long as the field you want to learn more about is not critical to the job you're interviewing for. Another excellent response is to refer to educational accomplishments: "My boss wanted me to have an MBA, so I enrolled in an MBA program and got my degree in two years. He liked that a lot, and encouraged me to cross train in other areas for which my new education qualified me."

Q28: Describe your personality.

A: The hidden issue here is often, "Are you stable, dependable, loyal, can you be counted on when push comes to shove?" You can prepare for the question by going through the self-assessment questions in Chapter One. Then you can answer, "I've been through a personality assessment, and it shows me to be a dependable, loyal individual with leadership potential," tailoring your answer to your self-assessment result.

Situational Questions

Companies are interested in your ability to handle situations that may arise on the job. Situational questions are designed to test your reasoning, thinking, and problem-solving skills.

Q29: When asked to describe a situation in which . . . , or to explain what you would do if . . .

... an employee became angry.

... you fired an employee.

... you were faced with a technical problem.

... a customer became irate.

... a dangerous situation threatened your fellow workers.

A: . . . then refer to your resume to select an accomplishment related to the particular situation. If it is a situation you have never encountered, you may respond by saying so and going on to describe your best judgment on how to handle the situation professionally and to ensure the interests of the company are protected. If it is a situation that should not be handled independently, be sure to include consultation with the appropriate staff. Remember team work in organizations is especially important in today's complex work environment. On the other hand, do not suggest that you would avoid or shirk taking responsibility for the situation when appropriate.

WORK UP ANSWERS TO THESE TOUGH QUESTIONS

Answers from Your Resume

In keeping with our concept of linkage, remember that many answers to the tough questions come from your resume, just as we discovered with situational questions. Examples of other common questions for which your responses can be crafted from your accomplishments include:

Q30: How have you increased sales and profits? How have you helped reduce costs?

A: Most people talk about broad, generalized responsibilities that mean nothing to the interviewer, who is looking for timely, specific references to what you have actually done in terms that relate to what the company interviewing you needs. You should state specific accomplishments related to sales and profits referring to dollars, percentages, market and industry growth. Specify results not only for your company, but also for your department, section, or group. Show how you met or exceeded budgets or profit goals. For example, "I restructured the international sales and distribution organization to effectively meet the demands of the changing competitive environment, resulting in a 14 percent gain in market share."

Q31: What are your five most significant accomplishments?

A: Your resume should state in priority order what your five most important accomplishments on your most recent job have been. State dollars, numbers, specific contributions to your job and your company. For example, "I managed salesmen and developed short and long range sales objectives for yearly sales of $60 to $70 million." "I increased efficiency by 10 percent by developing a computerized retrieval system." "I reduced administrative costs by 3 percent, by negotiating the lowest costs for suppliers."

Q32: How have you changed your job?

A: Here you want to state how you have improved, expanded, enriched, or enlarged your job to make a greater contribution to the company. Tell how you expanded your job description, set additional goals for success, brought new members into your department who made contributions to the company. Perhaps you brought in new technology, or brought in people with state-of-the-art knowledge who improved the technology or discovered new and innovative ways of doing things. Perhaps you looked at the competition and did everything you could to meet it today, tomorrow, and in the future. Or you developed ways of improving departmental procedures or expanded your responsibilities and skills.

Q33: Are you a leader? Describe situations.

A: Go through your accomplishments in priority order. Give specific leadership examples. "I conceived, researched, and supervised the introduction of a new product line which increased productivity of our department by 15 percent." In addition, give examples from your civic or professional associations, or refer to leadership roles in the military.

Q34: What was your greatest achievement in your most recent position?

A: Select your single greatest accomplishment in your most current position. Move from there to your second and third most important accomplishments, as required by the interviewer. In addition, you may also talk about a civic or association accomplishment, or about a professional accomplishment that shows your abilities. "On my own time, I have coordinated the Tenneco marathon." "I contribute personal time to the Boy Scouts." An answer like this shows that you are concerned about your community as well as your company.

Q35: In what ways can you make a contribution to our company?

A: Referring to your accomplishments and skills, outline a few examples. "As you can see from my technical skills, I bring capabilities in a number of software and hardware platforms. Not only can I perform independently in these areas, I can also help others in the department to enhance their skills."

Q36: How long would it take for you to make a contribution?

A: Your answer should be, "Immediately. I'll meet with all the key people and do a needs analysis," or "My proficiency in the areas you've outlined are such that I can contribute immediately."

Q37: What problems have you identified in your last job?

A: Respond with problems you have resolved stating how they were identified and resolved. Consider issues such as: was there a job description; were goals set for success in the job; was it a growth job; was it too easy; did it challenge you; did it lead to career growth; did you learn new and innovative approaches, techniques, ideas?

Following are additional questions with answers from your resume:

Q38: In your present job, what problems have you identified that were previously overlooked?

Q39: How large a budget have you been responsible for?

Q40: How many people did you supervise?

Q41: What are some of the most important lessons you have learned in your job?

Q42: Describe some situations in which your efforts have been praised?

Q43: What are the most important contributions you have made to your present employer?

Q44: What is your greatest potential for contributing to our company?

Q45: Why do you feel you have top management potential?

Q46: Describe some situations in which you have used initiative in your professional life.

Answers from Your Self-Assessment

The self-assessment in Chapter 1 is designed not only to assist in establishing your goals, but consistent with linkage, can be used in crafting powerful responses to interview questions.

Q47: Describe your ideal working environment.

A: Based on your style, you can answer this question from a number of perspectives. "The ideal environment is one in which . . . there is mutual trust; people feel free to communicate with each other; people are free to make mistakes as long as they don't repeat the mistakes; people are allowed to take risks in order to stretch themselves and do bigger and better things; people are trusted, respected, and given the opportunity to learn, to grow, and to achieve," or "The ideal working environment is one in which individual and team goals are set and met, and people are rewarded for stretching, growing, and achieving those goals." Or, "In the ideal environment, there is a career plan and a succession plan. People know where they are, where they are going, and how they are going to get there. People are given the opportunity to know where they are on their career path, and how they can improve and become better contributors."

Q48:   What are your goals?

A: Answer the question in a job-related fashion. If you say your goal is to be an Olympic runner, your interviewer may be thinking, "Runners come in late, run during lunch, and leave early to get to practice." The key here is to show that what you have done in your early career and more recent past has all led you inexorably to this company and this interview. Do not mention specific salary goals or job titles. "My future goal, based on all my past experience, is to become an excellent employee in the organization. I want to become all I can be."

Q49:   What are your five-year goals?

A: The key here is to make generic statements that do not threaten the interviewer. "I see myself as moving into the strategic planning area." "I see myself as continuing to grow in the engineering field. I hope that I might one day succeed in this company in an executive management position." Education, too, is a safe, non-threatening goal: "My objective is to get an MBA," "My objective is to cross train into the information systems field." Keep your answers growth oriented, and related to the goals of the company. Emphasize that you expect to earn any positions you may be promoted to in the future.

Following are additional questions with answers from your assessment:

Q50:   What do you look for in a job?

Q51:   What is your management style?

Q52:   What position do you expect in five years?

Q53:   How would you describe your personality?

Q54: What are your long-range (five-year plus) objectives?

Q55: What are you doing to reach these objectives?

Q56: What career options do you have at the moment?

Q57: What are some of the new goals you have recently established?

Q58: What are your most important concerns when seeking a position?

Q59 What are five unique features about you that contribute to your success?

Q60: How would you describe success? According to your description, how successful have you been so far?

Answers from Your Research on the Company

Doing your homework on the company with which you are interviewing can make or break the offer. You should revise your answers to these questions for each company with which you interview. In each question, consider some of the alternative issues to which you may respond in your answer, such as climate, culture and style of management.

Q61: What do you know about this company?

Q62: Why would you like to work for this company?

Q63: What does it take to be successful in a company like this?

A: Would you be happy working here? Do you know any people who work here? Have they told you about the company? Is your background appropriate; does it fit with the company? Do you understand the company's needs?

These are some additional questions you must answer for yourself prior to your interview. Study the company from every perspective possible: product line, annual sales, number of employees, geophysical locations, etc. Learn all you can in advance and then practice how you will respond to these questions.

Q64: What measures do you use to evaluate a company?

A: Is the company in a downturn or upturn? Is there a hiring freeze? If so, how do you get around it? Have you studied the annual report or read other literature? Is the firm profitable? What is its reputation in the industry? How you answer this question reveals your values and attitudes. Stay positive. Customize your response to the company for which you are interviewing.

Q65: Have you targeted specific companies you would like to join? (If so, list these companies and state the factors that attracted you to them.)

A: Always be prepared to suggest a few companies similar to the company you are interviewing, including competitors since this builds psychological leverage. If you are highly marketable, the company will not want to lose you to a competitor. Be careful, however *not* to reveal names of individuals with whom you are actually interviewing or to disclose any confidential information.

Q66: What position in our company are you applying for? Why?

Q67: What is your philosophy of management?

Q68: Describe your management style.

A: Before answering these questions, you will want to *determine the style of the company* with which you are interviewing and answer accordingly. Is the philosophy of the department consistent with the philosophy of the company? Do your homework using your network and if possible, talk to the person who had the job before you. In a progressive environment, your answer should be, "I believe in participative management, in common goal setting, in creating an environment of excellence in which people feel good about their contributions to the company, in which people want to achieve and succeed and move on to bigger and better things." Once again, practice your responses and make sure you score points.

Answers from Research on the Job Function

Q69: What are the frontier or leading issues in your field?

A: The interviewer is really asking if you've done your homework. Are you reading; are you staying current; are you in tune with what's coming down the pike? Are you aware; are you innovative; are you addressing state-of-the-art issues?

An interviewer who is a long range thinker will typically ask broad, open ended questions like this. Match your response to the style of the interviewer. Study the office, the secretary, the desk. Study the environment and shape your answers to fit the interviewer.

Answers from Research on the Industry

There is a *hidden agenda* for all the questions dealing with the industry. The interviewer is really asking if you have done your research. Is what you know consistent with the industry needs?

Q70: Why are you interested in this industry?

Q71: What kind of research have you done on this industry?

Q72: What in your opinion is the biggest problem in the industry?

Q73: What is the future of this industry? Short term/long term?

Q74: Where in your opinion is the greatest growth potential?

Q75: Where is the industry weakest?

Q76: How do you view the competition in this industry?

Q77: What do you consider to be the most important skill necessary to achieve success in this industry?

Q78: What important trends do you see in this industry?

A: Are you exploring the same industry that you are currently in? If so, what do you know about the industry? If not, what do you need to learn about the industry? Are there state-of-the-art issues? Is it a high-growth industry, a stable industry, a mature industry, a new industry? Does it have lots of ups and downs?

Management Style Questions

You probably have observed that the management style question has already appeared under the "Answers from Your Research on the Company" and

"Answers from Your Self-Assessment" sections. This is a complex issue that is very important to companies. Even if you are an excellent manager, responding to questions on how and why you perform managerial or supervisory responsibilities in certain ways requires thought and preparation. Here are a few questions to assist you in your preparation.

Q79: What do your subordinates think of you?

A: Do you get along with your subordinates? What is your leadership style? Are there letters of reference from your subordinates; if not, why not? Have you done appraisals on them? Have you had counseling sessions with them? Do you set team and department goals? Would they speak highly of you if asked? Are you a motivator? Do you create a climate of excellence? Do you bring out the best in people? Respond with all positives.

Q80: What kind of relationship should exist between managers and those reporting to them?

A: Find out what kind of environment exists in the company before answering the question. Is it authoritative, participative, old school, or new school? Some possible responses are:
       "A manager should seek to create a climate in which people get along, work well together and set specific team goals for the department. The climate should be one that is non-argumentative—one in which there is no jealousy and in which people strive toward individual goals that do not conflict in order to meet overall goals."
       "There should be mutual respect between managers and the people reporting to them. Subordinates should feel that the boss is willing to allow them to grow and set stretching goals, to train and learn, to have the opportunity to be the best they can on the job."

Q81: What qualities must a successful manager have?

Q82: Why are you a good manager?

A: "Successful managers must be easy to talk to, easy to relate to, and easy to communicate with. They must be honest, trusting, and respectful of their superiors, peers, and subordinates; they must be able to level with people regarding their strengths and their weaknesses and how those people need to improve; they must be willing to allow the time, energy, and money to train them; they must find the time to coach, counsel, and critique their subordinates, to help them be the best that they can be. Following these tenets is what has made me a successful manager."

Q83: What is the most difficult task of a manager?

A: "Having to terminate people." That's a neutral and positive response, much like blaming the economy. Go into the details: make sure that you don't give the impression that you're not willing to terminate people when necessary. "I understand the importance of the four-step corrective discipline process: oral warning, written warning, suspension, termination. I walk through all four steps, give the employee the benefit of the doubt; counsel, set goals, and give the employee time to improve; only as a last resort do I terminate the employee. And even with all that preparation, it's still not easy."

Another excellent response, "The most difficult task is managing in an uncontrollable situation, in an environment where I don't have control of budget, opportunities, product, service, resources or managing in a situation where possibilities for career growth for my subordinates just aren't there."

Q84: What do you look for when you hire people?

A: The trick here is not only to focus on technical skills, but on values and work ethics that are consistent with the organization. "I look for people who are one-percenters, team players, receptive to learning, open to constructive criticism, loyal, dedicated, and committed to excellence. I look for people who are willing to work harder, smarter, and longer to succeed." Notice the halo effect: The qualities you say you are looking for are presumed to be qualities that you also possess.

Q85: Have you fired anyone? How did you handle it?

A: If yes, "I handled it through the corrective discipline process: oral warning, written warning, suspension, termination—with counseling, goals, and an opportunity for the individual to improve at each step." Answer the question in terms of what you know an arbitrator will be looking for: "I documented all conversations, goals, and counseling sessions. I was firm, fair, and consistent. I handled it professionally." If you have never fired anyone, answer "No, but if I had to, I would walk the individual through the corrective discipline process."

Tough Questions too Tough to Categorize

Some questions defy categorization. Some are off the wall, some are curve balls, but your thorough preparation will ensure your ability to respond like a pro, scoring points as you master every salvo the interviewer can throw your way. Consider your positive responses to these challenges:

Q86: What are some important lessons you've learned?

A: "I have learned to expand my horizons, to strive to become 1 percent better every single day."

Q87: Will you be out for your boss's job?

A: Make sure you do not threaten the potential boss in any way. When asked what you are looking for in terms of future growth, never give a title, and never give a salary. Your response should be in general terms, such as, "No—I am interested in doing the very best job I possibly can in the position I'm interviewing for, and I'm confident that the company will reward me for it."

Q88: What do you like most about your current job?

A: Select an area of responsibility you now feel is of particular value for the position or company and expand on it as needed.

Q89: What do you like least about your current job?

A: "What I like least about my job is having to watch employees be terminated."

Q90: Why did you accept each of the positions listed on your resume?

A: Be sure your response is positive and focus on the learning or growth potential of each position. In addition, transition your responses by explaining promotional opportunities whenever possible.

Q91: Why haven't you found a new position before now?

A: If you have been seeking employment for an extended period, you should be prepared to share contract, project or consulting assignment, education, training or other meaningful activities in response to the question. Family or personal commitments can also be an acceptable reason, but suggesting that you preferred to "bum it" for six months is not an acceptable explanation for an employer.

Q92: Would you object to working for a woman?

A: You may respond, "Whether male or female, I respect management and their authority." If you are a man, do not say something flip such as, "Of course not. I love women!" *Do not joke* in response to this question. Companies take this question very seriously.

Compensation and Negotiation Questions

The key to successful negotiation is to delay it until you have an offer. For this reason it is important to handle early questions on compensation carefully. Also, never bring up the compensation question first—wait for the interviewer to do so. Following are typical compensation questions that the interviewer will ask early to get you to "tip your hand."

Q93: How much do you expect to make? or
       What salary are you looking for?

A: Deflect early and general compensation questions when possible until later in the interview: "That is a question I would be glad to answer once we've had an opportunity to discuss my capabilities and the position requirements. As you can see from my resume I've had extensive experience in . . . " or "I'm open to negotiation based on the position responsibilities." When you do respond with numbers, always give your range based on your research. To answer the compensation question, it is critical to do your research on salary norms in your industry, city, company, and function. Then give a range, "Based on my research, my salary requirements are in the $75,000 to $185,000 range." or "My total compensation package is in the $100K+ range." The latter approach accounts for salary, bonuses, profit sharing, and other benefits.

Q94: What was your salary in your last position?

A: If you are asked directly "What were you paid in the last position," tell them honestly and directly. Then follow with an explanation of your value and your required compensation range for the position for which you are interviewing. However, do not volunteer your previous salary in answer to a general question on your salary requirements or what you are looking for in the way of compensation.

       Call the company before your interview and talk to a peer to get the range. You need not ask the individual exactly what he is making—ask, "What is the range of your position?" Often, he will tell you exactly what he is making as a minimum. This is confidential information;

during your job interview, do not reveal your source. The bottom of your range should be what you are currently making as a minimum. Obviously, the salary you want is at the top of your range; but if you do have to negotiate down, you haven't lost anything. The exception to this rule would be if you are changing industries, changing locations, or making a trade-off due to geographical preferences. You may be moving from a low growth to a high growth company, and may be willing to take less money now for future growth opportunities, or opportunities to train on the job or go back to school. The key point here is that you *must* plan in advance what you are going to say and *stick to your answer*.

Q95:   Why aren't you earning more at your age?

A: "I don't consider age a primary factor in determining value or job satisfaction since enjoying my job is very important to me and the company."

Q96:   What do you feel this position should pay?

A: "My research suggests a range of $50,000 to $60,000," or if the position has not been well defined, "I'd like to learn more about the company's needs before we discuss compensation."

Q97:   What is the minimum you will accept?

Q98:   How much money do you need to make?

A: You're not interested in minimums—never give a figure less than your last compensation and once again state your required range.

See Chapter 9 for more on negotiating.

If you're like most people, you've skimmed over these questions. But be certain—now or sometime before you face an interviewer—to think through and write out appropriate answers to each of them. Only then will you be prepared for an interview. Although it's a long list, don't feel overwhelmed; one answer might cover four or five different questions.

BUILD YOUR SELF-CONFIDENCE

Ironically, all the time and effort you invest in prepping for these questions will have an implicit reward even more significant than your acquired ability to respond adroitly at every turn. When you've built a series of answers that links with your resume and letters of reference, you will be fully prepared. That preparation builds confidence, and confidence builds excellence under pressure. You will send nonverbal signals to the employer that you're a pro, ready for anything they can throw at you in the interview. We call this the positive expectation of success. Your nonverbal communication, dress, grooming, and confidence levels will close the credibility gap within fifteen to twenty seconds of the interview opening. Everyone walks in with this credibility gap. If you don't close it within a few seconds, you'll be struggling uphill for the entire session. Our clients close it. They know that they belong there; they know that they can perform in the interview. They expect to succeed.

There's more to successful interviewing than having all the right answers to the tough questions. Consider the following cautions and recommendations.

The Secretary

Your relationship with the employer's secretary in the interview process is as important as it was during your cold-calling. Treat her with courtesy, use her name, and ask her a few questions if there's time and opportunity before the interview. In many offices, the secretary is the first person an employer will ask for feedback following an interview. Make sure that she's on your side.

Affirmative Delays

We think one of our tiniest little tricks helps our clients beyond measure in interview situations. We all know that it helps you respond better to any question if you delay for a moment before answering. But in an interview, any lengthy pause can be destructive. It suggests lack of preparation on your part, and it allows negative energy to build in the room. So take your time to gather thoughts for an answer, but do it this way: As soon as the interviewer completes his question, affirm it but do not repeat it! For example, if you are asked to list your five greatest strengths, you immediately say, "Yes, Mr. Johnson, I'd be happy to." Then you can take a couple of seconds to get your brain in gear. But to the listener, you appear to be quick, bright, prepared, ready to go in any direction immediately. This is a key element in maintaining psychological leverage in the interview. And it's really very simple to accomplish.

Grooming and Dress

Much of our job search advice is predicated on the approach of custom-designing for each company's situation. So it is with grooming. Generally, be conservative, neat, clean, and understated. If there's a choice, always go for the more muted color, the more simple pattern. But dress differently for an interview on site at a chemical plant than you would in a bank or brokerage house. We suggest that you visit a day in advance of the interview to determine corporate culture, workstyle, and dress code. Every place has a dress code—

most often it's unwritten, but it's always there. When in doubt, dress professionally and conservatively.

Be Punctual, but Don't Be too Early

Don't show up 30 minutes in advance of your appointment. That suggests that you're a rookie who is desperate to get this job or that you have nothing else to do. Tardiness is *always* inexcusable, however, so here's our original proposition for interview punctuality: Arrive at the location 15 or 20 minutes in advance, and determine exactly where the interviewer is located and how long it's likely to take to get through the waiting area. (Is it a private secretary's office or a department full of visitors you might have to wait in line behind?) Having determined that, go to a coffee bar and spend a few minutes in last-minute preparation. Part of this preparation is a two-minute psychological drill. Tell yourself that you're the best candidate for the job because you've done your homework. You look right, you'll act right, and you feel good about yourself and about why you're there. Assert to yourself that you'll walk in with confidence. Then proceed to the interviewer's office. Time your arrival three or four minutes in advance of the appointment so that you'll be announced right on time. That's sharp and impressive. Again, the psychological leverage is evident. You've protected your interests by getting there in plenty of time to make the appointment. You've arrived on site only minutes ahead of time, yet you're calm, cool, collected, and ready.

INTERVIEW FORMATS

The traditional one-on-one interview continues to be the most prevalent format for interviewing in companies. However, panel or group interviews are becoming more common for selection of candidates at all levels in the organization. The flattening of the organization, the prevalence of a team approach to work, and concern over misrepresentation during an interview are reasons for this trend. In addition, on out-of-town interviews, companies will often save time in scheduling candidate meetings by using the panel approach. The dynamics of the group interview are more complex and can be more stressful than a one-on-one interview, making interview preparation even more critical to success. When an interview is arranged, be sure to ask who will be present, their titles and working relationships. This information will enable you to do some research on the interviewers. However, be prepared for changes in the interviewers and schedule for progressive interviews.

Another approach companies are using is a series of interviews including human resources, the immediate boss, team members and even subordinates, culminating with the department head or president. After a series of interviews, the interviewers will get together to compare notes—the consistency of your responses is crucial. Do not minimize the influence of any one interviewer because of level or relationship to the position for which you are interviewing.

Particularly common on university campuses is the video conference interview. Companies save on recruiting costs and have access to a broader number of campuses through this remote interviewing technique. As equipment becomes more accessible, video interviewing will become more common and will be used for recruiting at all levels when candidates are geographically dispersed. Using video to practice interview is an excellent technique for improving your interviewing skills and presentations in any situation, but is particularly important if you are asked to interview officially by video conference. Without practice, you will likely feel awkward and distracted during the interview.

Regardless of the interview format, preparation is the key to gaining the offer. Build your psychological leverage by expecting the unexpected, and preparing for every possibility.

KNOW YOUR INTERVIEWER

Let us offer a word of caution before we proceed. If you think there's enough material thus far to choke an army mule—or a job campaigner new to the task—stop now and begin digesting. Be sure that you have the basics down pat, because what follows is equivalent to a graduate course in interviewing.

Part of the process of a true commitment to excellence in interviewing is preparing and learning not only about yourself and the company but also about personality types of interviewers. If you can learn to read the person across the desk—how he lives, works, and thinks—you're really flirting with the stratosphere in the world of job search. There are four basic types:

- *The long-range planner:* Typically, this person, also known as the intuitor, is an economist, a forecaster, or occasionally a market or business developer. His job is to plan three to five years in advance, so that's how he thinks and talks. Your answers should focus on the big picture—where technology will take this industry in the next decade, how you picture yourself in that situation, and so forth.

- *The analytical, task-oriented type:* This very fact-oriented type of person is also called the thinker. Typically, the thinker is very neat, conservative, and well organized. Never use the word *about* with this person—deal in specifics, not generalities. If there are numbers in your resume, be prepared to defend them in detail. This person will tend to be very neat and controlled and immaculate in dress.

• *The people person:* This much more informal, more colorfully dressed interviewer is also called the feeler. Feelers are interested not so much in your analytical powers or skill levels but in whether you'll be a good fit for the company and the team. You're much more likely to be offered a cup of coffee, or even lunch, during the interview with this person.

• *The time-conscious, reactive type:* This person's environment is full of ringing phones and other interruptions. Also known as the senser, this individual really won't have time to allow you to create a full portrayal of your personality, skills, and background. Typically, the senser will have coat-off, sleeves rolled-up, and be harried. Always under the gun, caught up in the activity trap, with never enough people, never enough time, the senser will be looking for your ability to get things done quickly. The senser needs a doer—someone who doesn't waste time and gets right to the point.

This is typically a highly complex and sophisticated analysis, so don't deal with it unless you're ready. But if you are, you'll be able to structure your responses to mesh with the corporate style and the interviewer's frame of reference.

GO FOR THE OFFER

As we've mentioned before, we're not saying that you are going after a job during this stage of the interview. You're going all out for the *offer.* Then you will evaluate this company against the other offers you generate. If the environment is alien to you, obviously you may take another position. We're training you to survive in any interviewing situation, not push you into a corporate setting in which you can't cope and that you don't like.

THE INTERVIEW CLOSE

Be prepared to respond to a typical closing interview question:

Q99: Why should I hire you?

A: "You should hire me because my entire professional experience to this point has prepared me for this job. I've gone to school, received my education, and worked hard at determining the needs of the job, department, and company. As my resume suggests, my accomplishments speak to each of those needs, and I'm here because I am the best-qualified individual for the position. I will do an excellent job for you."

And the interviewer's possible finale:

Q100: How long will you stay with our company?

A: Your response should resound with dedication, "For the rest of my career" or "as long as I can contribute successfully to the company's goals."

Finally, at the close of the interview, in order to show the maximum amount of interest in both the job and the company, ask three questions:

1. Where do you see this job in three to five years?
2. Where do you see the company in three to five years?
3. And where can I get more information?

That's all. We don't recommend that you ask a lot of questions during the interview since it distracts interviewers from their agendas.

Avoid the common end-of-interview faux pas of asking for the job. This is amateurish and can have the opposite effect you expect! Do let the interviewer know your interest in and excitement about the position and the company. As you depart the interview, thank the interviewer(s) for their time and the opportunity to interview. Be sure to get their business cards and ask what their time frame for the selection process is so you can appropriately follow up.

THE THANK YOU LETTER

After the interview, as soon as possible write down notes about the interview, the position and company. Then craft a thank you letter to send out no later than the next day. The letter should reinforce important issues which were discussed and cover any areas you feel are important to getting the offer which were not covered. If research is needed to address these adequately, complete it as soon as possible. Timeliness of thank you letters is as important as their professionalism. Be sure to include all of your interviewers in the thank you letter either by separately addressed letters or by copying interviewers on your letter to the hiring authority. In order to do this effectively, it is important to get business cards of all your interviewers or write down their names and titles accurately. Exhibit 8.2 presents a typical thank you letter.

EXHIBIT 8.2
Thank You Letter

NAME
Address
City, State Zip Code
Office Phone Number
Home Phone Number

August 29, 199–

Mr. Michael Hearst
Vice President, Marketing
Energy Trading Corporation
Post Office Box
Houston, Texas 77088

Dear Michael:

It was certainly my pleasure to meet you today. The more I learn about Energy Trading, the more impressed I am. It is obvious that Energy Trading is striving for excellence in the position of Manager of the Southeast Region.

I am confident that my skills and experience are an excellent match with Energy Trading's needs. Initial contributions would come in the following areas:

- Expand the customer base of Energy Trading by offering a full range of service to customers. This would include spot and term proposals, taking advantage of gas futures, options and derivative products to meet the customer's pricing needs without exposing the company to risk.

- Create full market presence by exploring all supply options, taking advantage of transportation discounts and evaluating possible additional opportunities via split connections with alternate pipelines.

- Establish solid long-term relationships with customers by meeting their needs and solving problems quickly and efficiently.

- Continually search the market for new and profitable opportunities which will separate Energy Trading from all other trading companies.

I look forward to further discussions with you in the near future. If you have any questions or require additional information, please do not hesitate to call.

Sincerely,

Name

One of the most dynamic and convincing follow up letters to an interview is one we custom designed years ago and is called the *requirements/qualifications comparison* letter as demonstrated in Exhibit 8.3. Our clients have successfully used this strategy hundreds of times to win the offer and build their negotiating leverage. Potential employers are impressed by the comprehensiveness of this approach since it thoroughly states the requirements of the job much as a job description does. In many cases it reveals contributions the candidate can make which the interviewer had not considered. The thought and initiative that goes into preparing an excellent requirements/qualifications comparison letter alone can often make the difference in receiving the offer or not.

In addition to writing the thank you letter, if your references were provided to the interviewer, be sure to call each reference to apprise them of a potential call and to provide them with some background on the position. Here's an example of why you must prep your references:

> Sherry, having completed her interview and been asked for references, felt great about her chances for an offer. Unfortunately, she made two avoidable errors in the process—she failed to ask for the interviewer's business card, which made sending the follow-up letter difficult, and she did not call her references to prepare them. Later she learned that one of her references, without thinking about the consequences, had indicated to the interviewer her surprise that Sherry was being considered for the position since it was in a function and industry which was different from Sherry's experience. Sherry didn't get the offer.

Be sure too, to follow up by phone after the interview. Call within the suggested time, but if a return call is not immediate, try again within a couple of days. Waiting for a response can be frustrating, but keep in mind that the interviewer may have other priorities and the timing of the selection process often changes. In any case, never sit idle waiting for an offer! Continue networking and interviewing for other positions. Even if you get the offer, in keeping with linkage, you will want to bring as many offers to the table as possible before making a decision.

SOME LAST WORDS ON INTERVIEWING

Most Frequent Complaints about Interviewees

- Poor communication—talks too little, talks too much, rambles, is evasive, is nervous.

EXHIBIT 8.3
Requirements/Qualifications Letter

NAME
Address
City, State Zip
Office #
Home #

Date

Mr. Thomas W. Anderson
President
T.W. Anderson and Company, Inc.
P.O. Box
San Diego, CA 91718

Dear Tom:

I would like to take this opportunity to thank you for meeting with me on August 26th. The Institute's Executive Director position is very interesting to me, and talking about the position's responsibilities on a first-hand basis with you certainly reinforced that perception. Based on our conversation and the research that I have conducted into the plastics industry, I am absolutely confident that I can make a meaningful contribution to the industry as the Executive Director of the Institute.

After careful and thoughtful reflection on our conversation, I would like to propose that the committee consider the following points with respect to my background and qualifications for this position:

Your Requirements:	My Qualifications:
• Develop and implement the Executive Board approved programs for broadening the opportunities for the effective use of thermoplastic piping. Develop and recommend programs and budgets to meet the Institute's goals.	• Three years experience in strategic planning and implementing business plans. Full responsibility for an engineering compounds business unit, with staff budgets exceeding $300,000 per year.
• Manage the development and publication of technical and marketing literature. Manage technical, advertising and publicity programs.	• Over ten years experience developing technical and marketing literature, and publicity and market development programs.
• Manage the affairs of the Institute's Hydrostatic Stress Board, including its program for developing and listing recommended hydrostatic strengths of commercially available thermoplastic materials.	• Three years experience as a member of the Institute's Hydrostatic Stress Board and as a member of the Extrapolations Test Method development committee.
• Act as spokesperson for the Institute before code, standards, regulatory, trade and industrial groups, the public, the media, and outside organizations.	• Over twelve years experience as a company representative to the Institute, ASTM, NSF, FDA, UL, CSA, AGA, GRI, USP and various other industry and regulatory organizations.
• Develop and implement membership recruitment programs.	• Three years experience as membership chairman of the South Texas section of The Plastics Association (TPA) developing and implementing membership recruiting programs. Received TPA award for greatest membership growth for a large section in 1996.

EXHIBIT 8.3
(Continued)

- Supervise and give direction to staff: Establish work objectives for staff; ensure compliance to relevant TPA policies and procedures; assist and guide staff training and development; and periodically evaluate staff performance. Provide assistance and direction to the Institute operating units, committees, and working groups.

- Provide excellent customer service to members, people requesting information and other TPA staff. Interface with all the Institute/TPA staff and the Institute members; regulators (code and standard writing bodies); trade and industrial groups; manufacturers of piping materials and additives; engineers and consultants; other pipe associations and associations representing user interests; professional organizations; government organizations; and the public.

- College degree, preferably in a technical discipline. Graduate degree preferred.

- Special knowledge and skills: Understanding and appreciation of standards and code development. Demonstrated competence in effectively communicating with technical interests, special interest groups, industry members, the media, and the public. Excellent written and verbal communication skills. Effective staffing ability, conceptual (strategic) thinking, ability to delegate, enthusiasm for achieving objectives, tenacity of purpose, empathy and tact but firmness of purpose in dealing with and responding to adverse interests, and avoidance of overly ambitious or political behavior. Ability to work on a variety of projects simultaneously.

- Over six years management experience, with up to eight direct reports. Over thirteen years experience in working with task forces and quality teams. Extensive training in total quality management, team building and team facilitation.

- Over thirteen years experience in product development, technical service, marketing and sales areas where responsiveness to customer inquiries and interests was always top priority. Extensive experience in dealing with the media during the past three years while implementing publicity press releases, programs and trade show participation.

- BS in Chemistry and a PhD in Chemistry. 13 years experience in thermoplastics.

- These requirements reflect on my personality and character traits and can best be addressed through my references. Copies of my reference letters have been attached for review by the committee.

In summary, my background and experience presents the committee with a candidate for this position who can provide both technical and marketing leadership for the Institute and industry. Given this scenario, the committee may consider reducing the Institute's engineering management position in scope and responsibilities while expanding the executive director position in scope and responsibilities to fit my background and experiences and to take advantage of my talents and abilities.

Tom, I am looking forward to meeting with the entire search committee on September 16th at your headquarters. If you have any questions in the interim, please call me at the above number.

Sincerely,

NAME

- Poor preparation—asks no questions, has no information about company.
- Vague interests—lacks career goals, is unsure of job goals.
- Unrealistic expectations—is too concerned about salary, is immature, is inflexible.

Most Frequent Complaints about Interviewers

- Poor communication—talks too much, is unclear, rambles, is evasive.
- Poor preparation—didn't read resume, manages time poorly.
- Judgmental attitude—draws conclusions or makes statements that are inaccurate or unfair.
- Negative attitude—spends too much time talking about negative aspects of the job.
- Dumb questions—asks questions that don't relate to the position.

Your preparation and your ability to control the interview will enable you to overcome the weaknesses of a poor interviewer. Don't allow such an interviewer to cause you to lose your psychological edge. Gently lead the interviewer through the points you want to make, without letting on that you are aware of his ineptness. Like playing tennis with a rookie, if you get frustrated by the opponent's bloopers, you can easily throw the match.

Why People Are Hired

- Positive attitude and enthusiasm.
- Good presentation of skills needed by employer for the position.
- Professional in all contacts, including letter, phone call, and face-to-face contact; excellent verbal skills.
- Good rapport with interviewer, including good discussion.
- Past experience that supports qualifications for the opening.
- Provides knowledgeable questions and statements about company and job opening, thus proving commitment to research.
- Professional appearance, including appropriate dress, neat and clean personal grooming, friendly attitude.

Why People Are Rejected

- Bitter attitude based on previous employment experience.
- Limited presentation of skills, and abilities.
- Poor appearance and demeanor.
- Mistakes and misspellings in written correspondence.

- Lack of confidence during interview, including stumbling over answers and not portraying a positive attitude.
- Bad references or no positive references.
- Unqualified for the job or inability to communicate qualifications.

Look carefully at this list and observe that all of the foibles are *controllables* except perhaps the last—qualifications. Even that may be rectified with additional education or experience. The following case is an excellent illustration of how you can position yourself for the offer and success by controlling your presentation, appearance and attitude:

> Terry had been in the workplace for three years after graduation. He lost his computer programming job to a restructuring and also went through a divorce. Only 27, he felt that his whole life was falling apart. His defeatist attitude was reflected in his demeanor, body language and appearance. Long hair added to his disheveled look, even though he was particularly proud of it. He had been looking for a new job for several months with no success. Terry's father was in our program and asked if we could help. We welcomed Terry into the program and within two weeks he was a new man. The process of learning *The Total System* rebuilt his confidence. He began to walk and talk like a true professional. We suggested that a haircut would dramatically change interviewers' perceptions of him even if it had no bearing on his performance. Reluctantly he got a professional cut and amazingly, even his own view of himself was enhanced! Terry began networking and within two weeks had two offers. He placed successfully in record time.

This is just one example of how appearance and attitude affect the ability to market one's capabilities. Terry's talent hadn't changed in one month, but his outlook and marketing skills had. From head to toe, from resume to interviewing skills, he was an employer's dream candidate.

Your interview preparation will ensure that you avoid the points of rejection and emphasize the winning points of acceptance. The ball's in your court, so serve a winner and win the match!

CHAPTER 9

Negotiating the Deal You Want: Get the Money Now

As authors of this book, we have the easy job of teaching you the art of negotiating compensation even though it took us many years to learn and master this art form. To distinguish between interviewing and negotiating, we simply end one chapter and begin another. It's imperative that you, too, make such a clear-cut distinction between interviewing and negotiating in your campaign. Your task, however, won't be nearly so simple as concluding Chapter 8 and launching Chapter 9. Not only is negotiating a tough, complex, demanding proposition—it is, we think, the most difficult of all the steps in campaigning for a job—but it is also so subtle that it takes true discernment to know when to do it, let alone what to do. Of all the facets of looking for a new position, negotiating requires the greatest measure of discipline, preparation, and confidence on your part.

Interviewing usually gets preeminent ranking among the elements of job search. Resumes, networking, telemarketing, and research do nothing more than put your body in front of the hiring authority, with a chance at the job. Certainly, we agree with that. Negotiating compensation is typically considered a part of the interview process, and without question it's the most vital part of that interview. Throughout the pages of this book, we have attempted to instill in you the belief that getting "a" job isn't difficult or particularly noteworthy. We want you to find the "best" job for you. But if you cannot or will not negotiate the best available compensation package, what might have been "the" job may unfortunately turn out to be only "a" job. In fact, you'll probably never even know the possibilities of the position if you're not prepared to take negotiation to the limit.

THE SITUATIONS ARE REVERSED

Now that we've blessed negotiating with such an aura of significance, here's the reason we've separated it from interviewing: Despite the fact that negotiations may occur at the same time and place as your job interview, the interaction between you and the employer changes radically at that point. In fact, it represents a 180-degree position shift. Throughout all the hours of interviewing—in three, four, or five discussions—you have courted the employer with your ability to contribute to the bottom line. You've been selling, selling, selling.

When negotiations begin, the company has been sold. It wants you. Now the question becomes whether it is willing to pay enough to get you. At least, the events should be in that sequence. Don't ever let any discussion of compensation begin until it's clear that the company is making an offer. In some cases, you'll complete the final interview, get the offer, and shake hands on a tentative deal. Then the company will set up a subsequent interview to negotiate your entire compensation package.

In that scenario, the negotiating session will take on an entirely different tone from the employment interviews. Separating the two kinds of sessions, so that both sides can work toward a mutually satisfactory goal, is often best for both job hunter and employer. Unfortunately, job search reflects life, and the best of worlds happens all too infrequently. Consequently, once an offer is made, you'll have to help orchestrate the switch from your sales presentation to negotiations. And you'll have to do that in the heat of the interview. This is where subtlety, discernment, and confidence pay off. This is also why preparation for negotiating compensation is unrivaled in its importance to your successful job search.

One point here—stop and make certain that you buy into our philosophy of negotiating compensation as well as our challenge to you to make it happen. We hope that it's evident to you that this book is about self-help; it is not designed as a "feel-good-no-matter-what-you-do" journal. Our goal is to help your career, to challenge you to work hard enough to assume command of the events of your search. Not surprisingly, our position on negotiating is consistent with that stand. Of course, you can shake hands and smile, taking whatever first offer the company makes. That's safe, easy, and perfectly suited to the standards of slothfulness that dominate the field of job search advice. But we suspect that if you've answered the challenges set forth in this book, negotiating your own compensation package won't be such an imposing roadblock after all.

And negotiating is not reserved just for the manager or executive levels. Regardless of your level or years of experience, you too can negotiate. The following example illustrates this truth:

> Dick had graduated from college only a couple of years prior to losing his job as a computer programmer. Totally dejected and demoralized, Dick sought our help. After following the principles of *The Total System*, Dick succeeded in getting two offers, and a third possible offer. At first he wanted to take the highest offer, already 25% higher than his old job, but with our insistence, he played one against the other, creating psychological leverage and increased each offer. Ultimately, he negotiated a starting salary 40% higher than his last position, and got a signing bonus to top that!

Always remember that the level of compensation with which you begin your new position affects every dollar you'll earn with the company. When you shake hands on $65,000, all your future income will be calculated from that figure. Next year at this time, if the company determines that top achievers will receive a maximum increase of 10 percent, your increase will be $6,500 if you get the $65,000 you are looking for. On the other hand, if you settle for $50,000, your maximum increase just got a $1,500 cut a year in advance. Obviously, that shortfall widens every year you work at this company.

But arithmetic is easy. Negotiating is hard . . . unless you know what you are doing!

You don't just pick $65,000 out of thin air. If that were possible, why not ask for $165,000? The numbers are calculated from your research into the company and the industry—how your skills and experience are normally compensated, plus the demand for them in the current market. Back to the library. Back to the telephones. Without question, the skills required to research this question and then bring the research into action in negotiating are the most complex and require the greatest degree of precision of any you'll utilize in your search. Most important, you're relying greatly on linkage to make the negotiation process work in your favor.

The skills you acquired in the preceding chapters should have that employer leaning forward in his chair, ready to leap at the prospect of adding you to the team. However, if you've merely put on an OK interviewing presentation that convinces the company that you can do the job but nonetheless leaves you grouped with four or five other finalists, you don't have an abundance of negotiating leverage. When you've enhanced your marketability with a dazzling set of interview responses, that employer wants you. Now you're in the catbird seat, ready to negotiate with the power and authority in your corner.

NEGOTIATING COMPENSATION: MONEY FOLLOWS VALUE

Your value is subjective, of course. So your interviewing performance will prove your value to the company—or at least it must convince the employer that you're as valuable as your resume and your compensation expectations promise.

Make certain, though, that you back up your newly won authority and confidence with research and preparation. The proper numbers—$65,000 or whatever—are not based on what you fancy you'd like to earn this year. And most assuredly, you won't learn the right numbers from the interviewer. So you must reactivate all your networking and telemarketing skills to establish a negotiating position. In advance, talk to people with or formerly with the company, people in the industry, trade associations in your profession, as well as competitors and suppliers of the company. With your cold-calling skills, find out what your occupational skills will command today at that company. As much as we've belittled executive search firms, this is an area in which one you trust can help. It can be a source of accurate information about salary trends. At all costs, however, use the search firm for background information only. Do not allow the recruiter to be a surrogate negotiator. You'll lose every time. Obviously, such information has to be elicited subtly; if the search firm thinks that there is no incentive for sharing information, it won't be too open.

Besides talking with people, read. Library sources that can help in your salary research include the Occupational Outlook Handbook, the American Almanac of Jobs and Salaries, and the Salary Guide and Job Outlook. Don't forget periodicals; the best is the Wall Street Journal's National Business Employment Weekly (NBEW). In one issue each quarter, NBEW publishes comprehensive salary survey information by profession and industry. In addition, associations frequently conduct salary surveys.

When you get as much information as you possibly can, don't go in with only one number in your negotiating tool kit. Take the norms for the company and its industry and create a sliding scale of compensation upon which you plan to negotiate. Almost every company in American business—and every wise job hunter—structures compensation around a three-tier sliding scale.

For example, take the $65,000 figure. The company's figure results from a three-tier scale: high, low, mid-point. The high point might be $85,000, the low $60,000, with a mid-point of $70,000–$75,000. The offer,

$65,000, is well below the midpoint on the scale, which is typically where companies like to bring in new employees. If you take the offer, you'll fit nicely into the departmental budget, but you'll be about $5,000 to $10,000 poorer the first year, along with an expanding annual salary shortfall unless you provide a counter offer. You won't have gotten what a person with your skills and experience typically can command in the current marketplace.

Conversely, we're not suggesting that you shoot for the maximum salary on the scale right out of the starting blocks. If you drive such a hard bargain, the employer might leave the table with hard feelings that you held his feet to the fire, that you took advantage of his acute personnel need to bust a budget. In addition, keep in mind that if you hit the top of the scale to start, you have little room for increase in that position. You're boxed immediately, unless you can work your way into more job and more responsibility rather quickly.

So your goal should be to elevate that initial offer—to get into the upper range of the salary scale, but not to max out. When the interviewer mentions $65,000, you can respond with a statement such as, "I sincerely appreciate the offer, and I'm looking forward to working with an excellent company like yours. But based on my research, and how I can significantly contribute to your bottom line, I was looking at a figure in the high $70's." Again, of course, you must have a sound idea of the range of the three-tier salary scale from which the interviewer is negotiating. We can't tell you every word to say, because you must develop your own style. Moreover, your responses and statements will vary, depending on the personality and style of the interviewer. So scripting a conversation is meaningless. We know what works for us—you must learn what works for you. Plan that individually—but do commit now to the time and effort necessary to research and learn the scale. Then react to the first offer with a confident and professional transition into the negotiations.

Part of the negotiating process is identifying exactly what you are to do in the new company. One of the best ways to obtain the right job for yourself is to tailor it to your specifications! For example, when you're discussing a position with a firm during a sequence of interviews, you may custom-design a job description for the position based on how you perceive the company's needs. Of course, you would want to find out whether a job description already exists, but it is not unusual—even in major corporations—for there to be no job descriptions. Consider this example:

> In writing such a job description, Donna Holmes was able to create her "ideal job." She first presented it to Jim, the executive who was moving into a different division and whose job was available. Jim acknowledged

the accuracy of the description and was impressed. Donna then presented the description to her prospective boss, who responded so favorably that he even added some responsibilities that enhanced the position.

It should be pointed out that Donna was wise not to assume that Jim, the executive who was leaving, would pass the description on to his boss. Had Donna not taken the initiative to do so herself, it would not have become significant in the negotiations. In this case, Donna was offered not only a job, but the precise position she had custom-designed. In addition, by clarifying the responsibilities and authority of the position, Donna was able to increase the initial salary offered on the basis of the expanded scope of the job.

Never—*never*—meekly accept the first dollar figure offered. And always ask for the offer in writing. Similarly, do not accept a job offer on the spot unless the offer exceeds your wildest expectations and they must have your answer immediately. If the employer presses you, simply say that you must discuss the offer with your family or that you're evaluating several other offers from excellent companies like theirs (but never reveal who the other firms are). Offer to get back in touch as soon as possible and to let them know where you are in the decision-making process at that time. If an answer is required sooner, be flexible, of course, all the way down to a twenty-four-hour evaluation period. But under no circumstances (other than the one previously mentioned) should you be coerced into saying yes on the spot. Believe us, an interviewer who won't sit still for a twenty-four-hour consideration period may want you out of the marketplace where competitors can court you. Your decision time may be just the leverage you need to up the ante!

Which brings us back to the money. If you don't get it now, when your armor is spotless, when do you suppose you'll get it? The company wants you on the team, so this is your best chance—possibly your only chance—to negotiate your best deal, perhaps to transform "a" job into "the" job. And consider, if you don't get a salary commensurate with your skills and experience, you're more than just limiting income in the short range. Conceivably, you are retarding the progress of your career tomorrow and on over the horizon. Unless you have a sure long-range benefit in sight, a cut in salary will hurt you—and badly.

Are there exceptions? Of course—acceptable trade-offs for a substantially reduced salary include:

- A chance to run a business (less money but more power)
- A highly visible job, perhaps one in the national or industry spotlight

- A chance to join the start-up team of a hot new company (short-range loss for long-term gain)
- A radical career change
- A chance to leave a second-rate company to join an industry leader
- A chance to leave a declining industry that has built up a grossly overinflated salary structure during its boom years (for example, the oil and gas industry or the steel and auto industries)
- Extreme personal circumstances that dictate a geographic preference (for example, if your child has a chronic illness, and Armpit, Wyoming, has the only treatment facility in the nation, then it's Armpit, Wyoming, at almost any salary)

If you're preparing to accept a drastic salary reduction for any reason not listed, think hard. It's your career, your life—but you're making mistakes in interviewing and negotiating. And you're about to make a salary mistake that could hurt you for years into the future and from which your career may never recover. If you're rationalizing otherwise, you're blowing smoke on your own career. Go after the compensation that you're worth. We're not suggesting that you're there for a holdup, but don't settle for a dollar figure that is so low that it could cripple your career's progress.

One caution: You must realize that compensation encompasses a great deal more than salary. There are other, often better, ways than dollars on a paycheck to achieve your compensation goals. Consider these options, which can increase the value of your compensation package:

- *Benefits:* Standards here include health, dental, life, and disability insurance; retirement, pension, and deferred compensation plans; vacation and holidays; professional association fees; and perhaps educational and travel reimbursement. If your salary falls short, how about negotiating for a car? Credit cards? Stock options? Signing or performance bonuses? Relocation expenses?

- *Performance reviews:* Schedules are usually well established for employee performance evaluations. If you can't get the money on your initial agreement, how about an earlier-than-prescribed review of your performance on the job? (Just be sure that you get it in writing!)

- *Promotions:* Examine the firm's policy on promotions, and attempt to agree on a time table for when you can expect to move to a higher position. (This is another short-term loss for a long-term gain.)

- *Executive perks:* Another way to maintain your standard of living and your total compensation without cash is to negotiate perks, such as membership in health clubs and leisure facilities; discounts or business reimbursements on personal travel; tax, financial, and legal advice; publication incentives; and matching gifts.

Exhibits 9.1 and 9.2 provide employee benefit and relocation checklists to help you formulate a compensation package that meets your needs. With your written offer in hand, you can utilize these forms to develop your counter offer.

Our point is that everything is negotiable. This doesn't mean that you'll be successful on every item. But it means that whatever the company can do to increase the total value of your compensation is fair game to be placed on the table. For instance, benefits can dramatically affect how you come out financially. Smaller organizations may provide fewer benefits than major corporations. Here's an example of how you can use that to your advantage in negotiating:

> Kent Wilson recently moved from a large to a small organization. In negotiating his compensation, Kent was able to gain a 17 percent increase over his former salary because he carefully compared benefits and presented the differences to his new employer. On the basis of Kent's analysis, the new employer adjusted his initial offer to give Kent a total package that was substantially better than he had in his previous position.

Never assume "I can't get that" or "They have a policy against that." Remember, your challenge in the interview is to make yourself invaluable to that employer. If you've accomplished that goal, then you can approach negotiations with the mind-set, realistically, that your total compensation package should be in direct proportion to what you bring to the company's bottom line!

MAKE IT A WIN-WIN PROCESS

If you think that a tough negotiating session will alienate the employer, you're sadly mistaken—or maybe you're just copping out to evade a tough, demanding situation. In fact, the reverse is true. Our conviction is that weak, unprepared people hide behind that fear. Look at it this way. You're not out to hold up the company; you're out to join the team and contribute to a bolder bottom line for everyone. Of course, if you're rude, greedy, aggressive, and unprofessional during negotiations, you might jeopardize the offer or your future at the company. But who wants to be that way?

EXHIBIT 9.1
Employee Benefit Checklist

BENEFIT	COVERAGE	PREMIUM
Major medical insurance/health maintenance organization (HMO)		
Dental/optical insurance		
Annual physical		
Life insurance/supplemental life		
Accidental death and dismemberment insurance		
Disability insurance/long term care insurance		
Travel accident insurance		
Retirement/pension plans		
Vacation and holidays		
Educational assistance		
Dependent scholarships		
Professional certification/association fees		
Bonus plan/profit sharing		
Stock options/purchase plans		
Deferred compensation (401-K)		
Tax/financial/estate planning assistance		
Low cost loan		
Legal advice		
Company car/auto expense reimbursement		
Company credit cards		
Club memberships/entertainment privileges		
Publication incentives		
Matching gifts		
First-class travel		
Signing bonus		
Sabbatical leave		
Severance/employment agreement		
Outplacement program		
Spouse relocation assistance		
Others		

EXHIBIT 9.2
Relocation Checklist

RELOCATION BENEFIT	BENEFIT LIMITATION	COMMENTS
Home purchase	_____	_____
Home sale/purchase expense reimbursement	_____	_____
Advance of home equity	_____	_____
Mortgage interest differential	_____	_____
Temporary living expenses	_____	_____
Household goods shipment	_____	_____
Moving allowance	_____	_____
In transit expenses	_____	_____
Duplicate housing expenses	_____	_____
Storage of items	_____	_____
Income tax gross-up	_____	_____
Spouse employment assistance	_____	_____
Housing allowance (overseas)	_____	_____
Income tax equalization (overseas)	_____	_____
Other	_____	_____

The whole process should be a challenge for both you and the employer, but not a bloodletting. Reach for the best, and expect the same from the employer. Attempt to orchestrate not a win-lose scenario but a win-win equation for both the company and you. Consider these additional basic negotiation tactics to achieve those ends:

• Always negotiate with the hiring authority, not with the human resources department, because it is the hiring authority's bottom line that you are impacting.

• Let the employer name a salary figure first. Then ask them to put it in writing. While they do so, you can prepare your counter offer.

• Never answer the question, "What is the minimum you'll accept?" or "How much money do you need to make?" with a lower figure than your most recent compensation. (You're not interested in minimums.) State your required compensation boldly and confidently as you also address how you will dramatically impact their bottom-line.

- Orchestrate your potential job offers so that you can consider them simultaneously. This is another delicate, subtle process, but it pays off when it's done well. If you're under consideration for three different positions, it will limit your ability to evaluate each one objectively and compare them if you don't have all the details simultaneously. Insist that the first company to offer wait until the next week for an answer. If the process is slow in the second company, you can insist that you need all the details and the offer by Friday, with your answer forthcoming the following week. And so on with the third offer. It's difficult, but it's imperative if you're attempting to select the one best job for your future. (Exhibit 9.3 provides a form for evaluating offers. It will assist you in weighing factors that are important in the evaluation of multiple offers.)

To appreciate how beautifully this process can be orchestrated, recall the case of Joe Williams, the engineer who entered our program with no experience in job search. He couldn't even make a cold telephone call during his first couple of weeks. By the end of three months, he was placed in a better job from among three offers. And he skillfully arranged the sequence of events so that all three offers were on the table on a Friday afternoon. He took the weekend with his family, and selected the job he wanted. Speeding one offer up while you slow another one down is not easy, but if you apply yourself, you can adapt the proper techniques and make it happen.

Look at it this way—the entire process, whether you're negotiating compensation or orchestrating job offers to bear fruit simultaneously, really constitutes what might be called your first performance evaluation. If you're weak, unprepared, and easily overpowered—if you accept the first offer put on the table—the employer will walk away with a "victory." But believe us, it's a victory he'd just as soon do without. He will not be overly impressed with your ability. You've got the job, but not much else, and certainly not his respect.

In contrast, if you strap on your seat belt and accelerate for a mutually beneficial best deal, you'll have an ally, not an enemy. Just be sure that you keep it professional, and the employer will be impressed by your performance. You've proved that you're a formidable adversary, but he's lucky enough to have you as his ally. All the complexities and subtleties that you conquered in negotiating a win-win package will now be brought to bear in the marketplace for his company. Here's an example of how your negotiating skills increase your value to a company:

Cliff had transitioned from military officer to a corporate planning position, only to lose it to a reorganization. Still new to the civilian workforce, he was totally naïve about and apprehensive of the job

EXHIBIT 9.3
Evaluating Offers

For each offer, in column 1, rate each of the following criteria on a scale of 1 to 10 (1 low; 10 high) based on your personal needs. Column 1 will be the same for all companies. Then, in column 2, rate each criterion, again on a scale of 1 to 10, based on how well you feel the company satisfies those criteria. For each offer, multiply column 1 by column 2 and list that figure in column 3 (1 × 2). You can compare offers on the basis of their total scores.

CRITERIA	OFFER 1			OFFER 2		
	1	2	3	1	2	3
CAREER/PROFESSIONAL FACTORS						
Job responsibilities	—	—	—	—	—	—
Adequacy of staff/support	—	—	—	—	—	—
Title	—	—	—	—	—	—
Promotion/personal growth potential	—	—	—	—	—	—
Decision-making authority	—	—	—	—	—	—
Other	—	—	—	—	—	—
COMPANY FACTORS						
Size of company	—	—	—	—	—	—
Company/industry history and image	—	—	—	—	—	—
Management style (participative, directive, etc.)	—	—	—	—	—	—
Other	—	—	—	—	—	—
PERSONAL FACTORS						
Base salary	—	—	—	—	—	—
Bonus/profit-sharing/stock options, etc.	—	—	—	—	—	—
Benefits (pension, disability, insurance, vacation)	—	—	—	—	—	—
Perks (car, memberships, etc.)	—	—	—	—	—	—
Geographic location	—	—	—	—	—	—
Amount of travel	—	—	—	—	—	—
Commuting requirements	—	—	—	—	—	—
Special expenses (commuting fare, taxes, relocation, etc.)	—	—	—	—	—	—
Other	—	—	—	—	—	—
TOTAL SCORES	—	—	—	—	—	—

EXHIBIT 9.4
Sample Letter of Agreement

PETE BLUME
Address
City, State Zip
Office #
Home #

Date

Mr. Ted Bates
General Manager
Ace Company
Address

Dear Mr. Bates:

Thank you for clarifying the benefit question I raised earlier today. As I have voiced several times, I am interested in employment with Ace Company and particularly in working directly with you.

Upon receipt of a formal letter from you offering the following terms of employment I will be in a position to conclude my negotiations with the other companies with whom I have been talking and to begin the training process we outlined. Following are the terms we have discussed along with several additional items for your consideration.

- Base Salary - $90,000 per year, paid in 24 semi-monthly payments.
- Bonus Plan - To be written by Ted Bates and Pete Blume with agreed to targets and objectives paralleling the General Managers bonus plan. Ace guarantees a minimum bonus for 199__ of $15,000. The Bonus amount will be paid on Ace's normal bonus pay cycle.
- Car Allowance - $500 per month to cover the initial cost, taxes and insurance. Gasoline and normal maintenance, (i.e. oil changes, lubrication , etc.) will be expensed items outside the allowance.
- Insurance Coverage - Will begin effective May 15, 199__.
- Vacation Policy - Waived, to allow two weeks vacation during calendar year 199__ and 3 weeks for calendar year 199__ and beyond.
- Location Confirmation - Pete Blume will be allowed to fill this position without requiring relocation for at least 3 years.
- Employee Agreement - Will guarantee severance and outplacement including current base salary and benefits for a period of not less than 6 months after suspension of employment for "any reason" other than documented unsatisfactory performance and/or illegal activities carried on by Pete Blume.
- 401K Pension Plan - Please clarify the amount Ace matches 5% or 25%?
- Relocation Policy - Provide Ace's relocation policy and finances involved for future consideration of promotions which would require family relocation either domestic or International after a 3-year period.
- Office - Authorization to lease a furnished one man office outside of my home equipped with appropriate phone lines and electronics to conduct Ace business when not traveling outside of Houston.

I look forward to your careful consideration of the above points. If you or Ace Company require any clarification of these requirements, please contact me. I firmly believe a quick and positive resolution will ensure a solid and long lasting relationship and I look forward to receiving your offer in writing.

Sincerely,

Pete Blume

search process. Nevertheless, by applying our sound networking techniques, he received an offer with a small firm within one month. Feeling very lucky and really excited about working for an entrepreneurial company, he was about to accept a salary offer well below his last position. Upon hearing this, we convinced Cliff that the owner would be disappointed and would not respect him if he did not counteroffer. Skeptical, Cliff made the counteroffer, asking for a substantial increase. Without batting an eye, the owner reached over, shook his hand and said, "No problem, welcome aboard!"

If that alone doesn't convince you to get serious about negotiating, nothing will. Above all, trust in what we're telling you. This is a big step of faith, but if you do it our way, negotiating won't hurt your new relationship with the firm—it will enhance it.

For proof, look again to our firm's success rate. For many years we've guided displaced employees to placement in an average of 3.2 months—and we're usually counseling clients why they should not be taking certain jobs, or less money, rather than pushing them into quick acceptance of any offer. Even with our rapid turnaround figure, we're pushing no one into jobs. We guide them to the best jobs. Our system works. And it's best not only for you but for your new company, as well. Remember, by utilizing our techniques, every future job should be a better job, with a better company, for better pay.

Once you have negotiated the deal you want and have accepted your new position, it is wise to formalize your understanding with a letter of agreement. Some companies provide one automatically as part of their new employee procedures. If your new employer does not follow this practice, which we recommend, you can draft one yourself. (A sample letter of understanding is provided in Exhibit 9.4.) By putting in writing the agreed-upon terms, you ensure that no misunderstanding can rear it's ugly head six months or a year after you have joined the company. In addition, the agreement is the foundation on which you can build future negotiations.

CHAPTER 10

Your Curtain Call: Make It a Standing Ovation

It's up to you, now, to play out the scenario. You're the scriptwriter, director, producer, and star. If you fully utilize the job search techniques described in the preceding nine chapters, there is no question that you will be a hit. Before you begin your creative act, let's review the essential elements of a successful search.

- *The principle of linkage:* Each step of your search must be linked to the previous step and the one to follow. As smooth as a play's script, your job search should be planned and directed from resume to reference letters to networking to interviewing to negotiating. Link them all and increase your job search leverage.·

- *Positive thinking:* If you've ever performed before an audience, you know how debilitating stage fright can be. The effect is the same when you allow negativity to dominate your job search. You alone control your thoughts, attitudes, and actions. Use whatever techniques help you to reduce stress and maintain a positive frame of mind—motivational books or tapes, meditation, exercise, proper diet, discussing your successes with your friends and family, rewarding yourself for meeting daily goals, visualizing your new job, talking with positive people you admire, reviewing your accomplishments, and so forth. Whatever it takes, be positive.

- *Flexibility and realism:* In assessing your career options, leave no stone unturned. Changing careers, starting an independent business, exploring other industries, relocating—each option should be evaluated from the perspective of your interests, aptitudes, and personality as well as from the outlook of marketplace opportunities. If you merely skimmed the self-assessment questions in Chapter 1, take time now to think them through so that you know that your job objectives are on target.

• *Keeping your resume current:* By now you probably have your resume completed—if not, return to Chapter 3 PDQ! Recognizing that employers and employees no longer share undying loyalty and life-long career commitments, it is essential that you be prepared for your next inevitable job change. Maintain a file with your resume, performance appraisals, job description, and accomplishments. You'll find this file extremely useful for salary and performance reviews and when a new career opportunity presents itself. If you're still employed and looking, start this file now.

• *What not to leave home without—references:* Some people may be of the opinion that references are worthless, that no one puts stock in them, and that they are a pain to write. But if you follow our advice in Chapter 4, they become very meaningful and indispensable. Have them in your tool kit for situations in which they are required and to ensure that the individuals who are your references are properly prepared for that critical reference check.

• *Being a one percenter:* Use networking techniques to the maximum. It's okay to use search firms and answer ads—10 to 20 percent of jobs are found that way. But devote 80 percent of your time and efforts to networking. If you haven't started your personal and professional contact list, pull out those business card files, Christmas card lists, and alumni and association directories, and delay no longer.

Once you've placed yourself in your new job, be sure to send a thank you and announcement letter to your network. Maintain a networking file next to your current resume file and keep in touch with your contacts. Don't allow another five or ten years to pass—when you're in need of assistance again—before you call them. If your network is undeveloped now, vow to make it extensive for your next job search. It's up to you to be well connected.

• *Developing your personal marketing plan:* Get organized, set goals, and go for it. Pretend you're running the race of your life, because you are! You're at the starting block—on your mark! Fingers poised on the tape, you kick your legs and place them firmly in the blocks. Eyes focused on the finishing ribbon—get set! Every muscle tenses as adrenaline courses through your veins. The gun blast triggers your momentum, and you shoot off to the finish line. Can you win without training, without establishing goals, without desire? Throughout this book, we have provided forms to help you develop your personal marketing plan. It's not necessary that you use these particular forms, although we strongly recommend them, but it is essential that you develop some system with which you are comfortable—and use it.

- *Psychological leverage:* Whether you're on stage, in a tennis match, or running a race, your greatest advantage is being mentally prepared. Interviews are no different. Know your opponent. Anticipate every question. Beware of hidden agendas. Stay one step ahead, and use psychological leverage to keep the interview positive and general. Practice the tough questions in Chapter 8, and avoid the "red flags" at all costs. Interviewing success depends on your preparation and control.

- *Negotiating value:* Don't be afraid to ask for what you deserve. Whatever your concern, it won't hurt to lay it on the table. The offer is rarely "take it or leave it." If losing $5,000 on your house is what bothers you—let the company know. If your current medical insurance will lapse before the new policy comes into effect—let the company know. If your spouse would have to find a new job—perhaps the company will provide spouse relocation assistance. You are the "value"—don't sell yourself short!

- *Building a cycle of success:* Work hard, be confident, set and attain goals, be persistent, believe you will succeed. William James said it best: "Whatever the mind can conceive and believe, it can achieve."

That quotation appears in gold on a little gift we present to our clients when they succeed in achieving a new position. We call it our "touchstone." (For the practical-minded individual, it serves as a paperweight as well.) We have a tradition in our program to honor, with a special luncheon, each client who is placed. All clients are invited, and the "graduating" client is asked to speak to the group about his or her experiences during the job search—what we call "telling their story." It's an uplifting presentation for everyone, because it confirms that the system works. The newly placed client is rewarded for his or her success, and the other clients, who are still involved in the job search process, commit to succeed as well.

TESTIMONIALS TO SUCCESS

We have selected six successful placements in order to provide a cross-section of levels, functions, and experiences. All six clients told their stories at the traditional special luncheon, and their testimonials follow. If you have any doubt that what you have read in these pages works, you can believe these words—they were spoken by real-life clients of ours who found themselves in the same position you are in and who cast their doubts aside in order to succeed. (Names, titles, and companies are altered to maintain confidentiality.)

Testimonial 1

My name is Tom, and I was a director of geological services for over eight years. Over my career I have been laid off twice and have been nearly laid off two other times. I was working for XYZ Oil and Gas Company up until May 4, 5, or 6. I don't really remember the date—one that I never thought I would forget. We knew cutbacks were coming. When your boss calls you in, you know it's not to ask what you think about the weather that day. When he got done with me, he ushered me into a conference room, and there was an outplacement consultant saying, "Well, Tom, you have an opportunity ahead of you." I thought, "Right—like 10,000 other unemployed geologists!" But it turned out to be really true!

In the three months since I've been laid off, I have found that my commitment to the oil industry is strong enough to get through these tough times in the business. I've spent that time, first, letting people know—individuals I knew—that I was available. That's what networking is. I spent a lot of time, also, trying to put my own oil and gas deals together. As big as Houston is, it doesn't take long for the oil community to hear things like that. One of the people I had been networking through, who was recently promoted to a vice-presidency, decided that he needed a few extra consultants on his staff on a retainer basis. The company buys all the data that you need to generate oil and gas prospects, and then as you come up with these prospects, you are paid. It's similar to a commission basis. There are enough unemployed geologists in Houston that jobs like that are almost unheard-of. When he offered it to me, I was just in a state of shock! We negotiated back and forth on it. Fortunately, I convinced them that I am worth what I thought I was worth. I will be starting on October 15.

Most important, I think that what got me into this fortunate situation was keeping a positive attitude. Of all the things I learned from this experience, that was the most important. When I was cold-calling, I called just about every company that was left in Houston, and almost everyone was real polite. Some of the people I called were more down than I was, and that was real tough. For those of you who have a marketable skill that can be used outside of the oil industry, it won't be as bad; but for a geologist, really, the only thing you are trained to do is work for an oil company. Networking I found to be real easy. Everybody that I knew was always willing to help. I went through networking and cold-calling and answering advertisements, which works to a very small degree. I was usually able to keep that positive attitude.

I just came to the conclusion that I was going to make it, and I realized that it might take a little while. There was no period that I let myself get down for more than one or two days in a row. There were days that I just said, "Okay, today I'm going to be depressed," and I would just go through the motions. That helped me get it out of my system, and I was back doing something. If you keep after it like that, something really good will happen. This really is an opportunity. I know that sounds a little hokey; I know because it wasn't that long ago that I was where you are and somebody else was saying that to me! But honestly, it really does work. You get the picture.

One thing that helped me was knowing that I had a niche to fill, that somewhere out there was "the position" that was just what I was looking for. After being laid off this many times, I am very hesitant about going to work for a company on a regular 9 to 5 basis. What I wanted was to be a consultant on retainer, which is exactly what I found. Granted, the retainer isn't a total compensation package with benefits, but as the industry turns around, I'll be in a position to renegotiate. That's just what I wanted to do, and everything I did in my job campaign was in pursuing that goal. Whatever your goals, always keep them in mind. At the same time, keep your flexibility. What you get initially may not be precisely what you want, but if you get close, you can work your way into exactly what your want—which includes the beach house wherever.

I'll be happy to answer questions.

Q: Do you think you can match your previous salary on this retainer arrangement?

A: My income will depend on how many prospects a year I generate. If I get the kind of support I think I will get from the company, I will be looking at a 15 to 20 percent pay cut initially, for a twelve-month period. The thing about having a retainer is that in addition to the per prospect fee, you also get an override—that is, some percentage of the production of anything you find, right off the top. If you know anyone in the oil business who is really very, very wealthy, that's how they made it—having a percentage of something. I mean, that's how J.R. did it!

Thank you all.

Testimonial 2

My name is Dick. I am going to talk about my job search in two phases—what happened to me job-wise and emotionally. I was with St. Katherine's Hospital for twelve years. I lost my job as a pharmacist on June 13 of this year. The company made a decision that they were going to outsource my department. It didn't take long to figure out that my position would go away.

Fortunately, I learned what the "hidden" job market is. The way it worked out for me is that I had five job interviews with companies. Two came from ad responses and three, including the job I got, came from networking. Next Monday I start to work for Palmer Hospital. It may surprise you that the person who recommended that I talk to this group was my former boss! The job was never advertised. As a matter of fact, the hospital has a hiring freeze! Had I not worked aggressively to ask, "Who do you know—please jog your memory—do you know anyone that I might talk to," this probably wouldn't have surfaced. So I think it's very important that you go after the "hidden" job market, both cold-calling and networking, because either way it's a percentage game. If you go for the ads, you know the jobs are open, but you also know there's hundreds of other people coming in against you. If you cold-call or network, you know there is going to be only one in a hundred jobs open, but you are one of only a few who are coming in to apply for it. And if it's a networking situation, you may come in with the endorsement which is very strong. You have a leg up on any competitor.

The second aspect I wanted to talk about was the emotional side of the situation. I don't know how it was for you, Tom, or the rest, but the only way I can describe it is—it was hell. There is one thing in particular that I found helpful, which I'd like to share with you. Have you heard about the two frogs that fell in a bucket of milk? Two frogs one evening fell into a bucket of cow's milk down on the farm. And they were saying, "My gosh, what in the world are we going to do?! There is no way we can get up to the edge." They swam for about an hour, and they started to get really tired, and one of the frogs said, "Man, I'm so exhausted, I can't see why I should just keep swimming like this. The heck with it." He just quit swimming and sank; that was it. The other frog thought, "Well, I know what happens when I quit swimming, but I don't know what happens if I keep swimming, so I'm just going to keep swimming 'til it kills me." Well, through the long night, the frog swam so hard that the milk started to churn into butter. Finally, at dawn, he was able to get some footing and he just jumped out!

That's sort of the way I felt. In other words, I didn't know when this damn thing was going to be over, but all of a sudden I had footing and I jumped out and that was all. I knew what would happen if I quit swimming— I'd probably still be in the bucket of milk!

I don't know how each of you rewards yourself on a daily basis, but I know that when I get home if I really had a tough day, I like to drink a couple of beers and think about my accomplishments. At the beginning of my search, I thought, "Well I haven't accomplished a damn thing. I don't even have a job." I couldn't enjoy drinking beer or riding my bike or any of the things I like to do. Then I started to think, "I'm just going to churn as hard as I can. If I have a day when I know that I got up early in the morning and that I worked just as hard at my job campaign and churned as hard as I could— even though it didn't produce a job offer that day—then I deserve a couple of beers." Whether it is beer, ice cream, running, or whatever, reward yourself for each day of hard work. That carried me through, and I felt the sense of accomplishment. Every day, even though I didn't have the ultimate reward—which can only be defined as a new job—I felt that I had put in my eight or ten hours that day and I deserved a small reward. Some days are worse than others, but you do deserve that reward. Hopefully, that will be of some help to you. I know that if you just keep churning, all of a sudden— bam, it's over with.

Are there any questions?

Q: Could you talk about your networking techniques?
A: I mostly "warm-called" in networking. For instance, one of my interviews was over in San Antonio. I was referred by another man I knew in San Antonio. When I called, I didn't know this guy, but yet I was able to use the name of another acquaintance. To me that is a warm call. You are not just calling out of the blue. I had a name to drop, which got his attention, and that got me one interview. Initially, I wrote a letter of introduction to the person who offered me the job at Palmer. He didn't know me, but yet I started off with the name of my former boss, who he did know. I used other techniques, but again, the "hidden" job market was my main objective. If I had time at the end of each week, I answered the Sunday ads from the week before. That was my strategy. And it worked!

Thanks to everyone who helped me.

Testimonial 3

My name is Jerry. This is the moment I have been looking forward to. As of Wednesday, I have accepted an offer as vice president, marketing with Genetics Company. I'll be working for their international division and responsible for opening up new markets for their seed productions in Africa and some in the Mideast. It's interesting, because back in June, when we did our practice interviews, this was essentially the position for which I practice-interviewed. It just took a while to come together.

I was trying to think of some things that might be of interest as you are just getting into your job searches. A lot of very true and worthwhile things have already been said. I know my experience in the whole job search process was a learning experience for me. I had been with ABC Company for nine years and never had really learned to do an effective job search. I feel safe to say that I would probably still be at it or would have settled for a job at McDonald's by this point. I just didn't know how to go about it. I really feel that the best part of this whole process was learning about myself—what I want to do, how to clarify my career goals, how to market myself, how to communicate effectively. Those are skills that are universal in their transferability and are going to come in very handy down the road.

I would like to share an analogy of how I think of the stages of the job search. At least in my case, it worked sort of like taking a trip on an airplane. You start out and there are the emotional aspects of departure—breaking loose from family or wherever you've been, the flurry of activity associated with getting to the airport, of boarding the plane and settling in. This is similar to the emotional turmoil you experience when you lose your job. The slow, gradual ascent is analogous to the daily routine of making your calls and writing your letters. Then things begin to level off. Along about one month into the process, you are feeling pretty comfortable with it. It gets to be almost like any other job. Then, after about two months, things began to happen for me. That's analogous to the plane beginning to descend—things start to get a little bit turbulent, and there's just a lot of activity. People begin to respond to your letters or to your leads. Finally, just before landing, it gets very turbulent—and in my case, that was one of the most difficult parts of the job search. All these people start expressing interest—in my case, four or five. I started to wonder how I was going to put this guy off while I waited for these other offers to come in. But it all worked out very nicely. A few potential offers faded out of the picture toward the end, but I ended up with two strong offers.

The one I accepted with Genetics Company is really the ideal job for me. It combines most of my career objectives. The one drawback is that it involves considerable travel. I had a struggle with that as I got to the point of making a decision—really wondering, thinking it through with my wife. Did I want to be gone 35 or 40 percent of the time, overseas for three-week stretches? We don't know that answer yet. I guess the only way to find out is to jump in and do it. I decided that it is better to find out now rather than later regret not having explored it, because this is an area that I have wanted to be involved in really since college.

For me, the key to success was networking. All the leads that materialized were as a result of contacts with former work associates or people that I had contact with in other companies through my previous job. My job objective was market development or projects in agribusiness, which is a narrow field. Obviously, there are not a whole lot of positions advertised in that area, so I had to rely heavily on networking. Actually, I found no ads in my area of interest. I wrote a lot of letters to major agribusiness companies here in the United States. The "cold" letter route did not really work for me. I got a lot of very nice rejection letters. The amusing part was how many different ways people can tell you "Thanks, but no thanks." There were a lot of very original letters from personnel departments.

The thing that really was helpful for me was getting out to visit companies. I took three trips to various parts of the country—one up to the Midwest, one to Virginia, and one up to the Northeast. I lined up interviews along the way. Some of these interviews were with people I had written to, and they had told me they didn't have anything. But I called them back, thanked them for responding to my letter, told them I was really interested in the company, and just wondered if I could stop by since I was going to be in the area. And I mentioned that I would like to learn more about their company. That was very helpful for a number of reasons. One, it kept me current in the interview process. I got some new contacts from doing that and occasionally got a solid lead out of those interviews. This emphasizes the importance of getting out and meeting with people. I think it is a very effective technique.

I am very grateful for this opportunity. I think it's been one of the most positive experiences of my whole career thus far. I don't know how many people there are out in the work world who probably wish for this opportunity, who are not satisfied with their jobs. I wasn't with my previous job. The opportunity to get off the treadmill and step back, look at what you want to do, and lay down some long-range plans is, I think, a chance of a lifetime.

Are there questions?

Q: What are some of the techniques you used for negotiating?
A: Basically it was just asking for time to make a decision. I was going through a second or third interview with some of these companies, and they would say, "Well, we are getting very close to a decision stage. We would need you to make your decision here shortly." Well I became quite a bit anxious, and I wondered how I was going to hold off the other employers. Actually, that problem never materialized. The guy who said he was going to make a decision next week didn't end up making a decision 'til three or four weeks later. I think that may be practical wisdom—don't rely too heavily on what people say about when they will do something. In my case, the offers came through at least three or four weeks later than what they first told me. So just hang cool, and don't worry too much about it. The only other thing I would add along that line is, ask for time to make a decision. If they want you bad

enough, they will be willing for you to make a sound decision. In certain situations, I was very up front with people. I told them I was considering several other positions; if I felt it was appropriate, I would tell them very specifically what I was doing. They understood. They said, "We are willing to wait; we would really like to have you, so we'll just wait and see what you find out."

Testimonial 4

My name is Carol, and I was formerly with High Top Company.

I remember when I first sat in the outplacement seminar, especially that first Friday, there were two or three people who got up from previous groups who had just been placed. They spoke to us as we are speaking to you, and some of us were a little bit skeptical. I wondered if they were paying these people to get up and tell these nice things, since this is exactly what the consultant said in our first meeting at High Top Company—insisting how great things would be. I had doubts as to whether these things really happened as clients described them, but as the weeks went by and more and more people came here and talked to the group, I realized that everybody who spoke about their job search was just like I was. They were going through some very difficult time, but they stuck with it.

I'll tell you quickly what happened to me. I was manager of an audio/video production department for High Top. Of course, with the economic downturn—by the way I had that line down pat about the "downturn of the economy"—but anyway, my whole department was shut down. I won't say it was a shock to me. In service departments, you always run the risk of something happening. Within three weeks of being here, I decided that I wanted to start my own production company. I had looked around Houston, and there just did not seem to be an opportunity similar to what I had. I did send out resumes left and right the first couple of weeks, almost all of which were out of state. After about three weeks, I didn't hear anything back from all of the resumes I sent out. I decided that I would try starting my own production company—at least, give it the best shot I could. So for the next three months, that's about all I did, except for sending out resumes just to keep my options open. That's another thing the consultant talked about in the seminar—"Make sure you keep your options open, and don't close any door that might help you out down the road." So I kept looking on a small scale—which, by the way, also fulfilled my unemployment compensation requirements. I called on people to work on productions, individual slide shows, or whatever. And I developed a few contracts—I was at least getting some work and building that up.

Then, about a month ago, I got a call from a large bank in Florida to which I had sent a resume the week after I got laid off from High Top. About a week later, I called them and they told me that the position had been "filled." I didn't quite believe that line, since my background was perfect for the job description. Interestingly enough, they called me back a month ago and said that they would like me to interview if I was still interested. At that time, I wasn't even sure I wanted to go interview, since I was just so set on doing my own thing. Since I had started it, I was going to stick with it. But I thought, "Keep your options open. You don't know what there is out there—plus it's a free trip!" I decided to give it a shot. I went out there and interviewed with a different person every half-hour or so for about three and a half hours, one of which was an hour-long lunch meeting. That was seven interviews. The process was really an experience for me. I felt very prepared. Before I left, I reviewed my notes that I had taken in the seminar. I had written about five or six major points when we practiced interviewing, and I studied those. I felt very comfortable when I was there.

After I came back, they called me a day or two later and said that they were really interested in me and asked me to return for another interview. They were interviewing someone else for the job in about two weeks, but they were narrowing it down to the two of us. I almost hoped they wouldn't call me. I had spent money on stationery and business cards and called all these people and had people call me back about possible productions that I could do in Houston. They invited me and my husband to come for the weekend to talk to us a little bit more and show us the area, et cetera, et cetera, et cetera. I thought, "Well, okay, I'll keep my options open." I went there this past weekend, and they were just extremely nice to us.

On Monday, after I got back, they called me and offered the position. I still didn't know if I wanted to take it. After discussing it with my husband and establishing a minimum offer which could induce us to move, I told them, "No, thank you, but I can not accept the offer." They called back the next day and upped the offer. It was so good I couldn't turn it down. In fact Tuesday, when they called and upped the offer, I responded immediately. I said, "Okay, I accept the offer." The representative said, "What? You're kidding—you're taking the offer now? You don't want to think about it?" I replied, "No—you've been fair with me, I'll be fair with you."

One thing in particular about the negotiations is interesting. I had contacted a company in Chicago about a possibility of a job offer which never really came about. But since I had been talking with them, I used that as some leverage with these people. I told them I was talking to some people in Chicago. Well, when they came back on Tuesday to up the offer, the representative spent about ten minutes talking about the statistics between

Chicago and Jacksonville, Florida. She told me the difference in the price of housing—that the median price was 35 percent higher in Chicago than in Jacksonville. She gave me the cost of living index of the two cities, and the re-location index difference. I mean, there were about seven or eight categories that they were using to show why this was a better deal than going to Chicago. What was really a kick was that the lady expounding on Florida was from Chicago! I felt that having a little leverage really helped me. Even though I didn't actually have an offer from Chicago, I used that as a bargaining point.

Through all this, I did learn to keep my options open. I still would like to have my own business, which I am going to keep up. I've got some things I'm involved in which I can do on weekends. So I am going to keep that going just as a small business. If, down the road, things don't work out with this job, I'll always have that to go back to.

The last thing I would like to mention deals with networking ideas. I didn't know what networking was when I came here—except for ABC, NBC, and CBS. I quickly learned that you talk to your friends, your acquaintances, people who were former employers and let them all know what you are try-ing to do. You never know when they are going to find a friend or see some-thing that might be of interest. That gets down to how I knew about this job. A week after I was laid off, a friend in the employee communications depart-ment at High Top called me and said she had seen an ad in a trade publica-tion which I never read. She told me about it but had forgotten which issue it was in. Then, about a week later, the guy I was sitting next to in the seminar, who was another famous person from our group, told me about it. And he couldn't remember what issue it was in. Finally, after about two weeks, one of them found the magazine and sent me a copy of the ad. My point is that you never know where the possibility of a job will come from. That's why it's important to tell all your friends, your acquaintances, people you meet—don't be shy about it. If there is anything that is going to help you, it is be-lieving that the more people who know that you are looking for a job in a certain area and who keep thinking about you, the greater the possibility that they are going to find something and tell you about it.

Any questions?

Q: Do any of your clients need advertising help?
A: No, but I have a lot of business cards which I would be glad to share with you!

Testimonial 5

Hi. I'm Chris. Having just recently graduated, my plan was to enter medical school. Unfortunately, I wasn't able to start this year and was faced with a job search for the first time except for summer and part-time jobs. I was really at a loss until I had the opportunity to learn *The Total System*. I didn't even know there was a system to job search. In fact, I was so discouraged about not going to medical school I would have taken any job. Fortunately, I realized from *The Total System* that I have value to an employer, and that I can be in control of my future direction.

I had no idea how to target companies in particular industries until this experience. Once I investigated the medical research industry, I discovered that there were over 500 companies in this field. Using a CD-ROM database, I produced a list of about 100 companies and began to contact them. One of the leads I got from networking was for the DeBakey Heart Institute. Well, they suggested I contact a certain person at Baylor College of Medicine. When I contacted the person, she remembered that the DeBakey Institute had contacted them about a candidate. Anyway, for some reason she was under the impression that I was being recommended by Dr. DeBakey. She already had an interview set up for me.

So, that is how I got this job. It is with Dr. Sandra Shaw at the Doctor's General Hospital—Department of Pediatrics: Baylor College of Medicine. We are researching a "Preemie" newborn problem. When born prematurely, a baby's digestive system does not work properly. We are researching the problem and trying to find answers leading to a cure. We actually work with the babies at the hospital which gives me clinical experience, and we're working in a lab. I cannot tell you how perfect this position is! Aside from gaining experience in both research and clinical settings, I think that Dr. Shaw will be a great help in my application for school. I plan on going back to school in two years, the Physicians Assistant program, which happens to be at Baylor.

As you would guess, I am very excited about the whole thing. I could not have found a better job, even if I had researched all the possibilities and chosen my ideal position. The preparation of an A+ resume, networking, and practice interviewing gave me the confidence I needed to begin my career in the best possible position and environment. I owe a lot to *The Total System*— it works.

Testimonial 6

My name is Bill. I started my career as a chemical engineer in a refinery in Houston. I went from refinery to refinery, from chemical plant to chemical plant. Then I left the States and spent a long time in South America building refineries and operating refineries. Eventually I worked my way to Puerto Rico, to Pittsburgh, and back to Houston. I got out of the refining business and into the coal business, which had its ups and downs. Then I got out of the coal business and went into engineering and construction, which has its ups and downs, too. I worked here in Houston with two companies, then moved to Chicago where I had a nice tour of duty in the Midwest doing engineering and construction management. Then one of the nicest things I did was move to Washington. In Washington, D.C., I was president of a company that did public sector and government contracts, both engineering and construction. The company that I headed up got restructured, and then was restructured right out of existence.

At that time my wife, Glenda, and I talked about our choices. She could come join me in Washington and starve to death or I could come back to Houston. Since Glenda is president of her own company, the latter choice seemed most appropriate. We decided it was about time we stopped commuting anyway. It was a lovely decision and I'm glad we made it. I'm real happy now that I lost my job, got fired, came back to Houston and started over again. I'm also going to tell you that it was not easy. In fact, it was very hard on me to have to start over.

I remember the first day I was here, a consultant said, "Well, how do you feel about your situation?" That was the first time anyone asked how I felt about it and I determined at that point that I was going to be positive. So one word of advice—be positive throughout the ups and downs that you have in your professional career. So I started off on a positive note here.

I've always been a very pragmatic person, and I realized that I had to restructure the way I lived and the way I worked. It was very difficult. One of the things that I found very beneficial to me was that I arrived each day when the offices opened and I went home when they closed the doors. I didn't like using the telephone. The telephone was hard; believe me it was very difficult. But it's something that you must do. You have to overcome your stage fright and you have to overcome your reluctance to talk about yourself. I've done a lot of things successfully and I didn't want to tell people that I was unemployed. The sooner you get over that and get it behind you, the sooner you can move on. The seminar helped me get my feet on the ground and head out and start doing my work. I didn't get any interviews at the beginning. But I just kept plugging away.

You need those interviews—they are good for your ego. There was a point when Glenda and I talked about the possibility that it was time for me to retire. But after a while you realize all the money is going out and no money is coming back in and you've got to decide if you are going to sack groceries or just what you are going to do. Eventually the interviews came, and the job offers came, and what do you know—some of them were so low that I wouldn't consider taking them. Some of them were withdrawn! I'm going to tell you that one of you is going to get an offer, and you're going to call back the next day to find out more particulars, and discover that there is no job.

You're ready to negotiate, and they're going to withdraw the offer on you. And that's pretty hard to take. Memorial Day we had at least three jobs lined up—I just knew I would be working by July 1. Not one of them materialized. I worked with one company for weeks and I interviewed everybody from chairman down to project manager level. They offered a job once and withdrew it; then later they came back to me, and started talking all over again, but nothing ever came of it. And yet you need those interviews.

You need to talk to people. One of the things that I found very beneficial when I got to a real low level was to talk to people. You need their support. There are times when you just stop and talk over your situation and it helps you get through that day.

I did a lot of work at night. I did a lot of work on the weekends, and you need that. It is a full-time job. Don't let anyone tell you that it is not a full-time job.

I did some consulting work, but it didn't lead to a full-time position. I had one company that told me that they wanted to hire me but they couldn't get authorization. They wanted me to consult for awhile and then maybe they would hire me. It turned out that they took my strategic plan, which I put together for a business unit, and they are using it today. But at the end of the contract they said, "Well, I'm sorry but we can't get approval to hire you."

Another thing I would recommend is to keep in shape. You've got to be mentally in shape, but you also have to be physically in shape. Your appearance is also important. You've got to keep your wardrobe up, you've got to keep your body in good shape, and you've got to keep doing your work.

You've got to keep going—I can't emphasize that enough. I don't care how many interviews you get or how many job offers you get, you still need to be digging, going for a job, looking for those opportunities that are out there. Because you are going to have two or three interviews with one company and you are going to say, "Hey, this is it," and you will start neglecting your network, telephone contacts, your personal contacts. But if it doesn't work out, you've lost a lot of time.

The job that I have now is with an environmental remediation company. I selected it out of three offers. Along the way someone asked me if I had explored hazardous waste management. At the time I hadn't given it much thought, so I started working on it. As it turns out they found out about me from somebody else that eventually led to the interviews and that led to the job offer. So don't stop. Don't stop looking, don't stop working.

One of the other two offers I had was in Venezuela and I went to look at the job. Believe me, they needed help. They had all of their operations riding on three major projects in a country that needs a lot of work. The job is going downhill, and they are going to get thrown out of there if they don't do something about it. While I was looking at that job, a third opportunity developed. It was with another company here in town, where they wanted me to take over and run their engineering construction business.

I came back from Venezuela, and Glenda said, "You have an interview on Monday." She just told them, "Yes, Bill will be there to interview on Monday." It was Environmental Technologies, Inc., with whom I had been talking, and I didn't know if they were serious or what. As it turns out, they were very serious. I told them, "I've got to make a decision by Friday, and if you're going to play in this ball game, we've got to get with it." The vice president said it was a bad week—there were board meetings and this and that. I said, "Fine, you've got board meetings, I'll see you. If you want to talk to me, put your offer together and let's talk about it in detail. I need an offer by Thursday morning." At that point I was tired of fooling around; I had something I wanted and I was ready to take it. As it turned out they put it together and made me an offer on Thursday morning—he actually delayed it until Thursday afternoon because we ate lunch and talked about it. Because they were playing this game, they wanted to wear me out, take me out to the very end of the day. I decided to accept the job as executive vice president, business development; I will oversee things that are happening with their construction companies, their remedial companies and with their technology company. The company has big plans and is going places, and I plan to go with them. That is my story. Any questions?

Q: How do you feel now?
A: Great!

So there you have a few of the hundreds of testimonials we have heard. In a short time, you, too, can give testimony to a successful job search. Set your goal, apply the techniques, believe in yourself, and make it happen. That is how to create job search leverage. The one percent success factor is within you—use it to maximize your success. By the way, at your curtain call—when you've finished your script and attained your career goals—be prepared for a standing ovation. If you don't believe it now, perhaps then you'll know that rather than the worst thing, this is the best thing that could have happened to you! We wish you success, and we would like to hear your unique story when you've achieved your job search goals.

Ken & Sheryl Dawson

Appendix:
Sample Resumes

The following are 50 sample resumes that represent various categories of career situations, functional areas, organizational levels, and industries. For your convenience, a listing precedes the sample resumes. All of the samples are actual resumes from our client files. Names of applicants and companies have been altered to maintain confidentiality.

OBJECTIVE

Senior Executive Management - Power Project Development

SUMMARY

Over thirty years of bottom-line experience in sales, marketing, project development, and financing of major domestic and international projects with heavy concentration in power generation. Built beginning sales and development organizations into viable competitors with substantial backlogs. Experienced in all aspects of the development process, including contract negotiations and deal-making necessary to achieve successful financial closings including power sales, thermal sales, turnkey contracting, operations and maintenance, ownership structures, and arranging financing.

PROFESSIONAL EXPERIENCE

JB ENERGY SOURCE, INC. - Houston, Texas   1994 - 1995

General Manager, Business Development

Responsible for business development activities for Southern USA/Latin America region an independent power producing subsidiary of Public Service Enterprise Group, including development, acquisition, ownership and operation of power generation projects.

- Opened and staffed Houston office with development, financial, analytical and technical disciplines. Developed region plan and strategy, project screening and evaluation process, development process, and formulated business-getting strategies with staff.
- Closed acquisition of interest in existing gas turbine facility in Venezuela. Led negotiations for business deal and all agreements. Coordinated all aspects of due diligence and reviews, and presented to parent company board for approval. Formed joint venture with in-country owner to pursue other projects and developed business plan for new venture.
- Penetrated new markets in Colombia, Peru and Argentina, establishing in-country partnerships/ alliances to pursue greenfield projects and acquisitions. Developed deal flow from aggressive contact base. Obtained commitment for joint development of 100 MW project for major Argentina oil company. Pursuing major fuels driven projects in Colombia and Peru for near term close.

DEVELOPMENT E&C, INC. - Houston, Texas   1990 - 1994

Vice President, Corporate Development

Directed Corporate Development and Finance Department, providing project development, project finance, acquisition, divestiture, and financial analysis services to the company's eight business units for both domestic and international projects. Advised company's Office of the President on major projects and equity investments on a global basis.

- Promoted company's strategic investigation into the independent power market, domestic and international, which resulted in a re-focus of resources toward selected domestic targets and certain country targets and the closing of a 102 MW gas turbine cogeneration project in Ontario, Canada, for power business unit, its first project financed contract.
- Evaluated and recommended to company Office of the President and parent company the acquisition of a North Sea multiple support vessel costing over $40M, for offshore construction of production platforms and subsea facilities. Evaluated other acquisition opportunities which included a major international power engineering and construction firm ($250M).
- Authored "Turnkey Contracting Business Risks" to mitigate risks and increase margins.
- Promoted and recommended company's equity participation in a $320M toll road project in northern Virginia where subsidiary also won the $150M construction contract.

224

H&S ENGINEERING, INC. - Houston, Texas   1985 - 1990

Vice President/General Manager, Project Development
Specialized in the development, turnkey design, construction, operation, and maintenance of power generation facilities.

- Directed planning, sales, marketing, and project development activities, contributing to company growth from 35 employees to 350 employees.
- Negotiated and successfully closed twelve major lump sum turnkey gas turbine power plant project contracts in excess of 1000 MW and $600M, and developed sales and pricing strategies commensurate with assessed risks and competition.
- Led the company into development of a 235 MW project in Richmond, Virginia; provided project development services and recommended a total equity investment in the project.
- Supported developers in negotiation of power and steam sales agreements, fuel purchase contracts, obtaining permits, and project financing.
- Reviewed and evaluated joint venture equity investments in other projects, both domestic and international to share cost and risk.
- Developed extensive network of contacts among developers, utility subsidiaries, utilities, energy companies, vendors, and financial entities.
- Hired sales and support staff which achieved proposal activity in excess of $1 billion per year.
- Led investigation into municipal solid waste resource recovery projects and recommended against entry. Closed teaming agreement with electric utility for 18 MW gas turbine project; test marketed sales of services and marketing program for hydro projects and closed one $2M project.

MORRAY BUILDERS - Houston, Texas   1980 - 1984

Vice President, Sales & Marketing
Hired and managed a professional sales staff, developed business plans for pursuit of new markets including a Southeast Asia market study and a new business, a subsidiary company to develop, own, and operate power generation projects.

- Coordinated efforts that resulted in closing a major East Coast coal export terminal project valued at $115M.
- Created a "Guide to Marketing Plan Preparation" for all company operating units, which facilitated the planning process.

CONSOLIDATED ENERGY - Houston, Texas   1978 - 1980

Director, Project Development
Directed corporate diversification efforts into new areas of coal production, transportation, terminalling, and coal-fired cogeneration facilities.

- Hired and managed a professional development and marketing staff which pursued acquisition of coal properties, transportation systems, development of grass roots terminals, and solid fuel cogeneration projects.

PRIOR EXPERIENCE
- Marketing Manager for PowerSys Engineering, 1976-1978.
- Managing Partner for Development E&C/Johnston Interests joint venture, 1970-1976.
- Manager, Market Development for ApplianceWest, Pittsburgh, Pennsylvania, 1963-1970.
- Project Engineer and Industrial Salesman for O&G Exploration; Bayway Refinery; Bayonne Refinery; and Pittsburgh, Pennsylvania, sales district, 1956-1963.

EDUCATION

Master of Business Administration - Cornell University, Ithaca, New York - 1960
B.S. Civil Engineering - Purdue University, West Lafayette, Indiana - 1956

ADDITIONAL EDUCATION

Conversational Spanish; Quality Seminars - Deming, Covey, Wilson Learning

2) NAME
Address
City, State Zip Code
Office #
Home #

OBJECTIVE

Senior Executive Management

SUMMARY

Twenty-nine years of experience in petroleum refining and petrochemical industry. Possess excellent record of accomplishment in petroleum refining processes, project management, refining economics, LP systems, state-of-the-art software, crude oil pipeline systems, trucking operations, laboratory systems, and environmental, health, and safety regulations. Have demonstrated strong organizational, leadership, and decision making skills at the executive level which have contributed significantly to the bottom line.

PROFESSIONAL EXPERIENCE

CHAMBERLAIN REFINING CORPORATION - Houston, Texas   1969 - Present

Executive Vice President & Chief Operating Officer (1990-Present)
Responsible for crude oil supply and marketing functions, refinery operations, crude pipeline and trucking operations, short-term planning, corporate environmental, health, and safety activities, corporate purchasing activities, and corporate engineering technology for this $2 billion independent refining and marketing company with crude oil refining capacity of 155,000 BPD in three refineries, and approximately 1600 employees.
- Directed operating budget exceeding $175 million and capital expenditures of $35 million annually.
- Reduced Workers Compensation costs by 83% from $2.4 million in 1991 to approximately $400,000 in 1994.
- Managed safety program which reduced company's injury and illness rates to 70% below U.S. refining and marketing industry average.
- Directed Crude Oil Department purchasing including 180,000 BPD of crude oil and other feedstocks valued at $1.32 billion per year.
- Marketed over 65,000 BPD of crude oil, which generated revenues in excess of $400 million per year.
- Initiated a NYMEX crude oil trading program utilizing storage facility at Dell, Texas resulting in $1 million per year in increased revenues.

Vice President Refining (1987-1990)
Responsible for all aspects of refining operation at three plant locations (Texas, Louisiana, and Oklahoma).
- Achieved record safety, environmental, and health performance while reducing operating expenses and staffing. Reduced staff at one refinery from 270 to 200, which saved over $2.5 million per year.
- Operated all three refineries in 1989 without a lost-time accident.
- Achieved OSHA Star status at both major refineries and received numerous National Petroleum Refiners Association (NPRA) Meritorious and Gold Awards.
- Negotiated labor contracts at two refineries ensuring that promotions, demotions, and layoff were based on qualifications rather than seniority resulting in maximum utilization of personnel.
- Provided oversight for the engineering and construction of a 14,000 BPD UOP CCR Platformer, a 50% expansion of a UOP HF Alkylation Unit, and a new Butadiene Saturation Unit, resulting in completion on schedule and within budget.

Manager Mid-Continent Operations (1985-1987)
Responsible for the operation of a 10,000 BPD aliphatic solvents plant, 45,000 BPD refinery and two gas processing plants as well as all the duties of Director, Planning & Coordination.
- Negotiated gas processing agreements with large gas producers in the area, resulting in improved plant efficiency and profitability.
- Served as member of negotiating team which handled the sale of the gas processing plants, resulting in a plant sales price two times the sales goal.

226

Director Planning & Coordination (1983-1985)
Responsible for department which provided economic analysis for all company activities including crude oil supply, operations, and supply/marketing.
- Evaluated and selected new corporate Linear Program (LP) system resulting in over $5 million per year improved profitability.
- Directed branded marketing planning and pricing, which increased both sales and profits.
- Developed corporate five-year plan which enabled company to track progress and focus on goals.

Refinery Manager (1980-1983)
Responsible for 45,000 BPD refinery located in Desden, Louisiana.
- Reduced staffing by 15 positions with no adverse effect on productivity, saving $500,000 per year.
- Established strict procedures for security, operations, environmental, safety, maintenance, and technology which enabled company to meet objectives in these areas.
- Pioneered use of riser steam injection and metals passivation in company's FCC Units in 1980, generating revenues in excess of $3 million per year.

Project Manager (1977-1980)
- Spearheaded a $30 million modernization program for the Desden Refinery. Activities included development of required processing schemes for meeting unleaded gasoline regulatory requirements, contractor selection, organization, engineering, and construction. Project was completed on schedule.
- Recommended, initiated, and directed the first installation of electronic instrumentation on an FCC Unit without a costly pneumatic control system backup which resulted in significant cost savings to company.

Senior Project Engineer (1974-1977)
- Conducted project evaluation and development for three refineries; operated and maintained all refinery LP's; handled procurement and sale of refinery propane and butane streams.
- Conducted detailed process studies for refinery expansions and addition of new process units.
- Managed all field location activities for the construction of a new 17,000 BPD crude oil distillation unit including operator training and startup.

Senior Process Engineer (1969-1974)
Responsible for directing all process activities at a 35,000 BPD refinery in Desden, Louisiana.
- Created a process engineering department which provided technical services to operations.
- Established control limits for all operating units which improved yield and product quality.
- Coordinated all environmental activities, ensuring compliance with state and federal regulations.
- Served as startup team leader for new Phillips HF Alkylation Unit.
- Increased capacity of crude processing unit from 25,000 BPD to 35,000 BPD.

PRIOR EXPERIENCE   1964 - 1969
- MYERS, INC., Lake Charles, Louisiana - Administrative Assistant (1967-1969)
- MYERS, INC., Ponca City, Oklahoma - Senior Process Engineer (1966-1967)
- RUSSELL COMPANY, Alvin, Texas - Technical Service Engineer (1964-1966)

EDUCATION

Mid-level Management Course - University of Texas, Austin, Texas - 1985
Graduate Courses - Texas A&M University, College Station, Texas - 1965
BS, Chemical Engineering - Oklahoma State University, Stillwater, Oklahoma - 1964

PROFESSIONAL AFFILIATIONS

National Petroleum Refiners Association
American Petroleum Institute
American Institute Chemical Engineers
Leadership Oklahoma
Founders Club

227

OBJECTIVE

Healthcare Consultant

SUMMARY

Over seventeen years general and sales management experience with one of the leading healthcare companies in the world. Have a proven track record in turning organizations around in a short period of time. Have demonstrated the ability to develop and implement strategic business initiatives and plans. Team oriented, assertive style coupled with excellent business skills have significantly added to the corporate bottom line.

PROFESSIONAL EXPERIENCE

SMITH & BOLD, INC. - Houston, Texas   1994 - Present

President
Independent healthcare consulting firm which specializes in providing consulting services to healthcare professionals involved in the clinical and anatomic laboratory environment. Direct PAI's services providing clients expertise and assistance to effectively evaluate, develop, and implement plans and projects to increase revenue and improve efficiency, while decreasing overall operating costs.

MDP LABORATORIES INC. - Pittsburg, Pennsylvania   1978 - 1994

MDP Laboratories, Inc. is a division of MDP Corporation, with sales of $1.2 billion and 11,000 employees.

Vice President and General Manager - Dallas, Texas (1993-1994)
Led, managed and directed operations and sales activities for the Southwestern U.S. area with $135 million in sales and over 900 people. Established annual budget targets of 15% sales growth and 20% increase in profit, which exceeded corporate guidelines.

- Initiated continuous improvement projects throughout geographical area resulting in increased productivity of 12.9% and cost reduction of 6.1% within nine months.
- Developed and initiated plan for laboratory clustering resulting in a 23.7% increase in testing volume with no additional personnel.
- Led first successful venture for division in Mexico with first year sales projection of $2 million, which is currently on target.
- Flattened organization and broadened span of control optimizing utilization of personnel which led area to #1 position in Independent National Survey on quality and customer satisfaction.
- Directed team to a successful transition and consolidation of San Antonio facility which resulted in a 29% decrease in costs and a positive $1 million in additional profit.
- Negotiated management contract with a pathology group resulting in a $1.5 million contract which secured a #1 position for the company in that market.
- Developed new method of computing capitation rates for managed care accounts which added an additional $250,000 to area's bottom line.
- Aided in the development of a new procedure in toxicology which lowered costs by 20% and has become a corporate standard.

228

<u>General Manager</u> - Houston, Texas (1989-1993)
Directed operational and sales management for Houston and Southeast Texas area, with more than 200 employees and $35 million in sales.

- Developed business plan stressing strategic core competencies which led to sales growth of 288% over a 3-year period.
- Developed and initiated total quality management program with employee involvement groups resulting in annual 72% profit growth for three years.
- Led team to develop first successful hospital joint venture for company in the Southwest, which involved negotiating an arrangement with a major hospital resulting in a $3 million program, running 17% ahead of the proforma.
- Awarded President's Club status for achievement, given annually to 4 General Managers and 34 employees from the sales staff.
- Gained #1 market share among all companies in industry in 1993, by maintaining focus and involving all employees in vision.
- Achieved status as top performing facility in 7 of 10 measurement categories.

<u>Area Sales Director, South Central</u> - Dallas, Texas (1988-1989)
Directed sales for South Central U.S. encompassing four states comprised of four district managers and 28 sales representatives.

- Developed "No Excuses Selling" concept, resulting in #1 sales group within the division averaging 20% greater sales per month per sales representative than closest group out of 14 sales areas.
- Developed market specific sales training which became the core for National Training programs.
- Awarded "President's Club" status for significant sales and marketing achievement.
- Integrated sales force successfully following a major acquisition, resulting in less than 5% sales loss.

<u>District Sales Manager</u> - Philadelphia, Pennsylvania (1981-1988)
Managed, trained and directed sales force of 19 sales representatives.

- Developed hospital training program which resulted in highest dollar performance within division of 40 districts for four years.
- Developed managed care strategy, resulting in contracts totalling more than $5 million.
- Awarded district of-the-year honor 2 consecutive years.

<u>Territory Sales Manager</u> - New York, New York (1978-1981)
Sold clinical laboratory service to physicians.

- Achieved ranking of #1 territory in company for two years.
- Assisted in training and development of new sales representatives which ensured consistency and immediate productivity gains.

EDUCATION

M.P.H. - Public Health - William Paterson College, Wayne, New Jersey - 1981
B.S. - Biochemistry - University of Nebraska, Lincoln, Nebraska - 1971
External Law Studies - LaSalle University, Mandeville, Louisiana - (40 credit hours completed)

PROFESSIONAL AFFILIATION

Clinical Laboratory Manager's Association

CIVIC ASSOCIATION

Committeeman Houston Livestock Show & Rodeo

229

Address
City, State Zip Code
Office #
Home #

OBJECTIVE

Controller

SUMMARY

Over nineteen years of progressively more responsible experience leading to Controller, both international and domestic, with diversified accounting and financial experience including extensive involvement in financial reporting, cost accounting, taxes, treasury, internal control, budgeting and forecasting. Have demonstrated excellent managerial and interpersonal skills which have significantly impacted the corporate bottom line.

PROFESSIONAL EXPERIENCE

NTS CORPORATION - Houston, Texas   1979 - 199_

Deputy Group Accounting Manager, Energy and Transportation Equipment Group (1991-199_)

- Initiated hedging strategies across the Group which resulted in savings in excess of $2.0 million over the past two years.
- Implemented international tax strategies improving after-tax profits by more than $1.0 million in one year.
- Developed valuations and participated in due diligence activities of two acquisitions, one domestic and one Norwegian, adding $150 million in revenues to the Group. Assumed responsibility for assimilation of the domestic business into the company.
- Coordinated the consolidation of two commercial machinery groups into a single $550+ million Group which resulted in annual G&A savings of $2.0 million.

European Region Controller, Equipment Division - Edinburgh, Scotland (1988 -1991)

- Directed major restructuring of the accounting organizations in Scotland and France operations resulting in improved control and planning, while preventing reoccurrence of inventory losses in excess of $5.0 million.
- Dealt with foreign banks to establish bank guarantees, letters of credit, currency hedges, export insurance, and other various treasury functions.
- Prepared application, negotiated, and obtained an $800 million grant for a plant expansion from the Scottish Development Agency.
- Set up new sales/service offices in Oman, Nigeria, Norway and the Hague ensuring tax, legal, financial and accounting controls were adequately addressed.
- Guided in the installation of a new computer system in Scotland, and in France, supervised the in-house development of an IBM-based system which increased functionality. This improved accounting accuracy and timeliness of monthly closing while reducing accounting headcount by one third.
- Implemented percentage of completion accounting for the Scotland operation's expanding subsea project business, which facilitated tracking of $75 million in sales annually.

International Controller, Petroleum Equipment Group - Houston, Texas (1987-1988)

- Developed and implemented procedures and controls in newly formed operation in Jakarta, Indonesia. Installed a PC-based network accounting system and trained local accounting personnel.
- Directed the staffing and training of accounting department of Singapore operation after 60+% turnover in accounting personnel. Personally selected and hired Local Region Controller while filling the interim vacancy, resulting in significantly improved operational stability.

230

Division Controller, Control Division (1985-1987)

- Aided downsizing and eventual closing of California operation and consolidating all manufacturing and accounting into Texas operation. Reduced accounting personnel by 13 in California while meeting the challenge of reducing the Texas accounting staff by three.
- Led the turnaround of failed accounting controls and system to Class A level.
- Drove an effort which brought inventory accuracy from a 50% level to 99% in six months which greatly improved on-time delivery performance.
- Cured computer system deficiencies and subsequently led the conversion to fully integrated VAX-based system (MANMAN).

Manager of Cost Accounting and Billings, Equipment Division (1984-1985)

- Analyzed and developed ways through automation, to cut overhead costs significantly as capacity became underutilized in unforeseen market downturn. Strategies resulted in cutbacks at a sister plant and transfer of accounting support to Houston.

Manager of Financial Analysis, Western Region (1981-1984)

- Set up accounting systems for newly formed manufacturing operation in Venezuela. Recruited, hired and trained local controller, ensuring smooth start up.
- Introduced improvements in budgeting and forecasting by automating and revamping prior practices.

Senior Staff Accountant, Corporate Headquarters - Chicago, Illinois (1979-1981)

- Aided Arthur Anderson and Company on a three month consulting assignment to assess and improve internal management reporting and budget/forecast processes. Recommendations resulted in complete revamp of these processes.
- Conducted several internal audit reviews at the operational level and identified major control weaknesses at two locations.

TEMPO COMPANY - Chicago, Illinois   1975 - 1979

- Held a series of progressively challenging positions including Cost Accountant, Financial Analyst, General Accounting Supervisor and Senior Staff Analyst.
- Compiled and wrote financial sections of Quarterly and Annual Reports to shareholders and various SEC reports.
- Interpreted and implemented new FASB's including development of current cost accounting.

EDUCATION

M.B.A., Accounting, Bowling Green State University, Bowling Green, Ohio - 1975
B.B.A., Accounting, University of Notre Dame, Notre Dame, Indiana - 1973

PROFESSIONAL AFFILIATION/CERTIFICATION

Certified Public Accountant, State of Illinois
American Institute of Certified Public Accountants

TECHNICAL SKILLS

Strong PC Skills using Lotus 1-2-3, Freelance, Excel, Word Perfect, and Word

LANGUAGE FLUENCY

Working knowledge of French

OBJECTIVE

Executive Management

SUMMARY

Over twenty-five years of experience in management, sales, marketing and manufacturing of capital and consumable equipment serving the domestic and international medical imaging and dental industries. Have proven track record in trouble shooting with the ability to turn organizations around in a short period of time. Have demonstrated ability to operate and generate business growth in diverse areas of responsibility with results which significantly contributed to the corporate bottom line.

PROFESSIONAL EXPERIENCE

TIMMONS MEDICAL SYSTEMS, INC. - Newark, New Jersey   1973 - 199_

Timmons Medical Systems, Inc. is a subsidiary of Timmons Corporation with sales of $1.8 billion and 3,500 employees. Timmons AG is an international company with $48 billion in sales and over 391,000 employees and Timmons Corporation USA has $6.4 billion in sales and 35,000 employees.

Turnaround Consultant - Philadelphia District, Pennsylvania (1993-199_)

With the Philadelphia District in a turnaround position, was selected by the President and CEO to re-establish Timmons Medical Systems as a leader in the Philadelphia area. Developed, managed, and directed the sales, service and administrative office community of 90 employees, with profit and loss responsibilities.
- Increased district profit from $2.2 million to $5 million in one fiscal year.
- Developed and successfully implemented a sales marketing strategy that increased total district sales from $23 million to $50 million in one fiscal year.
- Achieved reduction in the district expense ratio from 34% to 23% of total sales in one fiscal year.
- Increased Timmons market share to over 50%, ranking number one in the market.
- Established the highest volume of sales in any district of Timmons Medical Systems.

FRAISER AND LAWRENCE - Greenville, South Carolina (1989-1993)
(Subsidiary of Timmons Medical Systems, Inc.)

President and CEO

Timmons purchased Fraiser and Lawrence in 1985. Due to company losses in 1989, was chosen by the Chairman and President of Timmons Medical Systems to turn the company around to profitability within three years.
- Led the company from a $7 million loss to profitability in three years increasing sales from $50 million to $65 million.
- Directed efforts to integrate the domestic sales force and focused on increasing international business from 10% to 20%.
- Negotiated with major dealers and customers, both domestic and international which maximized return while improving customer relations.
- Successfully implemented the consolidation of two manufacturing facilities into one location with changes in some of the production processes, ensuring state-of-the-art operations.
- Demonstrated the ability to work effectively with international colleagues and customers as evidenced by increased international sales.

232

TIMMONS MEDICAL SYSTEMS, INC.(1973-1989)

<u>Vice President, Senior Field Representative, Zone II Manager</u> - Atlanta, Georgia (1985-1989)

Selected by Timmons to increase sales, profit and market share. Planned, directed and coordinated the efforts of marketing, sales, services and administrative personnel to accomplish the corporate objective. The zone consisted of 6 districts in Central U.S.A. from Michigan to Florida.
- Achieved the company objectives for the zone which was ranked number one in sales profit and market share for Timmons Medical System three consecutive years.
- Increased profits from $2 million to $12 million.
- Managed the sales effort which increased sales from $57 million to $154 million in four years.
- Led the restructuring of the 6 districts which contributed to more effective sales penetration and improved utilization of personnel.
- Participated in the identification and hiring of sales, marketing and operations staff which supported more effective zone operations.
- Coordinated field effort and reported directly to President and CEO.

<u>District Manager</u> - Houston, Texas (1977-1985)
- Established a district office responsible for sales, service and administrative functions for southern Texas.
- Managed district which averaged 13.5% profit annually.
- Increased district sales on the average 36% annually from 1978 to 1982.
- Maintained district expense ratio at 18.8% of total sales annually.

<u>Senior Sales Representative</u> - Dallas, Texas (1973-1977)
- Ranked by company as one of the top medical x-ray salesmen in the United States.
- Achieved an average of $1.68 million in sales annually over a four-year period.
- Received a Million Dollar Club Sales Award for 1974, 1975, 1976 and 1977.
- Ranked as number one sales representative in accessories and supplies for company.

FAST MOTORS CORPORATION - Indianapolis, Indiana   1966 - 1973

<u>Manager of Production Control</u> (1970-1973)
- Participated as part of a start up team that implemented a new, centralized totally automated shipping plant.
- Planned production, coordinated processing of raw materials and managed inventory control resulting in improved operations.
- Coordinated engineering changes with manufacturing plants contributing to more efficient production.
- Scheduled production for 11 manufacturing plants and 145 departments.

<u>Manufacturing Supervisor</u> (1966-1970)
- Selected as one of 20 college graduates to attend company 6-month Training Program.
- Innovated a change in production to individual build and self inspection which contributed to increasing production by 15%.
- Developed knowledge of manufacturing process, employee relations and quality control.
- Promoted to production control.

EDUCATION

B.S. in Business Administration - Youngstown State University, Youngstown, Ohio - 1966

PROFESSIONAL AFFILIATIONS

Charlotte Forum Club
American Dental Trade Association
Supported Junior Achievement Charlotte
Charlotte Chamber of Commerce

Address
City, State Zip Code
Office #
Home #

OBJECTIVE

International Sales and Operations

SUMMARY

Over twenty five years experience in turnaround and expansion of business in multinational environment. Have a proven track record in leading efforts to develop and implement strategic and business plans. Have managed at the P&L level with results which contributed to significant improvement to the corporate bottom line. Have hired management and sales teams and directed the expansion of offices both inside and outside the United States. Have arranged numerous export and development project financings using sources from Europe, North America and the Far East.

PROFESSIONAL EXPERIENCE

ENERGY COMPANY - Brisbane, Australia   1994 - Present

President

Responsible for project development, execution and investment in Australia and the Far East. Managed regional headquarters of an organization composed of operations and project development professionals located in Australia and the United States. Total staff is approximately 150 people.

- Established Energy Company Australia in 1994. First year of operation produced a net operating income of A$30 million.
- Directed company's largest re-deployment of capital outside the United States (US$350 million).
- Identified in excess of $2 billion in investment opportunities for company and structured approach for pursuing.
- Negotiated agreements with state and federal governments in Australia for establishing Energy Company regional headquarters with government support.
- Established representation office in China.
- Negotiated co-development agreements with major oil companies and contractors for projects inside and outside Australia.

SIMPSON & CARLTON - Houston, Texas   1989 - 1993

Vice President

Served on a three member team responsible for the globalization of company's oil and gas, petroleum, and chemical business. Participated in all phases of the acquisition of Carlton to create Simpson & Carlton, a $1.3 billion company. Led work to create the company's international strategy, and to obtain the first contracts outside the United States. Managed an increase in international sales from virtually zero to over $150 million in revenue and $25 million in margin by 1992. As international business increased, assumed responsibility for project development, financing, and Far East regional management under a regional approach which divided the world into four operating sales regions.

- Participated in core team to develop strategy to expand worldwide business to more than $1 billion per year through internal growth and acquisition.
- Identified the $40 million Carlton acquisition and led efforts to create Simpson & Carlton.
- Negotiated joint ventures with Japanese and Korean companies to permit pursuit of business opportunities greater than would have been possible using only the company's resources. Directed bids on more than $1.5 billion opportunities through these joint ventures.

234

- Developed the start up strategy for company's entry into the Mid-east and Far east and then led efforts in all phases of the strategy. The strategy resulted in the Company's first international turnkey projects and the assignment of staff from the United States to execute the projects.
- Sold Simpson's involvement in the $3 billion trans-China pipeline project and negotiated the contract for this involvement. Established joint venture with China National Petroleum Company for project activities outside China.
- Arranged financing and counter trade to support $1 billion in company and worldwide proposals.

INTERNATIONAL INVESTMENT GROUP - Houston, Texas   1983 - 1988

Chairman/President

Formed company with a group of European lawyers and industrialists. Corporate offices were located in Houston and Paris with affiliates in Tokyo and Seoul. Worked on multinational development activities with financing and investors coming from Japan and Europe. Company was bought by its European partners in 1988. Its annual worldwide development activities exceeded $200 million.

- Developed the approach and financing for a major U.S. company to establish a Malaysian operation and pursue business in Southeast Asia.
- Established a venture affiliated with the company for building a log home in village in Japan using prefabricated homes manufactured in Canada. Financed the expansion of the Canadian factory with sources from Hong Kong.
- Directed the strategy and arranged financing for company's pursuit of various projects from waste to energy in the U.S. Midwest.
- Aided Japanese chemical companies to make acquisitions and establish operations facilities in the Southeast U.S.

THE TUTHILL CORPORATION - Kansas City, Missouri   1977 - 1983
(subsidiary of Korean Enterprises)

Vice President and Senior Managing Director: President Special Projects Division

Responsibilities included directing activities of both the U.S. operation and Korean parent. Work involved extended assignments to Japan and Korea. Directed the establishment of a special projects division which grew to 30% of total company revenues by 1983. Led preparation of the company strategic plans and managed key aspects of plan implementation.

BIG 8 ACCOUNTING, INC. - Cambridge, Massachusetts   1971 - 1977

Senior Consultant

Served as consultant to management in the chemical process and construction industries. Annual sales of consulting services exceeded 500% of budget. On occasions, this work included managing employees from the client organization. Managed project teams exceeding 100 people.

EDUCATION

Chemical Engineering (Minor: Business Management), Doctoral Level with MBA - 1974
Massachusetts Institute of Technology - Cambridge, Massachusetts

B.S. and M.E. Chemical Engineering - 1968, 1969
Texas A&M University, College Station, Texas

7) NAME
Address
City, State Zip Code
Office #
Home #

OBJECTIVE

Senior Investment Management

SUMMARY

Financial executive with over 25 years diversified experience in creating, developing, directing and managing investment advisory, mutual fund, pension, life, property and casualty insurance investments for major corporations.

PROFESSIONAL EXPERIENCE

INVESTMENT MANAGERS, INC. - Houston, Texas   1992 - Present

Managing Director
Reported to the President and Chief Executive Officer of a Phase II start-up institutional investment advisory firm. Responsible for its mortgage-backed securities, core portfolios and the development of new business. Also, served as Director of Research and Investment Strategist for affiliated institutional brokerage and investment banking firms.

- Achieved investment performance in first quartile.
- Participated in a consortium to privatize the Argentine Pension System and establish a government sponsored corporation to securitize Argentine mortgages.
- Negotiated terms resulting in the formation of a minority joint venture investment advisory company.

TEXAS CAPITAL MANAGEMENT CO., INC. - Houston, Texas   1989 - 1992

Senior Vice President and Chief Investment Officer
Reported directly to the Chairman of the Board and Chief Executive Officer of a major investment advisory company.

- Managed $18.8 billion diversified invested assets including money market, U.S. Treasury, mortgage backed, corporate, municipal, and convertible bonds and common stocks. Investment performance of money market and stock funds ranked in the top 5% of the relevant Lipper Money Market and Growth Stock Universes.
- Formulated and implemented new investment strategies optimizing High Yield Corporate Bond Fund and the Cortland Funds significantly lowering investment risk in the former and creating a more attractive and competitive product in the later.
- Initiated the design and spearheaded development of International Stock Fund and Adjustable Government Bond Fund facilitating the marketing of two new funds with exceptional earnings potential.
- Perceived unfavorable risk to reward ratio for the proposed Short Term World Income Fund and orchestrated a feasibility study resulting in identification of an unacceptable foreign currency exchange risk and product rejection.
- Improved relationship with third party advisory contract client contributing to annual fee retention of $1.8 million which represented 58% of Company's annual net income.
- Negotiated new custodian agreement resulting in a fee expense reduction for Company and increased investment returns to mutual fund shareholders.

ELNER & COMPANY - Hartford, Connecticut   1987 - 1989

Senior Vice President and Chief Investment Officer - Asset Management
Reported directly to the President/Chief Operating Officer of an international insurance service company. Managed $3.3 billion advisory and $1.5 billion active for client insurance companies.

236

- Actively managed $4.8 billion institutional client portfolios on a total return basis exceeding appropriate benchmarks.
- Instituted a new client advisory service which set objectives and analyzed client opportunities, created and implemented strategic and tactical plans and provided monitoring to ensure goal achievements. Resulting in immediate and successful marketing that increased assets under management by $800 million.
- Developed an asset-liability management program for the life and property and casualty industries which integrated insurance liabilities and investments; resulting in limited risk and enhanced opportunities for profitability facilitating successful marketing of services and increased fee revenues.
- Converted the Private Accounts Division's operating loss to profitability by implementing a program which reduced expenses, increased advisory fees and established a cost allocation procedure.

SOUTHERN CAL LIFE INSURANCE COMPANY - LaJolla, California   1985 - 1987

<u>Senior Vice President and Chief Investment Officer</u>
Reported to the President/Chief Executive Officer and was responsible for all life insurance investment functions including public bonds (investment and non-investment grade); direct placements; commercial mortgages; common stocks and real estate equities.

- Managed $3.5 billion of assets, investing $500 million annual cashflow and exceeded total return benchmarks.
- Served as Chairman of the Investment Policy Committee and Member of the Executive Council and Product Research and Design Committee.
- Evaluated overall competition in financial services for asset accumulation insurance products. Directed formulation of long and short term corporate strategic plans including investments, new and existing market driven products, capital adequacy, distribution systems and risk parameters.
- Organized and managed an asset-liability team of actuarial, marketing and independent consultants.
- Restructured $40 million impaired debt and equity securities to earning assets.

NORTHEASTERN FIRE INSURANCE GROUP - Hartford, Connecticut   1967 - 1985

<u>Assistant Vice President - Portfolio Manager</u>
Reported to Executive Vice President/Chairman of the Finance Committee of an international multi-line insurance company with $13.5 billion investment asset base.

- Achieved investment performance consistently above average as measured by dynamics earned spreads, budgeted net investment income (A.T.), market value differential and relative ranking of total return accounts. "New Money Rate" ranked NUMBER ONE in six of seven years in a universe of leading mutual and stock life insurance companies and the total return account of the Hartford Fire Insurance Retirement Fund ranked in the top 15% of a Fund Evaluation Service for a two-year period. The fund was NUMBER ONE among all pension funds of subsidiaries for the same period of cyclical economic change.
- Developed investment strategy, using state of the art techniques and managed $2.5 billion bond and preferred shares of four life insurance subsidiaries including segmented portfolios for universal life; tax deferred annuities; group pensions, guaranteed insurance contracts; group life-health; and structured claim annuities.
- Managed $3.5 billion municipal bond portfolio of the Hartford's property and casualty affiliates, the $100 million Northeastern Fire Insurance Company Retirement Fund and certain invested assets of foreign financial institutions under management by the Company's investment advisory subsidiary.
- Optimized the structured claim annuities portfolio realizing capital gains and a substantial cash take out which was utilized to rebalance the deferred annuities line of business across corporate entities.

<u>EDUCATION</u>

MBA - Investment and Taxation
BS - Accounting and Corporate Finance
New York University - New York, New York

237

8) NAME
Address
City, State Zip Code
Office #
Home #

OBJECTIVE

Marketing and Business Development

SUMMARY

Over twenty years experience in property and casualty insurance in company, brokerage and risk management. Broad working knowledge of program design, account management and insurance brokerage. Experienced in business plan development and execution with excellent communication and presentation and negotiation skills.

PROFESSIONAL EXPERIENCE

J. B. COMPANY - Houston, Texas   1992 - 199_

Senior Vice President

- Performed Account Executive duties for in-house clients, resulting in 9% increase in commissions for annual income in excess of $168,000.
- Produced and negotiated new client income of over $89,000 annually.
- Marketed $339,000 in new business commissions for agency producer staff.
- Negotiated contracts for five new insurance companies achieving new production objectives.

PHILLIPS & PHILLIPS OF TEXAS, INC. - Houston, Texas   1989 - 1992

Senior Vice President/Director of Marketing

- Directed the analysis, design and implementation of insurance programs; achieved success ratios of 70% on new business and 90% on renewals.
- Participated in direct client production representing the technical aspects of coverage, program design and marketplace evaluation.
- Personally marketed and negotiated insurance for medium to large clients representing commission income of over $1,500,000 annually.
- Developed and maintained relationships with top insurance company officials to ensure best market conditions and increased new business production.
- Negotiated contracts with six new insurance companies resulting in additional market capacity for the agency and over $200,000 annual income.
- Acted in an advisory capacity on a nation-wide basis to other offices on all items relating to Texas market conditions.
- Established all policies and procedures under which marketing activities operated to maximize efficiency and client satisfaction.
- Developed a departmental budget which met expense objectives and provided quality marketing for each client.
- Implemented two new Rent-A-Captive programs resulting in $90,000 additional annual commission.

TOM L. JAMES & COMPANY, INC. - Dallas, Texas   1987 - 1989

Vice President - Marketing Manager

- Directed merger of three agency marketing operations resulting in a 35% budget savings.
- Designed and implemented Agency/Carrier profit sharing management program which increased agency income by over $1,000,000 for 1988.
- Recruited and developed a highly productive marketing team which achieved in excess of $5,000,000 annual commissions, including a renewal to expiring ratio of 1.23%.
- Produced new client income of $175,000 over two-year period.

238

PHILLIPS & PHILLIPS OF TEXAS, INC. - Dallas, Texas   1983 - 1987

<u>Assistant Vice President - Marketing</u>

- Handled the renewal marketing of 14 Risk Management accounts and contributed a 12% growth in commission (1983).
- Assumed marketing management position in 1984 overseeing marketing staff and technical support units.
- Recruited 3 marketers direct from insurance company ranks with one achieving "Marketer of the Year" award in 1986.

SUN INSURANCE SERVICES - Dallas, Texas   1981 - 1983

<u>Vice President - Operations</u>

- Hired at the inception of the company to develop and oversee all marketing, underwriting, service and administrative operations.
- Provided risk management consulting and insurance services to the parent company.
- Developed clients, in addition to parent account, whose premiums grew to over $5,000,000 within two years.

COWBOY INSURANCE COMPANY - Houston, Texas   1976 - 1981

<u>Underwriting/Marketing Manager (Special Risks)</u>

- Hired as Senior Underwriter - Atlanta, and established new business production record of $1.22 million annual premiums.
- Promoted and transferred to Home Office (1978) to develop new large national account division; achieved written premium of over $40 million in large "fortune" type accounts over three-year period.
- Designed first captive insurance program which produced over $3.1 million new annual premium.

SOUTHERN INSURANCE COMPANY - Atlanta, Georgia   1973 - 1976

<u>Senior Casualty Underwriter</u>

- Served as Underwriter for South Georgia agents; represented underwriting, production and marketing for 65 agencies.

EDUCATION

B.A. Psychology - Lipscomb University, Nashville, Tennessee - 1967

ADDITIONAL EDUCATION

Texas Association of Compensation Consumers Annual Conference - 1989 and 1992
Training Program - Lloyds of London - 1990
Negotiation Skills Seminar - 1985

TECHNICAL SKILLS

Acknowledged Expert in Large Lines Casualty
Completed numerous insurance and management seminars
Skilled in design and marketing of Worker's Compensation Programs

PROFESSIONAL AFFILIATIONS

Licensed in Texas as Local Recording Agent
Past Member, Advisory Council for Home and Hartford Insurance Companies

239

9) NAME
Address
City, State Zip Code
Office #
Home #

OBJECTIVE

Senior Executive Management

SUMMARY

Over twenty-five years of bottom-line experience in management, sales and market development, both domestic and international, including thirteen years of senior level management. Have a proven track record in managing business opportunities to achieve superior financial results, realized through re-engineering multiple organizations dealing in the global market place. Demonstrated outstanding turn-around expertise which has resulted in significantly increased profitability through maximizing the productivity and efficiency of company employees.

PROFESSIONAL EXPERIENCE

INDEPENDENT MANAGEMENT CONSULTANT   1993 - Present

Specialize in analyzing prospective companies and corporations for acquisition.

PAULIS INDUSTRIES, INC.   1964 - 1993

<u>President and CEO (Paulis Products, Inc.)</u> - Houston, Texas (1988-1993)
Responsible for operations and activities of Products, Electronics, Automation and other operating divisions of Paulis Products during tenure as President. Operational budget was $25 to $30 million, sales were in the range of $80 to $100 million, with 650-750 employees.

- Realized $35-$40 million in after-tax profit on all operating groups combined during five years as President, which was more than twice that of the corporation as a whole.
- Re-engineered the organization, successfully achieving a rapid turnaround in profit in the largest revenue-producing segment of Paulis Industries from $750,000 in 1987 to $12.5 million in 1991.
- Evaluated and recommended changes in the Direct Paulis Products Sales Force/Representative Network, implementing change where necessary and restructuring the Sales Commission/ Incentive Program, which enhanced and increased revenues from $29 million in 1987 to $53.5 million in 1991.
- Established concurrent engineering concept, combining product and manufacturing engineering to increase efficiency and speed of developing new products and introducing to market, which resulted in 30% to 40% savings in development time.
- Expanded implementation of EDS Unigraphic, CAD/CAE/CAM systems providing advanced tools for new product development processes which tied manufacturing operations into a common database. Initiated computer integrated manufacturing (CIM), resulting in 15% to 20% decrease in rework and 15% increase in profitability due to shorter delivery time.
- Established through-put protocol for manufacturing and delivery of products, thereby replacing large-batch manufacturing and excess inventory, which reduced inventory costs by 10% to 20% and increased product profitability in excess of 15%.
- Installed flexible data network system which supported local area network (LAN) and enhanced overall flexibility and operational efficiency by 20% to 30%.
- Encouraged and guided aggressive development program for electronic products; replaced short-term "patch" approach with long-term evaluation of customer needs and company profitability, resulting in swing from ($1.3 million) loss to an estimated profit of $1 million fiscal 1994-1995.
- Analyzed and implemented replacement of inefficient and costly phone system, combining communications and information systems into a single point network, improving efficiency and communications, which resulted in long term savings of $2 to $4 million.
- Achieved ISO 9001 certification and registration resulting in immediate qualification approval with the majority of domestic and international customers.

240

President (Paulis Oil Tools Company) - Lafayette, Louisiana (1981-1988)
Responsible for sales/marketing and overall operations of Oil Tools Division with an operational budget of $1.5 to $2 million, sales in excess of $7.5 million and 100 employees.

- Re-engineered and restructured Paulis Oil Tools resulting in improved profitability.
- Revised sales/marketing philosophy from a "Gulf Coast Regional Sales Mentality" to worldwide-marketing concept, replacing domestic representatives with direct sales personnel and adding strong international representatives, which resulted in increased annual revenues of $2 million.
- Managed redesign of gas-lift products, entered marketplace with top quality products made of exotic alloys for superior performance in customer use, resulting in ongoing business viability during oilfield downturn between 1982 and 1988.
- Improved image of the Division by enforcing a rigorous Quality Control/Assurance program and improving quality and effectiveness, which resulted in increased profitability by 10% to 15% despite market downturn.

General Manager (Paulis Products Division) - Middle East (1976-1981)
Responsible for Top Oil account and coordination of all Paulis divisions involved in building the world's largest liquid and gas metering systems throughout the Middle East, with annual sales from $15 to $35 million.

- Directed and coordinated activities of fifty international and twenty-five domestic independent companies representing Paulis Industries worldwide during five-year period resulting in sales of $50 to $75 million annually.

Various Positions (1964-1976)

Served in positions of increasing responsibility including:

- Regional Manager (1970-1976)
- District Manager (1968-1970)
- Salesman (1964-1968)

NEWMAN OIL COMPANY   1957 - 1964

Held positions of increasing responsibility as Drilling and Remedial Engineer at various locations including:

- Oklahoma City, Oklahoma (1963-1964)
- Odessa, Texas (1961-1962)
- Ponca City, Oklahoma and Pampa, Texas (1957-1958)

EDUCATION

Bachelor of Science, Geological Engineering - University of Oklahoma - 1957

PROFESSIONAL AFFILIATIONS

Petroleum Equipment Suppliers Association (PESA)
PESA Board of Directors (1990-1993)
PESA Chairman of Manufacturing Committee (1990-1993)
Gas Supplier Association (1964 Present)

MILITARY EXPERIENCE

United States Air Force - Captain
Strategic Air Command (SAC) Intelligence, Walker Air Force Base, Roswell, New Mexico
Tactical Air Command (TAC) Intelligence, Itazuke Air Base, Fukioka, Japan
Honorably Discharged after serving from 1958 through 1961

10) NAME
Address
City, State Zip Code
Office #
Home #

OBJECTIVE

Senior Accountant

SUMMARY

More than seven years of professional accounting and financial experience with primary concentration in engineering and chemical industries. Extensive training and experience with work re-design projects and implementation of TQM. Have demonstrated excellent interpersonal, communication and team building skills as well as strong project management capabilities.

PROFESSIONAL EXPERIENCE

JAY'S POLYMERS INC. - Deer Park, Texas   1991 - 199_

Senior Project Accountant (1992-199_)

Promoted to supervisor and managed a three-member staff with responsibilities for transactions of four corporations with assets valued in excess of $700 million and an annual capital expenditure budget of more than $50 million.
- Facilitated the adjustment of the useful life and depreciation method of over 20,000 assets to realize a $12 million savings in depreciation expense for two corporations.
- Reorganized operations and developed computer programs which streamlined the effort of the capital projects accounting department by 33% for a savings in excess of $40,000 per year.
- Developed staff members by conducting cross-training of responsibilities for all positions which maximized individual performance and ensured increased productivity during heavy workloads.
- Coordinated resources to complete IBM mainframe mass maintenance of Dunn & Bradstreet software resulting in a savings of consulting fees in excess of $10,000.
- Analyzed construction labor contract changes and revised an existing labor system to accommodate these changes while reducing the volume of monthly reports by over 700 pages for a savings of over $8,000 per year.
- Instructed three-day team building courses and facilitated newly formed teams with the implementation of problem-solving methodology as part of a team which trained over 500 employees within two years and saved in excess of $800,000 in training consultant fees.
- Traveled to other accounting departments to consult and train department personnel on the construction-in-process system which reduced lengthy telephone calls by 90% for a $2000 annual savings in long distance expenses.
- Counseled subordinates during department reorganization resolving conflicts and allaying fears which ensured ongoing team effort and maintained high performance.
- Developed local area network (LAN) computer applications to report financial data which reduced hard copy report distribution by 30% and related costs in excess of $1,500 per year.
- Participated in the implementation of a paperless purchasing, receiving, and accounts payable computer system and administered the development of interfaces between the Hewlett-Packard paperless system and the IBM construction-in-process computer system which eliminated over 85 hours of data entry per month and saved over $25,000 per year.

Project Accountant (1991-1992)

- Led a departmental quality steering committee in the implementation of the TQM process and developed a system to ensure 100% participation which resulted in the elimination of two positions for an annual cost savings of $175,000.
- Analyzed the three-way matching process used in the accounts payable process and recommended alternatives resulting in a reduction of cycle time by 20 days and an increase in applied discounts of $50,000 in the first year in which the changes were implemented.
- Reviewed terms of payment compliance on accounts payable vouchers and reduced the margin for error to less than 2% representing a savings of $30,000.

242

- Audited construction contractors' time-keeping methods, tool room and warehouse inventory controls, and compliance with contract requirements which validated a $1.2 million annual expenditure.

HILCREST CORPORATION - Clear Lake City, Texas   1990 - 1991

Project Accountant

- Prepared raw material invoices for payment and maintained Superfund Rebate analysis which resulted in savings of over $1 million.
- Developed database programs utilizing Paradox software which reported project expenditures and maintained over 70 contract personnel records and reduced the time required to maintain these records by 25% representing a savings of $10,000 per year.
- Reconciled over 50 employee advance accounts which were more than a year in arrears and implemented a system to maintain current account reconciliation.
- Processed and reviewed in excess of 100 employee expense reports per week for payment and identified expenses in excess of $2000 which were non-reimbursable.

JOHNS, SILVER & ASSOCIATES - La Porte, Texas   1983 - 1990

Cost Analyst (1987-1990)

- Evaluated, selected, and installed accounting software for a microcomputer, and developed a chart of accounts for use with the new computer system which saved over $30,000 in consulting fees and yearly costs in excess of $50,000 for accounting services.
- Developed a computer-based job cost system for over 70 engineering and construction projects valued at over $20 million.
- Reduced operating costs by over 15% while reviewing accounts payable transactions for accuracy.
- Reviewed and interpreted corporate property and liability insurance policies, coordinated claims, and maintained records which ensured the lowest insurance costs possible.
- Updated a general ledger system resulting in timely statements for the first time in two years.
- Trained five new employees and coordinated their responsibilities which ensured efficient operations.

Clerk Typist (1983-1987)

- Produced proposals and correspondence utilizing desktop publishing software which contributed to obtaining over $10 million in construction and engineering contracts.
- Purchased materials and equipment for construction projects and service of existing fire protection systems. Placed from 20 to 50 orders per day and processed the resulting paperwork.
- Performed general clerical activities including greeting clients, answering phones, and filing.

EDUCATION

Anticipate pursuing MBA at University of Houston, Clear Lake, Texas - beginning September 199_
Bachelor of Science, University of Houston, Clear Lake, Texas - 1990
Associate of Arts, San Jacinto College, Pasadena, Texas - 1989

ADDITIONAL EDUCATION

Interaction Management (1993), Dale Carnegie (1993), PSM Training (1993),
Team Building Training (1991), Statistical Process Control Training (1991),
Instructor Training (1991), ISO Procedure Standardization Seminar (1991)

TECHNICAL SKILLS

Extensive knowledge of Lotus 1-2-3 (including Allways & WYSIWYG), WordPerfect, WordStar,
dBase, Paradox, Harvard Graphics, Freelance, Flow Charting, Windows, DOS
Mainframe software including Dun & Bradstreet, Access + Reporting, downloading to PC
10 key by touch, data entry

11) NAME
Address
City, State Zip Code
Office #
Home #

OBJECTIVE

General Management

SUMMARY

Over seventeen years of increasingly responsible operations management, accounting and auditing experience with companies of varying size, culture and specialization. Possess a unique blend of interpersonal skills, operational and financial management accomplishments and communications effectiveness. Have proven track record in managing business opportunities to achieve superior financial results and in leading management teams which have had a significant bottom line impact on overall company operations.

PROFESSIONAL EXPERIENCE

MEDICAL CENTER - Dallas, Texas   1989 - 1995

Manager, Operations (1993-1995)
Managed operational performance, financial results and personnel for four operational divisions. Supervised the Directors, Project Managers and Analysts responsible for 150 employees, $24 million annual operating budget and the parking, security, shuttle transportation and customer services provided daily for 35,000 physicians, employees, patients and visitors of the Center.

- Reported directly to President/CEO/COO serving as principal advisor on operational activities and their impact on the needs and customer relations issues associated with each of the 41 Center member institutions.
- Developed, presented to the President and participated in obtaining Board of Directors' approval of a $24 million annual operating budget which focused on aggressively reducing expenses rather than increasing revenues through rate increases deemed untimely in a cost sensitive health care environment.
- Established and maintained, through ongoing responsiveness and sensitivity, successful working relationships with executives of the 41 member institutions of the Center.
- Orchestrated and supervised consolidation of daily shuttle bus routes serving over 10,000 customers in remote parking locations. Adjustments to the transportation contract with METRO improved service efficiency, increased customer satisfaction and reduced annual contract expenses by 18% or $166,000.
- Created and led management team which developed and implemented a comprehensive customer service oriented training program, standardized performance expectations and counseling procedures, and eliminated over $150,000 of annual projected cashier overtime costs by centralizing shift scheduling procedures.
- Designed and implemented a deposit program which recouped annual access card inventory and set-up costs of $80,000 by encouraging customers to return cards for an immediate cash refund.
- Identified and eliminated potential employee theft transactions decreasing anticipated annual lost revenue by $165,000.
- Renegotiated $1.5 million third party security contract, converting fleet vehicle agreement from ownership to per unit fee arrangement, reducing annual contract expense by $40,000.
- Responded to and successfully resolved over 500 monthly customer parking complaints and violation dismissal requests through promotion of consistent, fair and courteous rule application.
- Coordinated outsourcing, through attrition of 33% or 30 cashier positions, eliminating recruiting, hiring and benefits costs associated with all open positions while increasing productivity of payrolled (non-contract) employees.

244

- Coordinated and supervised parking and security for special events held on the Center campus including the annual 4,000 participant Fun Run, the College of Medicine and University graduation ceremonies, dignitary and protocol visits of Heads of State, Ambassadors, Ministers of Health, and Consul Generals.
- Acquired invaluable historical, political and long range insight by regularly attending meetings of the Board of Directors and related Executive, Audit, Building and Lands, Finance and Forward Planning Subcommittees of the Center. Also attended Policy Council meetings and served as executive representative on the Parking and Mobility Advisory Council and the Student Affairs Advisory Council.

Director, Parking Services (1992-1993)
Managed four customer service offices and the headquarters access control center responsible for sales, activation and maintenance of 27,000 monthly parking contracts.

- Developed and implemented sales strategy increasing contract parking revenue by 36% or $3.9 million in two years.
- Developed, presented for Senior Vice President/Chief Operating Officer approval and met $15 million annual operating budget.
- Developed and implemented capacity monitoring system enabling facilities to be oversold by over 200% while eliminating garage/lot closings due to full capacity status.

Assistant Director, Purchasing (1990-1992)

- As acting Director, planned, directed, reviewed and controlled the activities of the Purchasing Department for Center and Center Housing corporations.
- Wrote and established clear purchasing procedures that strengthened internal control and served diverse multi-division operational needs associated with fifteen departments and a $26 million combined operating/capital budget.

Senior Staff Accountant (1989-1990)

- Saved corporation over $13,000 of sales tax late fees by obtaining due diligence waivers from the Texas Comptroller of Public Accounts.

TEXAS COMPTROLLER OF PUBLIC ACCOUNTS - Houston/Austin/Dallas   1978 - 1988

Tax Auditor

- Conducted sales tax, franchise tax, motor vehicle tax and hotel/motel tax audits on Fortune 500 corporations, partnerships and proprietorships throughout the United States.
- Developed and implemented training programs for field audit personnel, providing technical instruction and audit supervision.
- As Industry Liaison, presented seminars for professional associations providing tax information and compliance guidance.
- As Policy Liaison, analyzed legislative tax changes and developed agency policies in cooperation with industry representatives.
- Conducted audits on over 400 entities which generated over $7 million in tax revenue as well as immeasurable goodwill and voluntary compliance for the State of Texas.

EDUCATION

B.B.A., Accounting - The University of Texas at Austin - 1978

Address
City, State Zip Code
Office #
Home #

OBJECTIVE

Senior Counsel

SUMMARY

Over twenty-five years experience as an attorney with both direct and oversight responsibility in the areas of regulatory, general corporate, business, energy and international related law. Experience includes representation of these companies in various legal matters with emphasis on the negotiation and preparation of documents and contracts, litigation management, regulatory work, international operations and general corporate practice.

PROFESSIONAL EXPERIENCE

BRIGADE COMPANY - Houston, Texas   1980 - 199_
(International Group, Megar Industries, Inc. - Houston, Texas)

General Attorney/Assistant Secretary

Responsible for legal matters relating to the mining, production, distribution and marketing of the company's products and services on a worldwide basis.

- Successfully supervised and settled a lawsuit seeking damages in excess of $1 million for breach of mining agreement and mining claims and leases, reducing exposure to $150,000.
- Prepared and negotiated credit/loan agreement, security agreement and related instruments, together with personnel work agreements for subsidiary's operations in Kazakhstan.
- Prepared and implemented use of standardized forms and basic contracts for field personnel, resulting in time savings in contract preparation while ensuring proper substantive content.
- Supervised local counsel and prepared and negotiated documents for joint venture mining operation in Nigeria.
- Prepared and negotiated agreements and instruments for purchase of barite processing plant, prepared documents and assisted the company in negotiations with labor unions and principals to realize substantial cost savings through related plant consolidations and closing.
- Supervised local counsel, in dismantling barite mining and related subsidiary company operations in Thailand.
- Prepared and assisted management in negotiation of agreements for lease of fluids process equipment and services in Venezuela, Columbia and Ecuador valued in excess of $1 million.
- Prepared and advised management in connection with worldwide customer master work/service agreements valued in excess of $50 million.
- Supervised and advised management in the closing of specific domestic operating areas and in their place, the establishment of independent distributors and agents resulting in annual cost savings of approximately $500,000.
- Supervised local counsel and prepared documents in connection with the reorganization of the company's operation in Venezuela resulting in significant savings.
- Contributed as part of a team in Brazil in connection with the negotiation and establishment of a joint venture mining, manufacturing and marketing operation in Brazil.
- Successfully established subsidiary operations in the Ivory Coast, Cameroun and Gabon.

246

- Supervised outside counsel and established litigation plans in connection with a series of labor claims and suits in Brazil resulting in significantly reduced liability.
- Successfully handled (both directly and through outside counsel) mineral patent applications (Bureau of Land Management) covering barite and bentonite reserves valued in excess of $100 million.
- Advised management in negotiation of and documented the company's financing and participation in operator exploration and development programs.
- Prepared documents, negotiated and advised management in the long-term supply of bentonite to Japan (Nissan, Toyota) valued in excess of $4 million.
- Supervised local counsel and prepared documents in connection with establishing subsidiary operations in Colombia, Peru and Ecuador.
- Represented the company on creditor committees, supervised counsel and documented various claims and bankruptcy proceedings valued at over $25 million.

TOT, INC. - Tulsa, Oklahoma   1978 - 1980

Senior Attorney

Primary responsibility in connection with aspects of oil and gas production, regulatory matters, pipeline, natural gas processing, storage and marketing operations.

NATURAL GAS COMPANY - Houston, Texas   1969 - 1978

Attorney

Primary responsibility for regulatory matters, pipeline, natural gas processing, storage and marketing operations.

PUBLIC SERVICE COMMISSION - Austin, Texas   1967 - 1969

Attorney/Hearing Examiner

Conducted administrative hearings, issued written opinions and orders and advised Commission members concerning rail, truck and utilities (telephone/electric) rate and certificate matters.

FEDERAL TRADE COMMISSION - Washington, D.C.   1966 - 1967

Attorney

Assigned to Bureau of Competition.

EDUCATION

J.D., University of Nebraska - 1966
B.S., Business Administration, University of Nebraska - 1964

PROFESSIONAL AFFILIATIONS

Nebraska State Bar Association
Oklahoma Bar Association
State Bar of Texas
The Houston Bar Association

Address
City, State Zip Code
Office #
Home #

OBJECTIVE

Business Development Management

SUMMARY

Over fourteen years experience in business management, sales, marketing, application development, product development, technical service, and R & D of plastics. Have a strong record in new product development and business development emphasizing value added products with significant contributions to corporate profitability. Excellent interpersonal and communications skills emphasizing the team approach have contributed to many successful projects and accomplishments. Have proven management skills with experience managing product development and technical service groups.

PROFESSIONAL EXPERIENCE

THE PLASTICS ASSOCIATION - New York, New York   1993 - Present

Executive Director

- Creating and implementing programs which promote the effective use of plastics piping systems.
- Contributing to the development of standards and regulations, educating designers, installers, users and officials.
- Preparing and publishing up-to-date technical reports, presented recommendations and statistics on plastic pipe, serving as a liaison with industry, educational and government groups and providing a forum for problem solving and innovation with plastics piping products.

PLASTICS CONSULTING SERVICES COMPANY - Houston, Texas   1993 - 1994

Consultant

Provided consulting services to the chemicals and plastics industries.

- Wrote market analysis of polyethylene pipe markets for a plastic pipe manufacturer.
- Developed training programs for a plastics manufacturing company which taught a general introduction to polyethylene plastics and how polyolefins degrade and how they can be stabilized to prevent degradation.
- Conducted market analysis for a major division of a Fortune 500 chemical company interested in introducing a new chemical additive into the polyolefins industry.
- Analyzed engineering plastic alloy product line for a client company.
- Conducted analysis of the engineering plastics industry for a major foreign plastics company.

JAY'S POLYMERS INC. - Houston, Texas   1980 - 1993

Application Development Specialist (1990-1993)
Engineered Compounds Group

Responsible for profit and loss and business development, including sales and marketing of Jay's Engineering Compounds in North America for four product lines: IXEF polyarylamide compounds, IXEF M modified polyarylamide compounds, EREF polypropylene-nylon compounds, and PRIMEF polyphenylene sulfide compounds. Managed a budget of $ 340,000 in 1992.

- Increased sales by 450% in 1992. Projections for 1993 were for 300% growth.
- Identified applications with potential sales of over 4 MM lbs ($12 MM).
- Managed product promotions. Wrote and coordinated the release of product announcement, coordinated and managed industrial trade shows.
- Developed and managed a product literature program which responded to more than 2700 inquiries in two years.

Group Leader - Polypropylene Extrusion Applications (1987-1990)
Product Development and Services Department

Managed six professionals and four technicians. Directed the product development and technical services activities for Biaxially Oriented Polypropylene (BOPP) film, cast film, blown film, sheet, thermoforming, fibers and strapping applications.

- Developed nine film resins for which sales grew by 1250% from 1987-90.
- Developed five controlled rheology fiber resins and reformulated the entire fiber product line (seven grades). Sales in 1992 were 85 MM lbs.

Group Leader - Polyethylene Extrusion/Injection Applications (1984-1987)
Product Development and Services Department

Managed two professionals and four technicians. Directed the product development and technical services activities for pipe, sheet, thermoforming, geomembranes, injection molding, rotomolding and monofilament applications.

- Developed seventeen new products for pipe, sheet extrusion and thermoforming applications resulting in increased sales of 535% from 1983 to 1989. In 1992 sales in these areas exceeded 220 MM lbs.
- Developed two new resins which resulted in increased sales for injection molding applications by over 176% from 1985 through 1988. Sales of products for these applications exceeded 250 MM lbs in 1992.

Research Chemist - Polypropylene Research and Development Department (1980-1983)

- Developed new products for extrusion applications.
- Promoted to Research Chemist after two years as a Polymer Chemist.
- Developed blowmolding and specialty extrusion grades for which sales exceeded 38 MM lbs in 1992.

EDUCATION

PhD, Chemistry - 1980
Rensselaer Polytechnic Institute - Troy, New York

BS, Chemistry - 1968
Boston College - Chestnut Hill, Massachusetts

TECHNICAL SKILLS

PC Software:
WordPerfect, Lotus 1-2-3, Graphwriter, dBase, PC Write

Mainframe Programs:
HP E-Mail, HP Word, Laboratory Information Management System (LIMS)

14) NAME
Address
City, State Zip Code
Office #
Home #

OBJECTIVE

Health Care Administration

SUMMARY

Over sixteen years experience in all aspects of Health Care ranging from Staff Nurse to Administrative Director, including inpatient and outpatient services, marketing and fiscal administration, program development, construction and design. Have demonstrated a unique blend of interpersonal skills, financial management and clinical expertise.

PROFESSIONAL EXPERIENCE

SAINTS HOSPITAL - Houston, Texas   1980 - 199_

Director of Clinical Observation Unit (1990-199_)

- Coordinated the design, planning and construction of new 20-bed Observation Unit which included managing a construction budget of over $1 million dollars and interior furnishing budget of $500,000.
- Formulated new policies and procedures for expanded service which resulted in a smooth transition of staff responsibilities.
- Determined the needs and controls required to meet contractual cost, schedule, procurement and operating requirements of the project which resulted in minimizing costs and increasing productivity.
- Modified plans, procedures and work activities when necessary which overcame obstructions to project progress resulting in on-time completion of construction.
- Developed patient classification system for outpatients based on acuity which set standards, improved customer satisfaction, and increased revenue by 15%.
- Prepared and monitored annual budgets for three departments in excess of $2.5 million dollars.
- Established a comprehensive quality assurance program which met regulatory requirements to improve documentation and was adopted by other departments resulting in improved communication and patient outcome.
- Created telemetry bed criteria for expanded Cardiology services which increased physician satisfaction and increased Cardiology admissions by 25%.
- Streamlined admission process for observation patients having radiological procedures which decreased waiting time by one hour and improved consumer satisfaction.
- Developed discharge waiting area concept which increased bed turnover resulting in expanded services and efficient patient flow.
- Contributed as a member of the Hospital Information Steering Committee which coordinated the planning, acquisition and installation of a new Hospital Information System.
- Participated actively in university and hospital committee which addressed many issues including infection control, quality assurance, new products, nurse appreciation, retention and recruitment.
- Reviewed and analyzed monthly statistics to prepare monthly financial reports which justified staffing and identified clinical service requirements.
- Increased contribution margin by $200,000 (18%) over a two year period by marketing outpatient services, limiting expenses and maximizing outpatient charges.
- Served as Director of Otolaryngology and Dermatology 1991-1992 which provided continuity and enhanced service.

- Formulated and implemented internal education programs for staff which expanded knowledge base, improved morale and promoted retention.
- Instituted comprehensive cross training with the Otolaryngology and Dermatology clinics which strengthened services and expanded clinical expertise.
- Surveyed consumer needs and attitudes which led to consumer satisfaction and greater staff accountability.
- Assisted in preparation of quarterly and annual reports reflecting economic growth or decline by clinical service which resulted in expanded clinical service and increased fiscal responsibility.

Otolaryngology Coordinator (1986-1990)

- Coordinated clinical services for patients and assisted physicians with procedure.
- Maintained clinical schedules for six resident physicians and eight attending physicians.
- Counseled, sedated and observed pediatric patients for Audiology testing.
- Developed, produced and distributed monthly education calendars for Ambulatory Care.
- Assisted physicians with outpatient surgical procedures.
- Formulated and implemented educational teaching of adults and pediatric patients with tracheostomy tubes resulting in greater patient confidence and reduced problems when discharged home.
- Assisted in the preparation and review of quarterly and annual financial reports.
- Monitored Central Supply items, sterile packs, pharmaceutical supplies and maintained inventory through direct vendor requisition.
- Organized and taught internal staff development and education programs.

Staff Nurse (1980-1986)

- Delivered direct patient care in a critical care environment, including physical and emotional support of surgical and trauma patients.
- Served as relief charge nurse for 20-bed unit.

EDUCATION

Bachelor of Science Candidate - Anticipated completion December, 199_
Prairie View University - College of Nursing, Houston, Texas

Associate Degree - Hinds Junior College, Raymond, Mississippi - 1976

PROFESSIONAL AFFILIATIONS

National Association of Female Executives
Texas Nurses in Business

CIVIC ASSOCIATIONS

March of Dimes Teamwalk Medical Chairperson (1986-Present)
Volunteer In Public Schools (VIPS)

LICENSURE AND CERTIFICATION

Registered Nurse, State of Texas
Basic CPR, American Heart Association

251

15) NAME
Address
City, State Zip Code
Office #
Home #

OBJECTIVE

Electrical Engineer, Software and Hardware

SUMMARY

Five years of professional computer and electrical engineering experience, with extensive experience in the following areas: semiconductor assembly, quality improvement, specification coordination, new product refinement, test program generation, device application, device failure analysis, customer new device qualification and training in water fab process operation.

PROFESSIONAL EXPERIENCE

FINE COMPUTERS, INCORPORATED - Houston, Texas   1988 - Present

Product Development Engineer (1989-Present)

- Generated test software and associated hardware for development, characterization, production and failure analysis of memory devices and surface mount memory modules.

- Performed characterization of prototype memory devices, collected data from characterization, and analyzed data for device refinement.

- Generated software routines for characterization of memory devices reducing engineering time spent on data collection.

- Conceived and created weekly/monthly production yield report which aides analysis of yield improvement for surface mount production.

- Performed trouble shooting for customers' systems which utilize application's specific memory.

- Evaluated, revised and improved new product technical data sheet aiding customer application of the product.

- Accepted short term overseas assignment to provide technical support for assembly rework of high volume customer return and the rework was completed in less time and with a higher yield than targeted.

Product Engineer (1988-1989)

- Coordinated new device customer qualifications achieving qualification by several major customers in record times.

- Served on quality improvement team focusing on customer failure analysis cycle time and shortened the time from 45 days to 15 days.

- Participated with device failure engineers to perform customer failure analysis and provide feedback to wafer fab for effective process and improvement quality.

- Maintained, reviewed and updated computerized manufacturing specification flow.

252

- Conducted and presented a study of device parametric shifts under corrosive environment as part of the analysis to determine device reliability.

- Trained overseas for 6 weeks in assembly operation and new device internal qualification.

QUALITY HOSPITAL - Houston, Texas   1986 - 1988

Computer Operator

- Performed daily back up of accounting data file for Digital PDP 11/44 and IBM 340.

GOLDEN SEMICONDUCTOR CORPORATION - Austin, Texas   1985 - 1986

Computer Assistant

- Assisted design engineer inputting plots of VLSI communication microcontroller schematic Into PC databases for auto routing and logic simulations.

- Worked with layout engineers in performing file transfer and maintenance on Unix system with VAX/VMS computer.

EDUCATION

B.S. Electrical and Computer Engineering
University of Texas at Austin, Austin Texas - 1986

ADDITIONAL EDUCATION

Completed 9 hours in graduate electrical engineering
University of Houston - Central Campus

Wafer Fab Process Training
Juran on Quality Improvement
Total Quality Awareness
Seven Quality Control Tools
Statistical Quality Control
Design in Reliability
Failure Analysis Training
M16A/C Tester Software Training
Colt III/III A Tester Hardware Training

TECHNICAL SKILLS

Software: M16A/C, Colt III/III A Programming languages, PASCAL, FORTRAN, BASIC, C, Motorola 6805 and Intel 8085A Assembly Languages, Lotus 1-2-3

Hardware: Microprocessor and Perpheral Interfacing, PLL Modem Link, Microwave Communication, Digital Logic Design, Regulated Power Supply, Oscilloscope, Spectrum Analyzer, Curve Tracer

253

16) NAME

Address
City, State Zip Code
Office #
Home #

OBJECTIVE

Senior Project Engineer / Manager

SUMMARY

Over nine years of broad engineering experience with increasingly responsible positions in R&D - Product design, process design, quality and total manufacturing systems within the medical field.

PROFESSIONAL EXPERIENCE

FT MEDICAL INC., Cardiology Division - Houston, Texas   1990 - 199_

Senior Manufacturing Engineer

- Managed the successful manufacturing start-up operations of the PTA (Angioplasty) Catheter over a 9-month time period.
- Developed and implemented the following management systems and procedures: process design and process flow for the Just-In-Time (JIT) system; Statistical Process Control (SPC) and Total Quality Management (TQM); equipment and manufacturing documentation Standard Operating Procedure (SOP); cost management and unit cost reduction which resulted in approximately 30% savings; plant layout and assembly technology; design tooling and material handling.
- Updated company validation procedures to ensure compliance with current GMP and FDA validation guidelines.
- Developed and implemented a special team building session within the PTA Project which enhanced team work and was subsequently adopted throughout the plant.
- Developed and implemented processes which dramatically reduced product cost by 40%.
- Established the product cost and cost reduction forecast for 5-year planning projections.
- Conducted process and equipment validation resulting in greater efficiency and safety.
- Participated in the development of product and packaging design to improve marketability.
- Served as a key contributor in transferring process technology from R&D to full-scale manufacturing.

CARDIAC SYSTEMS - Los Angeles, California   1986 - 1990
(Division of Jones and Co.)

R&D Process Engineer (1989-1990)

- Served as a key member in the transfer of a new fixed wire catheter from R&D stage into full scale manufacturing.
- Developed and implemented catheter design and modification, process design and process flow for Just-In-time (JIT) inventory, statistical process control and total quality plan, as well as equipment and manufacturing documentation (SOP).
- Conducted process and equipment validations for new and existing catheters.
- Supervised pilot production to resolve process problems during pilot build.
- Performed the introduction and coordination of new catheter design, transferring from R&D to pilot and full scale manufacturing.

254

R&D Project Engineer (1986-1989)

- Served as a key engineer in designing new products including initial component parts and material specifications; procured materials and developed process; wrote disclosure to patent attorneys; provided information package for FDA filings; and developed the introduction to marketplace.
- Managed project from conceptual design through final debugging and animal/clinical testing resulting in a new business unit within the company.
- Provided technical training for the pilot supervisor and assemblers for new catheter design to initiate the pilot program and manufacturing, which resulted in successful product introduction.
- Planned and conducted initial manufacturing and quality specifications.
- Provided technical support to clinical research and physicians during clinical tests.
- Developed and implemented test design changes resulting in the use of Design of Experiment (DoE) throughout the company.
- Provided information to marketing department to assist in positioning the product and developing brochures.
- Maintained up-to-date information on competitive products and advised project team on technical strategy to enhance the product.

NEW TECHNOLOGY - Kansas City, Missouri   1984 - 1986

Quality Control Engineer

- Assured quality supplies from vendors and established quality requirements for purchase orders; qualified vendors; inspected semiconductors to meet specifications.

EDUCATION

M.S. Industrial Technology - Concentration in Automated Manufacturing
B.S. Mechanical Engineering Technology
Central Missouri State University, Warrensburg, Missouri - 1985

ADDITIONAL EDUCATION

Massachusetts Institute of Technology - Cambridge, Massachusetts
Cardiovascular Pathophysiology for Engineers - 1989

California State University - Fullerton, California
Practical Application of Process Validation for the Medical Device Industry - 1989

PROFESSIONAL AFFILIATIONS

Society of Manufacturing Engineers (SME)
Industrial Management Society

TECHNICAL SKILLS

Auto-CAD/CAM
Lotus 123
Excel
Micro Project Planner
Design of Experiment

255

Address
City, State Zip Code
Office #
Home #

OBJECTIVE

Senior Staff Engineer

SUMMARY

Over thirty years experience in engineering/design and manufacturing of pressure containing components. Extensive experience solving difficult thermal expansion problems with bellows expansion joints.

PROFESSIONAL EXPERIENCE

THE LANGER HILL CORPORATION - Houston, Texas   1976 - 199_

Chief Engineer's Staff (1979 - 199_)

Performed as an expert consultant in mechanical engineering to engineering managers and clients on special mechanical problems, including corrective measures for field problems.

- Devised unique internally insulated bellows expansion joint design for catafin process MTBE plant, avoiding elevated temperature design. This resulted in a cost saving of $1,882,500 (56%) over original pricing.

- Negotiated stainless steel piping material specification alternate with the MTBE plant licensor, which permitted a higher B31.3 Piping Code design stress. This converted to a $1,265,000 savings (24%).

- Solved field problem with piping mitered elbows at Kuwait LPG plant for B31.3 Piping Code compliance, Kuwait Oil Company. Field fix prevented plant shutdown for welding and replacement of 2000 large diameter elbows.

- Designed (by analysis) the primary quench exchangers for a number of Millisecond ethylene furnaces, resulting in satisfactory life performance for severe service (1650°F in 1200°F out application).

- Conducted stress and life cycle analysis of delayed coking units for TECH Oil. The results of this study showed the client sufficient remaining life in the coke drums to proceed with a plant revamp.

- Performed finite element heat transfer and thermal stress analysis of cat cracker ring forging connecting stripper, disengager and regenerator. This analysis provided the client with design integrity assurance for a non-standard size cat cracker.

Staff Consultant - Civil/Mechanical Engineering (1976-1979)

- Developed quick design calculation method for external loads on piping and vessels, such as nozzle and trunnion loads.

- Provided stress and life cycle analysis leading to the successful development of the Millisecond ethylene furnaces.

256

- Designed heat exchanger channel flanges for PEP Company ethylene plant. These designs resulted in leak tight flanges complying to ASME Sec. VIII Div. 1.

- Designed heavy wall flanged and flued heat exchanger shell bellows to ASME Code allowable stresses.

IFP, Inc. - Chicago, Illinois   1954 - 1976

Performed in various positions of increasing responsibility including:

- Test Engineer (four years): Performed testing and development of aircraft and missile ducting systems.
- Supervisor, Analytical Engineering (10 years): Supervised a stress engineering section of 10 engineers on NASA space program hardware for Saturn I and V booster launch vehicles.
- Supervisor Expansion Joint Design (two years): Supervised design group of six engineers and draftsmen.
- Manager Product Design (two years): Supervised product design group of 20 engineers and draftsmen.
- Project Manager: Managed the design and manufacturing for major LNG piping expansion joints including Brunei (Borneo) LNG, Columbia LNG (Cove Pt., Md.), Elba Isl. LNG (Savannah, GA), Distrigas LNG (NY) and Pertamina LNG (Badak, Borneo).

EDUCATION

B.S. Engineering Science
North Central College, Naperville, Illinois - 1952
Additional Engineering Courses, Illinois Institute of Technology

CERTIFICATION

Registered Professional Engineer, Texas and Illinois

PROFESSIONAL AFFILIATIONS

Member American Society of Mechanical Engineers
Member ASME B31.3 Chemical Plant and Petroleum Refinery Piping Code Committee
Past Member, ASME B31.10 Cryogenic Piping Systems Code Committee
Member Sigma Xi - The Scientific Research Society
Past Member, Technical Committee, Expansion Joint Manufacturer's Association

TECHNICAL SKILLS

Proficient with ANSYS Finite Element Analysis Program
Conducted numerous finite element heat transfer and stress analysis
studies on pressure vessels and piping

PUBLICATIONS

Kellogg Report SIP-128 "Stress Due to Local Loads on Cylindrical Shells"
"Bellows Expansion Joints Pressure Loads, Anchors and Guides"
presented at 4th International Pressure Vessel Conference, London, 1980
"Flow in Corrugated Hose", Product Engineering, 1963

NAME, P. E.
Address
City, State Zip Code
Office #
Home #

OBJECTIVE

Senior Environmental Management

SUMMARY

Over twenty-seven years experience in environmental engineering for a wide range of industries and government facilities including steel, petroleum, petrochemical, commercial hazardous and solid waste disposal, chemical, aluminum, food, plating, and Department of Defense Air Force and Army bases. Have demonstrated strong record of innovative and cost-effective resolutions for remediation projects and wastewater treatment facilities. Have broad experience including process development, studies, detailed design, turnkey projects, construction observation, permitting, business development, strategic planning, management, and administration. Have gained in-depth expertise in regulatory and contractual negotiations. Possess proven capability in business development resulting in significantly increased revenues and profits.

PROFESSIONAL EXPERIENCE

HAMMOND-SCIENCE - Houston, Texas   1990 - 1993

Vice President and Office Manager

Responsible for office of 45 professionals with peak revenues of $12 million. Organized and implemented business development and strategic planning programs. Provided technical and financial oversight for projects and maintained client liaison. Developed office protocols for technical, financial, and administrative activities.

- Increased office staff from 12 to 45 in 1.5 years with resultant increase in revenues from $2 million to $12 million.
- Re-established relationship with major client to retain multi-year project resulting in increased project revenues from $14 million to $25 million.
- Achieved client and project diversification including Department of Defense, hazardous waste disposal companies, and remediation projects with resultant sales exceeding $15 million in two years.
- Performed expedited remediation of 20,000 cy of material and re-design of wastewater treatment plant (WWTP) to avoid RCRA regulation with savings in excess of $30 million.
- Developed machine to remediate contaminated gravel, reducing the cost from $8 million to $2 million (patented by client).
- Completed study and innovative design to obtain agency approval to construct WWTP upon an impoundment closure resulting in the preservation of valuable land space for production facilities.
- Developed exemplary inter-company relationship for joint project completion resulting in remediation revenues exceeding $40 million and studies for capital projects totalling more than $100 million.

HAZARDOUS WASTE MANAGEMENT - Chicago, Illinois   1983 - 1990

Environmental Manager / Remediation Manager

Responsible for line management of commercial disposal sites remediation activities as well as consent agreement negotiations, consultant management, contractor selection and oversight, selection for remediation alternatives, and supervision of site staffs for post-closure activities. Annual budgets exceeded $30 million. Provided environmental oversight of hazardous waste treatment and disposal sites including landfills, incinerators, treatment, injection wells and fuels reclamation facilities. Responsibilities included permitting, agency liaison, overview of proposed treatment processes, and health and safety program management for facilities with more than $200 million in revenues. Developed environmental programs with staff of 60. Participated in strategic planning for facilities and pre-acquisition environmental audits.

258

- Negotiated consent order for remediation of commercial HW site which resulted in excess of $50 million in savings and produced a favorable agency precedent.
- Obtained one of the first interim status expansions of commercial landfill disposal capacity which will provide for revenues of more than $100 million and which received national and state awards for design excellence.
- Served as key participant in the development of the company-wide ground water monitoring program for more than 1200 wells with annual costs exceeding $20 million and obtained agency agreements to reduce costs by $7 million per year.
- Obtained timely procurement of HW and TSCA permits for eight commercial treatment and disposal sites and for commercial remediation division projects to allow uninterrupted operations.
- Obtained some of the first clean closure approvals for land-based HW disposal units, eliminating future liabilities and post-closure care costs exceeding $10 million.

ENVIRONMENTAL COMPANY - Chicago, Illinois   1969 - 1983

Vice President/Technical Director/Project Manager

Provided technical oversight for staff of 140 professionals. Served as Project Manager for studies, design, construction observation, turnkeys for industrial and municipal WWTPs. Performed business development, and client liaison activities, construction observation, start-up services, and operator training.

- Developed and designed innovative, patentable physical-chemical WWTP for first facilities to meet Best Available Treatment standards for blast furnace/coke plant wastewaters, which was installed at two grass-roots facilities.
- Expanded a $5,000 study for a food industry client into a $2 million turnkey project and achieved $1 million in savings through innovative design and reclamation of salable by-product.
- Designed filtration plant for 60,000 gpm steel mill wastewater to reduce costs by more than $10 million versus conventional filter design, which allowed construction without interruption to operations.
- Performed planning studies for several integrated steel mills for environmental control systems with capital costs exceeding $200 million.

JONES CORPORATION - Chicago, Illinois   1966 - 1969

Project Manager / Engineer

Responsible for process development and design of industrial wastewater treatment, water supply, and solid waste management systems. Design projects included physical-chemical plants up to 50,000 gpm capacity, unique facility for deep well injection of coke plant liquors, and in-mill process water systems for steel manufacture. Conducted treatability and pilot plant studies for a variety of physical-chemical and biological treatment systems in the steel, aluminum, plating, specialty metals, and other industries.

EDUCATION

MS Water Resources Management, University of Wisconsin - Madison, Wisconsin

BS Civil Engineering - Sanitary Option, Marquette University - Milwaukee, Wisconsin
Honors: Tau Beta Pi (Engineering Honor Society), Chi Epsilon (Civil Engineering Society)

REGISTRATIONS

Registered Professional Engineer: Illinois, Indiana, Texas, Oklahoma

PROFESSIONAL AFFILIATIONS

American Academy Environmental Engineers, Diplomate
American Institute of Chemical Engineers
Air and Waste Management Association; American Water Works Association

19) NAME

Address
City, State Zip Code
Office #
Home #

OBJECTIVE

Director of Health, Safety and Environmental

SUMMARY

Over eighteen years experience primarily in directing proactive safety programs for international land and marine seismic operations, cable and heavy equipment manufacturing and in managing corporate security of domestic and international facilities and field operations. Have established a proven track record in developing and implementing programs resulting in increased safety awareness, reduced accidents and lost time injuries.

PROFESSIONAL EXPERIENCE

CONSOLIDATED SAFETY SERVICES - Houston, Texas   1992 - Present

Owner
Provide domestic and international loss control services for the geophysical, oilfield services, construction and transportation industries. Services include audits, training and establishing total loss control services to prevent injuries, asset losses and to maintain compliance with policies and regulations.

NOR COMPANY - Houston, Texas   1974 - 1992

Director of Safety & Security
Responsible for Safety and Security Management of data processing centers, land and marine seismic operations, domestic and foreign. Extensive hands on experience with U.S. Department of Transportation (FMCSA - USCG), OSHA, EPA, Texas Water Commission, Bureau of Alcohol Tobacco and Firearms and Workers Compensation regulations and programs.

- Created a Safety Training Division and developed a Safety Management Course which resulted in reduced lost time injuries by 25% annually for 1990 - 1992.
- Produced 5 multi-lingual safety training videos which ensured effective communication of safety programs to all employees.
- Contracted with certified Crane Operator Instructor and Certification company to train and certify crane and lift truck operators in compliance with federal regulations.
- Created a safety advisory program. Experienced supervisors and managers were trained in safety policy, procedures and management, which they shared with crews on a global basis. Successful safety advisors returned to operations with an advancement.
- Developed a safety manual which received recognition from management and client companies as one of the best in the industry.
- Contracted with and monitored programs of accredited institutions and academies for marine fire fighting, offshore helicopter survival, explosives handling, helicopter passenger safety, crane and forklift operations and first responder, emergency medical training.
- Instituted a driver selection, training, rollover protection and safety belt program resulting in reduced injuries and the risk of deaths. Program included training for Commercial Drivers License (CDL) and compliance with U.S. Department of Transportation regulations.
- Developed a Crisis Management Plan to deal with natural disasters, criminal acts, such as kidnapping, and political emergencies in foreign countries.
- Contracted with a highly recognized trauma center to provide emergency medical consultation with offshore and land personnel in remote environments.
- Customized an accident, injury and illness statistical reporting program which resulted in up-to-date measurements of safety performance.

260

- Served as Chairman of International Association of Geophysical Contractors Safety Committee; assisted in the organization of a blue ribbon task force which revised the industry safety manual and training guidelines adopted by oil production companies.
- Managed a Drug/Alcohol awareness program which included employee testing and searches, significantly reducing drug use and on-the-job injuries.
- Coordinated with Architects, Engineers and Contractors in planning, selection and installation of security programs and systems in all new data processing facilities and on marine seismic vessels.
- Conducted environmental audits for compliance with state, local and federal regulatory agencies resulting in bioremediation of contaminated soil and a hazardous waste disposal program.
- Investigated accidents and property losses, breaches of security, and implemented or recommended corrective action to management.
- Managed a Department of Defense Security Program for a facility which was cleared as secret level by D.O.D.

LOUIS & ASSOCIATES - Houston, Texas   1972 - 1974

Investigator

- Investigated accidents, personal injuries, corporate fraud, thefts, will contests and anti-trust matters as assigned by corporate defense law firms.
- Appeared before Grand Juries which resulted in indictments and recovery of large sums of monies for corporate victims.

EDUCATION

Houston Community College, Houston, Texas - currently enrolled
Cameron Commercial College, Temple, Texas - Graduated

ADDITIONAL EDUCATION

British PTF-ICI Nobel Explosives Training Course
Travelers Insurance - Fleet Safety Management - Ergonomics
DuPont Training Division - Explosives Handling & Safety
Shell Oil Co. - Safety Health & Environmental Management
Texas A & M Ext. Service - Hazardous Waste Management - All Updates
Texas Education Agency - Defensive Driver Instructor Development
IBM - Protection for Data Processing Facilities
American Red Cross - First Aid/CPR Instructor Development Course
Bell Helicopter - Helicopter Safety
American Truckers Association - Transportation Regulations

PROFESSIONAL AFFILIATIONS

Texas Safety Association
National Safety Council
American Society of Safety Engineers
Gulf Coast Safety and Training Group
American Truckers Association Safety Council

LANGUAGE FLUENCY

Bilingual - Spanish

261

20) NAME
Address
City, State Zip Code
Office #
Home #

OBJECTIVE

Employee Benefits Consulting

SUMMARY

Twenty years experience in human resources and employee benefits management with in-depth knowledge of the corporate benefits function. Hands-on experience in benefits design, communication, financing and planning. Self-starter, alert to problem solution using quality management techniques.

PROFESSIONAL EXPERIENCE

REAL COMPANY - Houston, Texas   1989 - 199_

Manager, Health and Welfare Plans

- Managed a $20 million Flexible Benefit Program for this quality driven international engineering company. Achieved $250,000 annual savings from re-engineered work process activities.
- Developed and implemented a vendor search for a health plan claims administrator resulting in $1 million savings in reduced fees and medical cost management techniques.
- Developed communication materials for the Flexible Benefits Program including an award-winning Summary Plan Description document which contributed to improved employee understanding and participation.
- Analyzed health plan utilization and claims information, initiated design recommendations and established annual budget and long-term plan pricing strategies to meet company's objective.
- Negotiated service contracts and performance standards with administrators and vendors which ensured maximum return on investment. Consulted with management and employees on benefit issues which enhanced management/employee relations.
- Managed plan compliance activities, assuring legislative conformance and timely reporting to the Internal Revenue Service.

INSURANCE SERVICES, INC. - Dallas, Texas   1987 - 1989

2nd Vice President, Corporate Benefits

- Managed 21 corporate-sponsored retirement plans and 40 health and welfare plans for over 25,000 employees and agents and 8,000 retirees.
- Implemented a pre-tax contribution plan under IRC Sec. 125 incorporating cost-containment features for a $35 million medical program.
- Developed a corporate Benefit Cost Analysis for creating long-term, corporate health care strategies and establishing a base-line measurement.
- Consulted with in-house management, legal and actuarial personnel regarding benefit plan funding and administration issues. Coordinated purchase of $65 million annuity contract.
- Developed a consolidated retiree database for pension plan valuation and administration which improved response time to inquiries and increased efficiency.

RAINER SERVICES, INC. - Houston, Texas   1971 - 1987

Director of Human Resources (1985-1987)

- Managed the human resources and benefit functions, reporting to the Senior Financial Officer during a period of major downsizing activities.

- Developed benefit plan communications and employee presentations following spin-off, sale or shut down of subsidiary locations which contributed to effective implementation of corporate changes.
- Reported to the Plan Administrative Committee to manage the termination and total distribution of the defined contribution savings plan and the partial termination and surplus recapture of pension plan assets.
- Recruited and coordinated orientation of corporate office staff for new headquarters located in Dallas, Texas within 60-day period.
- Directed corporate outplacement and relocation activities during shutdown of Houston office resulting in a successful transition.

Manager of Employee Benefits (1980-1985)

- Managed the corporate employee benefits function for this highly diversified energy corporation during its peak financial years. Successfully merged three defined-contribution plans.
- Set-up an in-house health claim processing unit resulting in significant plan cost reductions.
- Implemented a pre-tax, premium conversion plan (IRC Sec. 125 plan) for health benefits resulting in significant FICA savings.
- Created self-insured Long-term Disability Benefit Trust under 501(c)(9) of the Code which ultimately became fully funded.
- Effectively interacted with senior company management and outside plan trustees, consultants, actuaries, legal counsel and group health providers.
- Developed employee communications and conducted employee presentations for a diversified industry group of corporations including offshore drilling, financial services, engineering consulting, pipeline and coal mining.
- Assisted regional management and their local health-care physicians and hospitals in Southern Kentucky to establish preferred-provider relations.

Manager of Personnel Systems and Services (1976-1979)

- Managed the implementation of a corporate Human Resource Information System for a diverse employee group within 16 subsidiary companies.
- Interfaced with corporate data processing and subsidiary-company users to determine system and user requirements.
- Developed standard and specialized reports for consolidated personnel and benefit reporting.
- Developed user training and documentation materials to ensure data integrity.

Personnel Generalist (1971-1976)

- Administered the company's group insurance plans; recruited non-technical office personnel; assisted in the development of personnel policies, EEO and AAP programs.

EDUCATION

BBA, Personnel Management - Texas Tech University, Lubbock, Texas - 1970

ADDITIONAL EDUCATION

CEBS Life, Health and Other Group Benefit Programs - 1989
CEBS Retirement Plans: Basic features and Defined Benefit Approach - 1989

PROFESSIONAL AFFILIATIONS

Houston Area Health Care Coalition
Former Member, Houston Personnel Association

TECHNICAL SKILLS

Lotus 1-2-3, WordPerfect, Harvard Graphics, Easyflow

21) NAME
Address
City, State Zip Code
Office #
Home #

OBJECTIVE

Information Systems Management

SUMMARY

Twenty years of diversified information systems experience including programming, systems design, application development, customer support and staffing, communications, estimating and scheduling.

PROFESSIONAL EXPERIENCE

UNIVERSITY OF TEXAS M.D. ANDERSON CANCER CENTER - Houston, Texas   1992 - Present

Systems Analyst III/Project Manager
Reported directly to the Associate Vice President and Chief Information Officer of Information Services (CIO).

- Conceived, obtained approval and implemented a computer services contractor vendor list resulting a reduction of lead time for contract employment from 3 months to a few days.
- Solicited bids from 200 vendors for qualification on computing services vendor list; coordinated review of bid responses with IS directors utilizing groupware software system; coordinated vendor interviews for selection of 30 finalists. Evaluation process was successfully completed in 4 months.
- Conducted search for computer-based Patient Record Project Partnership (CbPR) partner with hospital providing orientation training, including creation of an orientation manual, for prospective partners.
- Provided summaries for the project steering committee which facilitated the decision making process.
- Conducted a computer-based Patient Record Patient Data study to evaluate percentage of patient data recorded electronically versus manually which was part of a feasibility test to understand the amount of system integration required to complete a computer based patient record.
- Compared hospital functional requirements to industry literature which provided a computer-based patient record industry requirements comparison. Co-authored paper with CIO.
- Served as Project Manager for executing a computer-based patient record project, successfully establishing institutional goals, strategic plans, and selecting vendor of choice.

THE J. BOB COMPANY - Houston, Texas   1980 - 1993

Manager, Information Systems - Human Resources (1991-1993)
Directed support and development of Human Resources and Benefit departments computer systems with a staff of 6 team members.

- Expanded the use of existing applications by justifying and installing a Novell network which interconnects IBM, VAX and microcomputer platforms, saving the company over $50,000.
- Managed the development of a savings investment plan system which will improve service to employees and will decrease costs to the plan by over $100,000 annually.
- Integrated VAX retiree database into IBM welfare database to save company overhead costs in tracking welfare on two separate systems.
- Supervised the design of a service award data base reducing administration expenses by over 50%.
- Implemented the use of xBase to respond to ad hoc queries on employee information database eliminating a bottleneck which was dependent upon mainframe programming.
- Reduced data entry costs by 50% with the implementation of spreadsheet applications in the salary review process.

Manager Information Systems - Information Center (1989-1991)
Directed Information Center staff of 15 team members. Responsible for providing customer support on IBM mainframes, DEC VAX's and microcomputers to 4,000 company employees worldwide.

- Established hardware and software microcomputer standards for the company, which are still in use, through program development and product evaluations.

264

- Managed computer training activities which increased employee proficiency through improved computer skills.
- Coordinated help desk supervision with department to quickly resolve reported problems and maintain high productivity of company employees.
- Managed systems support group which expanded the integration of microcomputers into company and a wide area network.

Supervisor, Information Systems - Information Center (1985-1989)
Developed support services in the Information Center for microcomputers and their integration with IBM and VAX computer systems.

- Implemented the use of microcomputer networks resulting in $100,000 savings.
- Designed a material tracking system for overseas projects in remote areas used by jobsites to save inventory dollars and improve construction costs.
- Created and implemented a field inspector system that expedited communications between the home office and the field expediters.
- Managed purchases, installation, tracking and maintenance of $2 million of computer equipment.
- Originated satellite office and vendor communications to VAX and microcomputer systems which eliminated data entry and rework on projects.

Systems Engineer, Systems Engineering (1980-1985)
Responsible for transient analysis calculations through the use and maintenance of a Fortran developed computer system.

- Trained engineering staff in the use of company computer systems.
- Designed and implemented hand held computer programs which saved the company mainframe computer expenses and improved engineering productivity.
- Conceived and designed civil engineering programs to calculate underground piping specifications which eliminated 75% of the manual effort formally applied.

- Engineer - Risk Management WEATHERFORD INSURANCE COMPANIES   1976 - 1980
Houston, Texas

- Systems Engineer - Linde Division UNION CARBIDE CORPORATION   1976 - 1978
Tonawanda, New York

EDUCATION

B.S. Mechanical Engineering, Newark College of Engineering - 1976
Post-Graduate Business Administration, University of Houston

TECHNICAL SKILLS

Hardware: IBM 30XX, Four-Phase, DEC VAX, IBM PC/AT and PS/2, Compaq, AT&T, Toshiba, Apple, 3Com/Enterprise (Bridge) and Novell ethernet networks, IBM 3270, Hayes and MNP type modems.

Software: IDMS, VSPC, ATMS, TSO, VMS, Culprit, Intergraph, DEC office automation products, Mass-11, Recital, Basic, Fortran, MS-DOS, CP/M, Lotus 1-2-3, dBase III+/IV, Clipper, FoxPro, Wordstar, Crosstalk, Kermit, Xmodem, pcLINK, SIMPC, Reflections, Freelance Plus, MS Chart, MacDraw, Excel, Write, Paint.

Group Systems: Facilitator, IS Decision Room, groupware application

PROFESSIONAL AFFILIATIONS

Information Center Managers Association
Houston Area League Users Group
Tesseract Users Group
Health Care Information Management Systems Society

Address
City, State Zip Code
Office #
Home #

OBJECTIVE

Vice President, Operations

SUMMARY

Over twenty-six years of diversified experience in the development, operations and maintenance of open pit mines and mills. Excellent track record in managing a wide variety of disciplines through strong team building efforts. Successfully met cost and production requirements during growth and depressed economies.

PROFESSIONAL EXPERIENCE

GOLDEN BEAR COMPANY - Houston, Texas   1965 - 199_
(Formerly Kingman Corporation - Tucson, Arizona)

Operations Manager - Denver, Colorado (1988-199_)

- Developed an inexperienced work force to be competitive in the mine and mill operations and maintenance. This group achieved the lowest production cost per ton ($0.90 to mine and $4.65 to mill) in the company, even under adverse conditions.
- Established a guideline for supervision and management to treat all employees fairly and equally, creating opportunities for the employees to excel based on their attitude and abilities.
- Negotiated both construction and utility agreements ranging up to $15 million, with a total project capitalization of $60 million.
- Coordinated major mine and mill construction, bringing both mine and mill production on line simultaneously from grass roots development, which included all support groups.
- Initiated and organized the reclamation and environmental plan for the project, resulting in minimum long term liability for the company.
- Guided supervision and department heads through an employee evaluation program and the development of job descriptions.
- Implemented a comprehensive communication skills training program for supervision and department heads and strongly supported a Safety Program which resulted in zero severity rate in injuries.
- Instituted plant revisions to increase production by 12% with minimal capital expenditures.
- Managed 4000 acre Irrigated Farm from close to receivership under different owner to projected positive cash flow for 1993.
- Participated in preparing 5-year, annual and semi-annual business plans.

Mine Superintendent - Hilltop, Nevada (1980-1988)

- Reduced mining costs by 33% during first three years on site.
- Increased mine production by 30% per year, successfully meeting short and long term production requirements.
- Contributed support to developing a program which won the Centennials of Safety Award from the Mine Safety Health Act (MSHA), the highest National Government award given for safety performance.
- Inspired and successfully coordinated a preventative and planned maintenance program for increased equipment availability.
- Developed supervisors and general foremen using various techniques involving supervisory skills training and resource management maximizing their contribution to the organization.
- Restructured the mine department to cross-train employees and establish goals and objectives resulting in improved performance and productivity.
- Pioneered four ore bodies into production from grass roots development.

266

Mine General Foreman - Tucson, Arizona (1976-1980)

- Unified work force in the mining operations to work together as a team, allowing mine to meet and exceed productivity goals.
- Mined at costs which were typically $0.10 per ton or 13.5% less than the costs of the company's other mines.
- Implemented and taught duPont's "Stop to Observe and Prevent" safety program, which led to the mine department winning the MSHA Centennials of Safety Award.
- Scheduled work force and equipment to meet and exceed production requirements.
- Evaluated all salaried employees in the entire mine department to maximize personal growth and development.
- Coordinated the annual and five-year business plans for capitalization and expenses.
- Assisted the mining department in developing two ore bodies into production, while actively running a production mine.

Mine Supervisor - Tucson, Arizona (1969-1976)

- Created an atmosphere of motivation for the work force through trust and communicating a sense of urgency, which enabled the crew to set a production record of 30,000 tons or 50% over plan in a shift.
- Organized and planned the major repairs of off-road haul trucks and electric shovels.
- Delivered safety training to employees resulting in an improved safety record.
- Conducted meetings with employees to open two-way communication for a thorough understanding of needs and goals.
- Assigned and scheduled crews of up to twenty-five employees.

Equipment Operator - Tucson, Arizona (1965-1968)

- Built roads and dumps with dozers, graders, loaders and electric shovels for mine production, drill sites, benches and mine development.
- Trained fellow employees in the operation of mining equipment and milling equipment at 16,000 ton-per-day mill and 25,000 ton-per-day mine.

EDUCATION

Dan Ammerman's Experience - Media Relations - 1990
University of Nevada, Reno, Nevada - Project Management - 1987
Northern Nevada Community College - Electric Construction - 1984
Mine Safety Health Act - Certified Instructor - 1976
Mojave County Community College - Communication/Supervision - 1972 & 1979
Paramount High School, Paramount, California - 1961

PROFESSIONAL AFFILIATIONS

Board of Directors - Colorado Mining Association
Member - Nevada Mining Association

CIVIC ASSOCIATIONS

Chairperson, Lander County School Board - 1982-1986

23) NAME
Address
City, State Zip Code
Office #
Home #

OBJECTIVE

General Management

SUMMARY

Over twenty-seven years experience in the petroleum industry with progressively more responsible supervisory and management positions in operations, refining, training, human resources and marketing. Have demonstrated strong organizational development skills emphasizing bottom-line contributions. Have proven management skills with excellent interpersonal and communications ability emphasizing teamwork and goal attainment.

PROFESSIONAL EXPERIENCE

MILLS ENERGY, INC. - Houston, Texas   1986 - 1996

General Manager, Marine Fuels - New Orleans, Louisiana (1992-1996)
Responsible for $3 million budget with 38 employees which encompassed profit and loss, marketing, operations and administration for seven (7) terminals in Southern Louisiana. Responsibilities included supplying diesel, lubricants and chemicals to drilling, inland marine, shipping and commercial industries which generated over $30 million in annual sales.

- Developed and implemented market strategies that resulted in $20 million increase in sales from $9.5 million to $29.6 million in one year.
- Directed changes in operations procedures resulting in a 50% reduction in down time on marine equipment, translating to $70,000 annual savings on maintenance and $1.1 million in increased sales annually.
- Additionally accepted responsibility as Commercial Manager for credit approval up to $50,000 per customer.
- Initiated upgrading and reorganized the accounting area to handle increased sales without increasing staff, resulting in savings of $20,000 to $40,000 annually.
- Expanded operations from four (4) to seven (7) terminals in one year, resulting in $4 million in increased sales.
- Compiled statistical data and aided in the negotiations for the sale of the division, consisting of barges, tugs, trucks, trailers, terminals and inventory, resulting in $5 million profit on the sale.
- Coordinated the transfer of $1 million in assets and inventory to purchaser of the division and controlled the orderly close-out of $3.2 million in receivables and all outstanding payables.
- Managed the sale of the remaining assets and inventory of divested division, resulting in a savings of over $200,000 to the company.

Operations Manager, Marine Fuels and Asphalt (1986-1992)
Managed operations for a department with over $100 million in annual sales which included directing resupply, blending and delivery of fuels from two (2) terminal locations including activities of schedulers and administrative staff.

- Expanded operations to port of New Orleans, effectively increasing market potential by $45 million.
- Aided in the redesign and directed changes to the New Orleans facility which reduced blending time by 50% resulting in the potential to increase sales by $1.1 million annually.
- Negotiated day rate charters for tug boats and barges, resulting in 12% rebate on freight rates or $108,000 annual savings.

268

- Aided in the design and justification for a $6 million terminal achieving approval that resulted in increasing sales by $7.2 million annually.
- Controlled expansion of operations capabilities by 600,000 barrels per month translating to $5.7 million in monthly sales.
- Developed procedures for inventory control, cost control and administration resulting in $350,000 annual savings.
- Aided in the development of an associated business resulting in net profits of $600,000 annually.
- Participated in the development of marketing strategies, resulting in increased sales of 600,000 barrels per month.
- Researched and participated in the assessment and acquisition of a $2.2 million privately owned company.

SMITH OIL COMPANY - Houston, Texas   1979 - 1986

Operations/Marketing Representative, Marine Fuels (1981-1986)

- Improved communications between marine fuels and refinery operations, reducing loading delays and improving sales potential by $7.2 million annually.
- Researched historical trends and market statistics to develop world-wide marketing strategies.
- Trained to replace Marketing Manager and Operations Manager during their absence.
- Contributed to the development of blending methods, resulting in opening new markets previously unavailable to the company.
- Scheduled, coordinated and issued blending instructions for the supply of fuel to ocean vessels.

Training/Labor Relations Manager (1979-1981)

- Justified and participated in the development and approval of $500,000 training facility.
- Aided in the development and implementation of a maintenance training program, resulting in a $500,000 cost savings in the first six months of operation.
- Designed and developed operations and new hire training programs resulting in improved performance.
- Negotiated and achieved designation as a field test facility for American Petroleum Institute sponsored training programs, thereby acquiring the latest training programs at no cost to the refinery.
- Evaluated job applications and conducted employment interviews resulting in selection of best qualified candidates.

PREVIOUS EXPERIENCE   1967 - 1979

Held the following positions of increasing responsibility:
- Smith Oil - Quality Control Supervisor (1978-1979)
- Smith Oil - Start-up Operator, FCC Unit (1977-1978)
- Sharp's Oil & Gas Company - Operator, Udex and FCC Unit (1967-1977)

EDUCATION

Electronics & Management Major - (110 Semester hours)
San Jacinto College - Houston, Texas

Plan to complete Bachelor of Arts, Business and Administration (Projected Graduation 199_)
University of Houston - Houston, Texas

TECHNICAL SKILLS

WordPerfect, Lotus 1-2-3

24) NAME

Address
City, State Zip Code
Office #
Home #

OBJECTIVE

Operations Manager

SUMMARY

Twenty-three years retail management experience in convenience grocery/gasoline and restaurant management. Positions included operations, merchandising, marketing and personnel responsibilities. As strong problem solver, self-starter and proven leader, have excellent record of growth and accomplishments.

PROFESSIONAL EXPERIENCE

CROCKETT CORPORATION   1987 - 199_

Operations Manager - Houston, Texas (1991-199_)

Responsible for budget attainment of $42,000,000 merchandise sales through 400+ employees.

- Accepted operational and marketing responsibilities for 78 convenience stores when company downsized due to restructuring. To improve P&L deficiencies and low employee morale, began an immediate program of training, development and progressive motivational techniques.
- Established minimum acceptable store standards for cleanliness, in-stock conditions and customer service. Because each team member was involved in setting these standards, compliance was immediate. Rating system was greatly responsible for an increase of 13% in merchandise sales.
- Challenged and assisted supervisors and store managers to develop programs on a store-by-store basis for increase in gasoline sales and profit. Strategy resulted in a 13% increase in gallonage and 22% increase in gross profit dollars.
- Negotiated better costs and promotions from wholesalers allowing company to lead competition in promotional activity. This resulted in an 11% gross profit increase in grocery.
- Reduced store salaries 10% by training supervisors and store managers in proper techniques for interviewing and screening of prospective employees to reduce turnover. Hiring part-time employees became policy resulting in a 38% decrease in overtime hours.
- Evaluated cause of high repair/maintenance costs. Established system holding repair personnel accountable for all hours worked. Hired an "in-house" gasoline repairman. Total savings resulted in a 32% decrease in monthly repair costs.

Division Manager - Houston, Texas (1989-1991)

Responsible for budget attainment of $175,000,000 merchandise sales through 1800+ employees.

- Directed operational and marketing activities for 300-plus stores located along Gulf Coast from Lafayette, Louisiana, to Brownsville, Texas.
- Decreased inventory loss from 2.25% to 1.05% through emphasis on training and development of district managers and store supervisors. In seven cases, supervisory management was given written objectives, emphasizing need for improvement. Of the seven supervisors, six succeeded.
- Implemented guidelines for negotiations and relations with vendors to decrease costs and increase profits by $200,000 in the first three months in position.
- Established consistent evaluation system to identify "performers" for recognition for advancement.
- Increased sales and gallonage by 15% through ongoing communication and training of management personnel.

270

Division Manager - Tulsa, Oklahoma (1988-1989)

Responsible for budget attainment of $160,000,000 merchandise sales through 1700+ employees.

- Managed over 300 stores in five states involving extensive travel and highly efficient communications. Stores were located in Oklahoma, Kansas, Missouri, Arkansas and Texas.
- Revised promotional strategy of soft drinks and beer, encouraging wholesalers to offer deeper discounts, resulting in 17% increase in sales and 12% increase in gross profit dollars.
- Reduced inventory loss from 2.29% to 0.97% of sales by establishing increased training expectations and holding management responsible for results.
- Increased gasoline gallons by 14% through establishment of different gasoline strategy developed and implemented by supervisors throughout the division.

District Manager - Houston, Texas (1987-1988)

Responsible for budget attainment of $23,000,000 merchandise sales through 240 employees.

- Assumed responsibility for turnaround of 45-store district which had been without a manager for one year. District was behind previous year in sales and gasoline gallons. Supervisors and store personnel were lacking in direction and motivation.
- Established structured guidelines for all personnel to insure that standards for conduct, store conditions and profitability were met. Sales increased by 26% and gallons increased by 19%.
- Implemented accountability at store and supervisory levels to achieve established goals. Inventory loss decreased from 3.10% to 1.09% in 60 days. Customer complaints decreased by 264% due to emphasis on customer service.
- Promoted two supervisors to position of District Manager who had been previously targeted for replacement.

HAYES FOOD SERVICE - Houston, Texas   1985 - 1987

Sales Associate

Assigned to geographic area with only 12 accounts, generating negative sales growth. Through consistency, determination and superior customer service, grew business to 67 accounts in the first year.

SHERMAN CONVENIENCE STORES - Houston, Texas   1980 - 1985

District/Zone Manager

Progressed from store associate to store manager in three months. Promoted to supervisor responsible for eight stores after six-month tenure with company. Promoted to District Manager (45 stores) at 18-month tenure and Zone Manager (185 stores) at two-year tenure as result of outstanding performance.

GOURMET RESTAURANTS - Baytown, Texas   1972 - 1980

Manager-Partner

Joined family business and assisted in growth from one location to three. Due to ill health of parents, dissolved partnership and pursued new opportunities.

EDUCATION

Del Mar College, Corpus Christi, Texas
Business Administration

OBJECTIVE

Materials Management

SUMMARY

Over eighteen years experience in international and domestic purchasing and materials management, operations, financial analysis and administrative management. Have extensive knowledge of procurement procedures, with strong analytical abilities and excellent communication skills. Have demonstrated ability to interface effectively with all levels of management as evidenced by successful negotiations and materials management achievements which significantly contributed to the bottom line.

PROFESSIONAL EXPERIENCE

ACME MEDICAL INSTITUTE   1994 - Present

Director of Materials Management
Responsible for all aspects of materials management for three hospitals and six satellite clinics with a staff of 25 and an annual supply budget of $35 million.

- Initiated proposal, presented action plan to senior management, and spear headed the implementation of a centralized purchasing and distribution center for three hospitals within Columbia Corporation. This combined inventory will result in an initial savings of $325,000.
- Reduced annual costs by $278,000 on the top twenty warehouse items through aggressive negotiations and product utilization through corporate contracts.
- Served as Chairman of the Product Standards Committee which produced savings of $100,000 through research and evaluation of highest quality, least cost, and product standardization.

INTERNATIONAL OIL SERVICES, INC. - Houston, Texas   1989 - 1994

Procurement Specialist
Responsible for purchasing over $1.2 million in material on an annual basis for integrated oil and gas partnership in Indonesia which included travel to Java and Kalimantan to monitor operations.

- Initiated and participated in purchasing and logistical support actions which resulted in achieving 18% lower prices through aggressive negotiations.
- Created actions to address savings through consolidations of material which resulted in savings of $600,000 over three years.
- Created the company Purchasing Guideline and Procedures Handbook for the purpose of standardizing and enhancing procurement and materials management activity which eliminated redundancies and improved overall efficiency by 15%.
- Supervised seven professionals and clerical staff in absence of Purchasing Manager for frequent periods of three to five weeks contributing to a 10% increase in productivity.

BEST HOSPITAL - Houston, Texas   1987 - 1989

Lead Buyer
Responsible for procurement of all materials for 37 departments, including the Emergency Room and Life Flight with an annual budget of $32,560,000.

- Created vendor selection grid analyses and procedures to document and analyze incoming bids which improved quality of service by 25%.
- Researched, developed, and implemented new transcription system for entire hospital saving $350,000 the first year and significant amounts on a continuing basis.

- Reduced hospital expenditures on rental, lease, and service agreements through negotiations which resulted in savings of $525,000 and additional savings of $100,000 in capital equipment purchases.
- Travelled throughout the United States to evaluate potential new product lines and vendors which saved an average of 20% on capital and operational expenditures.
- Participated in fund raising for the Life Flight program. Initiated and participated in public speaking engagements to area rotary clubs and other business associations resulting in increased consumer awareness and a sponsored golf tournament.
- Advised other buyers in major acquisitions, trained and directed clerical staff on special projects resulting in increased efficiency and effectiveness which ultimately saved 20% on projects valued at over $6 million.

GEOLOGICAL CONSULTING, INC. - Houston, Texas   1986 - 1987

Business Manager
Responsible for all aspects of establishing a small geological consulting business including contract negotiations, bookkeeping and procurement.

- Analyzed and determined pricing schedules. Prepared all proposals and quotations resulting in annual sales of $150,000.
- Negotiated and purchased all equipment, supply and service agreements saving over $10,000.

OFFSHORE DRILLING INTERNATIONAL - Houston, Texas   1984 - 1986

Principal Buyer
Responsible for coordination of all procurement activity for 10 offshore drilling platforms located worldwide, including extensive negotiations involving repair and maintenance.

- Prepared material values associated with inventory disposition enabling asset recovery of $500,000.
- Served as Authorization for Expenditure (AFE) administrator which included interfacing with operations, engineering and accounting on capital projects resulting in effective coordination and compliance.
- Achieved savings of $200,000 annually through vendor contract negotiations.
- Resolved all vendor invoicing and shipment discrepancies, resulting in on-time payment to vendors and decreasing lead time to the field by 75%.

PRIOR EXPERIENCE   1976 - 1984

- Lead Expeditor for SOS Oil and Gas, Houston, Texas (1980-1984)
- Buyer/Expeditor for PV Offshore, Houston, Texas (1977-1979)
- Buyer/Expeditor for Thomas Supplies, Inc., Houston, Texas (1976-1977)

EDUCATION

B.S. Political Science - University of Texas at San Antonio, San Antonio, Texas - 1976

ADDITIONAL EDUCATION

Marine Well Control School - 1985
Medical Technology
Various Seminars: Supervision and Management
National Association of Purchasing Conferences

PROFESSIONAL AFFILIATIONS

National Association of Purchasing Management
National Association of Purchasing Management of Houston, Inc.

TECHNICAL SKILLS

Computer and PC literate, WordPerfect 5.1, Microsoft Word, Excel
Purchasing/Expediting/Traffic Management System

273

26) NAME
Address
City, State Zip Code
Office #
Home #

OBJECTIVE

Process and Catalyst Development Chemist

SUMMARY

Over twelve years experience in process research, product development and coordination of experimental products on commercial lines of polyolefins (HDPE and PP). Expertise includes inventing/developing commercially important catalysts to improve resin performance, new resin development through additives formulation, process/product quality improvement, technical marketing and service and manufacturing troubleshooting. Gained expertise in engineering resins, specifically polymer blends and property improvement of polybutylene terephthalate (PBT). Have demonstrated effective supervision, team leadership and participation.

PROFESSIONAL EXPERIENCE

BEST POLYMERS, INC. - Deer Park, Texas   1989 - 199_

Senior Chemist - Catalyst and Polymer Development

Served as the chief liaison between Polypropylene Production and the Product Development and Services group. Responsibilities include scheduling, planning, and coordination for all experimental product campaigns, final approval on all experimental products specifications, catalyst and process troubleshooting, liaison with company's Technical Group in Europe for all catalyst and technology transfers and initiation of quality improvement measures for production processes.

- Conducted over 140 experimental production trials which resulted in the commercialization of 40 new products.
- Coordinated and edited the Product Development Department ISO-9002 level 2 manual and wrote six procedures for the level 3 manual. Company passed the audit and was certified for ISO-9002.
- Developed a non-sticky masterbatch formulation which resolved feeding problems for six products totaling 50 million pounds-per-year and improved production quality by 50%.
- Participated on a Quality Improvement Team for Polypropylene Film Resins to address quality problems in production which were identified and corrected in the first quarter of 1993.
- Studied the detrimental effects of processing additives on clarifiers in polypropylene resulting in identification of new solutions. Four new products are under development which will enable company to compete in the clarified polypropylene market.
- Investigated the effects of different additive combinations on the molecular weight and its distribution changes during compounding for better control which will significantly increase the quality of 60% of the entire product line (250 million pounds).
- Initiated and led a Quality Team to streamline the product specification system which resulted in a 20% reduction in time required for product approval or changes in product specification.

274

HALBERT COMPANY - Houston, Texas   1981 - 1989

Senior Resin/Product Development Engineer-HDPE (1987-1989)

- Spearheaded the technical defense of the DuPont litigation (1978 PMA patent) against company and all company licensees. At least 10 billion pounds annual production of HDPE in the US were affected. The defense included: A.) the development and field testing of ethylene/butene copolymers in blow molding, injection molding, and rotational molding applications; and B.) the development and customer trials of new resins out of the scope of the claim range through new catalyst technology. The successful technical defense secured the confidence of company management and contributed to winning the case.
- Developed high performance blow molding HDPE resin with lightweighting advantage. Conducted extensive field evaluations which resulted in significant improvement in productivity.
- Developed a blend of HDPE and styrenic polymer to control bubble stability in blown film.
- Developed low density PE film with superior impact resistance through catalyst technology and conducted extensive customer evaluations. This resin is being commercialized and will be introduced to the market in late 1993 as the first LLDPE using company technology.
- Developed a single modal high molecular weight polyethylene film resin to compete with bimodal high molecular weight polyethylene film resin.

Process Research Chemist (1981-1987)

- Invented a group of catalysts which control polymer fines through "chemical coating" resulting in a reduction of the safety hazard due to polymer fines and improving the fluff transfer rate in the plant.
- Improved the productivity of an existing commercial polyethylene catalyst by 60%.
- Demonstrated the criticality of the terminal vinyl group in the current crosslinking product.
- Reduced taste/odor of polyethylene resin by cocatalyst control and controlling finishing conditions.
- Initiated the development program of poly (4-methyl-1-pentene) by publishing a review article on both the technical and market aspects of this high performance polyolefin which later led to a extensive development program.
- Developed propylene/butene copolymer used as impact modifier.

PARADOX COMPANY - Indianapolis, Indiana   1979 - 1981

Research Chemist

- Developed PBT/PET blend to achieve balance of processing and properties.
- Developed an efficient method to quantify amino groups on fillers used in plastics.

EDUCATION

State University of New York, Syracuse, New York, 1979
Post doctoral work in ionic polymerization with Professor M. Szwarc

Purdue University, West Lafayette, Indiana, 1978
Post doctoral work in biopolymer with Professor M. Loudon

Ph.D Inorganic Chemistry - Rutgers University, Newark, New Jersey - 1977
M.S. Organic and Organometallic Chemistry - University of Texas, El Paso, Texas - 1972
B.S. - Tunghai University - Taiwan - 1969

PATENTS

Five U.S. patents issued and three patents
pending in the area of polyolefin catalysis and property improvement.

27) NAME
Address
City, State Zip Code
Office #
Home #

OBJECTIVE

Project Director

SUMMARY

Over 30 years of professional experience with expertise in all phases of project management. Performed extensive program/project management responsibilities with both owner/operator and engineering and construction companies.

PROFESSIONAL EXPERIENCE

E&C COMPANY - Houston, Texas   1989-199_

Project Director

- Managed as Director of Alliance Operations, the engineering and construction operations for a major soap and detergent manufacturing client.
- Organized and directed establishment of a satellite office to meet clients engineering requirements, resulting in a $6-per-engineering-hour cost reduction compared to previous engineering hourly costs in Houston.
- Established relocation and personnel policies to attract qualified professional staff resulting in relocating key staff position requirements from Houston and successfully recruiting additional 60 position requirements from local community. This saved the client over $120,000 in relocation costs.
- Introduced and obtained approval for commercial approach which saved client $3 million in capital costs without risk to company profit margin.
- Led engineering and construction effort for multi-site plant modernization and expansion program. Projects completed on schedule within approved budget enabling client to achieve market capture objectives.
- Reduced engineering costs expressed as a percentage of total installed cost by 23% in a 12-month period.
- Managed individual projects with capital value from $20 million to $300 million.

CENTURY - Greenville, South Carolina   1985-1989

Project Director

- Directed major engineering and construction projects for various clients.
- Led home office engineering on projects requiring from 50,000 work hours to over 1 million work hours.
- Represented the company in all contractual dealings with clients, ensuring positive relationships.
- Successfully negotiated contracts limiting contractor liability for construction management requirements resulting in 30% reduction in insurance costs.

276

- Developed recovery plan for an in-trouble project and led engineering/construction of project to completion within reforecasted budget and schedule.
- Organized and directed project task forces of both home office and field personnel achieving job quality, effective cost control and compliance with project schedule.
- Managed individual projects with capital value from $50 million to $400 million.

RAYFORD, INC. - Alexandria, Louisiana   1980-1985

President

- Managed self-owned company providing business development and consulting services to major engineering and construction companies, with emphasis on Middle East markets.
- Served as member of Board of Directors of Haitham Enterprises, Inc. in Dhahran, Saudi Arabia and to Steiner Fabricators, a Mobile, Alabama, shipbuilding and fabrication company.
- Established Houston-based company to develop U.S. firms for market representation in Middle East markets, resulting in contracts for 20 U.S. manufacturers who became active in the Middle East market.

PYRAMID OIL CO. - Dhahran, Saudi Arabia   1974-1980

- Advanced through several management positions from Senior Project Manager to Department Manager with consistent increasing responsibilities for directing project management programs.
- Provided major interface for company with international engineering and construction companies for contract negotiations and administration.
- Managed and directed project teams overseeing major contractors work on power and utility projects.
- Completed 500 kilometers of 230KV power line substations and turbogeneration facilities in time to support early development of the crude and gas expansion program.
- Managed and directed project teams for producing, refining and utility projects; conducted major program involving approximately 60 projects with capital value ranging from $50 million to in excess of $1.0 billion.
- Established single page reporting format for monthly executive review of cost and schedule performance for major projects. Format provided for early identification of potential problems allowing time for corrective action.
- Set up standards for performance measurement and progress reporting used by major projects, resulting in a 20% reduction in time required to produce reports.
- Assisted in reducing contract negotiation and execution period by six months by establishing consistent language and contract terms for all contractors.

PRIOR EXPERIENCE   1961-1974

- Filled successive positions of increasing scope and responsibilities in process engineering and project management. Focus on a career in project management began in 1965.
- Employed by: Johnson Chemical Company, Royce Chemical Company, and United Chemical Company.

EDUCATION

B.S. Chemical Engineering - Louisiana Polytechnic Institute - Ruston, Louisiana
Executive Development Program - University of Houston - Houston, Texas

277

NAME
Address
City, State Zip Code
Office #
Phone #

OBJECTIVE

Corporate Communications

SUMMARY

Over twenty years experience as a communications professional with corporate, government and non-profit organizations in media relations, project management, financial communications, employee communications and public affairs. Creative problem solving and negotiating skills have been used to develop and implement successful communications programs to help instill employee understanding and loyalty; develop and strengthen the customer base; create an appreciation of corporate goals, strategies and programs by special publics.

PROFESSIONAL EXPERIENCE

SMITH AND MYERS - Denver, Colorado   1993 - Present

Vice President
Counsel with clients of this international public relations firm on communication strategy for bottom line results and building and enhancing community, constituent and client relationships.

- Counseled energy client senior management on disclosure guidelines during successful acquisition of a competitor.
- Supervised execution of crisis communication training for several industrial companies ensuring crisis preparedness.
- Developed strategy and communications programs for major international energy company to show its commitment to energy projects in North and South America, resulting in significant media coverage and industry understanding of its goals and objectives.
- Developed and supervised execution of a PR strategy for personnel management company which facilitated its expansion to markets outside of its headquarters location.
- Positioned client as a leader in its industry through strategic alliances with key community and business activities and strengthening customer communication program.

OIL FOR LESS, INC. - Houston, Texas   1990 - 1993

Director, Corporate Communications (1992-1993)
In consultation with senior management, developed and implemented community and media relations strategies to enhance the corporate image of this Fortune 50 company with $10 billion in assets.

- Counseled with senior management for several key business units on media relations and community relations issues, developed appropriate communications programs and served as a company spokesperson in response to media inquiries, resulting in consistent reporting of corporate information.
- Developed a trade press program for identified business units and wrote and placed articles in targeted publications to broaden marketing opportunities for the corporation.
- Drafted a communications plan for a proposed 800-mile natural gas pipeline system in the Southeast. Participated in the plan's implementation, resulting in positive feedback from both key state environmental groups and the news media.
- Directed oversight of community relations program for company's largest U.S. refinery. Set up press conference for county officials to announce a significant company environmental project, resulting in both favorable news coverage and successful implementation.
- Developed the strategy and received senior management approval to introduce a new company marketing and capabilities video at the annual meeting, resulting in unprecedented video requests for both internal and external use here and overseas.

Eastern Regional Director, Corporate Communications (1991-1992)
Developed media and community relations counsel to East and Southeast refining/marketing and coal business units to enhance the company's image as a responsible corporate citizen.

- Strengthened a community relations program for the company's largest U.S. refinery, resulting in higher visibility of refinery management and significantly improved relationships with county and city officials.
- Established a refinery tour program for key decision makers including federal elected officials, enhancing their understanding of how an industrial site and its specific needs fit into local, state and national legislation.
- Formulated and prepared company positions on proposed state legislation for use by company officials which resulted in favorable legislation to both parties.

Director, Media Relations (1990-1991)

- Contributed to the development and implementation of a crisis communications plan for a Corpus Christi, Texas industrial facility, resulting in increased credibility and trust by city government.
- Monitored media coverage from strategic areas of the country which facilitated accurate and effective reporting of company activities.

WEST TEXAS OIL AND GAS CORPORATION (West Texas Corporation)   1987 - 1990

Manager, Media Relations and Advertising
Managed three professionals in the development of programs to strengthen awareness by news media and other publics of strategic goals and objectives for one of the nation's largest integrated natural gas pipeline companies following its $3.2 billion purchase of West Texas.

- Implemented a schedule of media visits and news releases on significant company activities, resulting in greater understanding of Company's activities as evidenced by positive media coverage and enhanced information flow throughout the company.
- Supervised planning and execution of special events such as legislative receptions and open houses, for stronger ties with elected officials through better understanding of company programs.
- Wrote and supervised annual report production, achieving a 15% reduction in production costs.
- Received management approval to redesign the quarterly report, resulting in an award-winning publication providing more pertinent information for the financial community and other publics.
- Developed theme and prepared speeches for employee meetings and supervised an award winning employee communications program.

PUBLIC RELATIONS COUNSEL   1983 - 1987

- Coordinated fund-raising newsletter and media events during construction of the $70 million fine-arts entertainment center to enhance donations during Houston's severe economic downturn.
- Developed and implemented the international media relations activities for inaugural season of fine-arts entertainment center and achieved the target goal of very positive worldwide media coverage for both the City of Houston and the arts.

PRIOR EXPERIENCE

Prior to 1983, held increasingly responsible corporate, energy, industrial and government positions in media relations, financial, internal and marketing communications.

EDUCATION

B.A., Journalism, University of Iowa

PROFESSIONAL AND COMMUNITY AFFILIATIONS

Accredited member, Public Relations Society of America

Chairman, Marketing Committee, San Jacinto Girl Scouts Council
Board of Trustees, Theatre Under the Stars

OBJECTIVE

Banking Consultant

SUMMARY

Twenty-five years experience with commercial banks and savings and loans in the assessment, negotiation and modification of large, complex real estate transactions. Nine years intensive work dealing with distressed loans based on a 16 year foundation in commercial banking.

PROFESSIONAL EXPERIENCE

CONSULTING AND CONTRACT POSITIONS - Houston, Texas   1991 - 199_

Consulted with the following institutions in due diligence, loan portfolio review and grading, foreclosure and charge-off recovery analysis: Al Bank FSB, T & T Savings Association, Passbook Savings Bank FSB, First Savings and Loan, Southwest Savings, Total Savings Bank, Bank-On-It Inc., and Fidelity Bank.

- Developed computer programs to facilitate due diligence, loan and portfolio review resulting in recommendations for remedial actions and regulatory compliance.
- Conducted loan negations and implemented collection strategies as Vice President, Special Assets Real Estate Loan Department, for an 85-loan portfolio consisting of commercial real estate and Small Business Administration guaranteed loans at Fidelity Bank, a $52,000,000 independent bank.
- Achieved unscheduled collections of $987,158 within six months and restructured an additional $2,232,478 while managing foreclosures and settlements.
- Directed staff of six in liquidating assets of First Savings Association as Asset Disposition Manager. The assets consisted of loans, real estate and personal property totaling $330,000,000.
- Assumed control of a 60-loan real estate loan portfolio of $127,314,000 as Commercial Workout Officer. Within five months, $6,220,000 was resolved through collection, modification, reinstatements and payoffs.

TWIN TOWERS BANKING CORPORATION - Houston, Texas   1990 - 1991

Vice President, Portfolio Manager, Real Estate Managed Assets
Directed as unit manager a staff of five officers and two secretaries responsible for the management, collection and resolution of a $157 million loan portfolio consisting of 222 loans. Supervised negotiations with borrowers, approved business plans and collection scenarios of 5 loan officers in an effort to maximize the cash flow of this Texas based subsidiary of Twin Towers Corporation.

- Collected $15,300,000 during the initial 13 months of operations.
- Resolved an additional $23,313,000 through foreclosure, deed in lieu of foreclosure and settlement.
- Facilitated the formulation of collection suit strategies and approved bankruptcy negotiation tactics.
- Pursued collections aggressively while avoiding governmental inquires and lender-liability lawsuits.
- Assessed officer performance, promoting, counseling and directing as necessary.

CAPITAL SAVINGS - Houston, Texas   1987 - 1989

Vice President, Real Estate Division, Special Assets Department
Analyzed problem loans and assessed borrowers' position, evaluated the lender's options and probable outcome. Negotiated modifications and pursuit of legal remedies for this $3.5 billion savings & loan.

- Consolidated 41 separate real estate loans into a single master modification of $16,000,000 and obtained $2,400,000 in interest payments.
- Collected $1,477,000 in interest payments while delaying borrower bankruptcy filing 17 months.
- Secured a $12,000,000 deficiency judgment on an $18,000,000 transaction.
- Conducted an investigation resulting in a criminal referral against a savings and loan owner, a high profile developer and a Certified Public Accountant.
- Initiated and controlled an out-of-state bankruptcy action which concluded in 6 months with full repayment of $2,800,000 and payment of all legal fees by the borrower.
- Developed a lawsuit against a powerful real estate syndicator, prevailing in bankruptcy court and thereby preventing a forced write-off of $4,500,000.
- Negotiated a below market interest rate with a coalition of lenders which spread required write-downs of $5,200,000 over 21 months.

EWING SAVINGS & LOAN ASSOCIATION - Dallas, Texas   1986 - 1987

Vice President, Real Estate Division
Analyzed distressed real estate projects and restructuring alternatives. Negotiated various workout scenarios with borrowers, attorneys and other creditors at this $780 million savings and loan.

- Instituted arbitration which led to deed in lieu of foreclosure and savings of $30,000 in legal fees.
- Negotiated the settlement of an $11,000,000 apartment complex loan.
- Initiated an asset inspection procedure for distressed projects ensuring monthly review.

DOLLAR SAVINGS & LOAN ASSOCIATION - Dallas, Texas   1983 - 1986

Vice President, Commercial Real Estate Loans
Solicited, analyzed, documented and closed commercial real estate loans and land acquisition/ development transactions at the Dallas Loan Production Office. Reworked problem loans and supervised closings as well as foreclosure activities at this Houston based $1 billion savings and loan.

- Developed a matrix tracking system for an $86,500,000 loan portfolio insuring appropriate action in a timely manner.
- Preserved the return on a $12,000,000 asset through collection of $1,100,000 in payments.

SUNSET BANK - San Francisco, California   1980 - 1983

Assistant Vice President, Assistant Branch Manager
Negotiated, documented and closed real estate construction loans. Underwrote, obtained approval and implemented equipment acquisition loans and revolving lines of credit for this $115 million San Francisco based regional bank.

- Achieved annual goals for delinquency, growth and new business each year which enabled the branch to meet annual budgets and profitability targets.

GOLDEN GATE BANK - Los Angeles, San Francisco, California   1968 - 1980

Assistant Manager, Operations Officer
Managed six branch offices with approximately 60 employees for this $72 billion international bank.

- Recommended approval of loan commitments for a 33 branch division.
- Controlled branch operations, staffing and cash control, meeting profit and expense goals.

EDUCATION

BSBA - California State University, Los Angeles, California - 1968

30) NAME
Address
City, State Zip Code
Home #
Alternate #

OBJECTIVE

Architectural Management Training Position

SUMMARY

Recent college graduate with business and architectural experience. Have demonstrated leadership, as well as, team work capabilities in co-curricular activities and in organizational positions.

WORK EXPERIENCE

BROWN & SMITH CONTRACTORS, INC. - Corpus Christi, Texas   1995 - 199_

General Draftsman

- Drafted for small architectural office resulting in precise and neat drawings.

- Performed variety of duties including lettering, title block layout and redlines, which were completed on a timely basis.

- Reproduced office prints ensuring quality copies.

- Performed deliveries and pickups for the office which ensured timely business transactions.

PROPERTY MANAGEMENT, INC. - Austin, Texas   1994 - 1995

Assistant (Part-time)

- Researched commercial and residential property records.

- Delivered and picked up office documents and prints.

- Designed displays, maps, charts, and graphs resulting in professional presentations to clients.

- Performed routine maintenance on rental properties which contributed to tenant satisfaction.

EDUCATION

BS, Architectural Studies - 1996
The University of Texas at Austin - Austin, Texas

ACTIVITIES & HONORS

Supreme Court Justice for the Student Council, Texas A & I University
Vice President of Senior Class - H. M. King High School
Member, SIGMA CHI Fraternity
Member, Recreation Committee - University of Texas
Varsity Gymnastics and Golf Teams - H. M. King High School

282

31) NAME
Address
City, State Zip Code
Home #
Alternate #

OBJECTIVE

Administrative Assistant

SUMMARY

Over four years administrative and customer service experience while obtaining BBA in Office Management. Have demonstrated excellent computer skills and ability to work independently and as a team member.

WORK EXPERIENCE

EAST TEXAS STATE UNIVERSITY - Commerce, Texas   1995 - 199_

Student Assistant, Department of History

- Assisted in managing all office functions which enabled instructors to focus on teaching priorities.

- Operated an IBM PC accurately producing articles and instructor research documentation.

- Assisted students in meeting academic needs which resulted in reducing student frustration.

- Answered the telephone and professionally responded to callers' requests and questions.

- Handled and distributed incoming/outgoing mail on a timely basis.

PUBLIC LIBRARY - Palestine, Texas   1994

Summer Student Program

- Assisted with the Youth Reading Program which contributed to improved reading abilities of students.

- Provided customer assistance with a friendly and professional manner, locating materials and processing library books for check out and in.

- Shelved books and maintained orderly collection.

JOE'S RESTAURANT - Palestine, Texas   1991 - 1992

Cashier

- Operated cash register while providing courteous customer service.

- Prepared food which ensured a high quality meal.

- Awarded "Employee of the Month, July 1992" for excellent performance.

EDUCATION

Bachelor of Business Administration, Office Management - 1996
East Texas State University, Commerce, Texas (GPA 3.5)

SUPPLEMENTAL INFORMATION

TECHNICAL SKILLS

Computer Literate
IFPS, Lindo, Lotus 1-2-3
Word Processing - WordPerfect
Typing - 63 wpm

ACTIVITIES AND HONORS

Awarded Canadian Pacific Enterprises Scholarship for Academic Achievement
Administrative Management Society High Achiever Award - 1996
Society of Alpha Chi - 1996
All-American Scholar Collegiate Award - 1995
President's Honor Roll Fall 1995 and Fall 1996
Outstanding College Students of America - 1994
Gamma Beta Phi Society Award of Appreciation - 1994
Member, Chi Omega Sorority
Member, Beta Gamma Sigma Honorary Society
School Newspaper Staff
Yearbook Staff & Photographer
National Association of Accountants, Buffalo Chapter
Association of Graduate Business Students
Internal Revenue Service (Volunteer Income Tax Assistance)
Syracuse University Graduate Scholarship & Graduate Assistantship
Boys Club Volunteer
Captain of Bobsled Team - 1990-1991
Longhorn Cheerleader
Dean's List (four semesters)

AFFILIATIONS

Administrative Management Society
Member - 1993-1996, Treasurer - 1995

Gamma Beta Phi Society
Member - 1994-1996, Vice President - 1995-1996
Reporter/Chairman of Publicity Committee

Intercultural Affairs
Texas Editor - 1995-1996

LANGUAGES

French (Fluent)
Spanish (Working Knowledge)

284

OBJECTIVE

Natural Gas Transportation/Supply/Market Representative

SUMMARY

Over two years of progressive career experience in the petroleum and natural gas industries, including natural gas transportation, volume management, and transportation fee maintenance. Have proven organizational skills in solving problems and achieving results in pressure situations.

PROFESSIONAL EXPERIENCE

GAS, INC. - Houston, Texas   1994 - 1995

Analyst, Gas Scheduling
- Coordinated the nomination, confirmation, scheduling, and allocation activity for various Northeast US pipelines and local distribution centers.
- Analyzed and executed gas transportation routes, determining the most cost effective path.
- Recommended and negotiated prices based on actual and forecasted cashout prices leading to greater profit margins.
- Handled supplier and market inquiries and requests for service resulting in improved customer satisfaction.

MYER NATURAL GAS, INC. - Houston, Texas   1993 - 1994

Analyst, Transportation & Exchange
- Maintained the gas marketing management database by researching and inputting pipeline transportation rates and adjustments.
- Created and sustained mandatory records which documented and verified transportation rates, fees, and adjustments necessary for gas valuation.
- Amended, researched and serviced long term supply contracts ensuring accuracy and appropriate distribution.

WERNER ENTERPRISE - Houston, Texas   1992

Treasury Department Summer Intern
- Received and invested daily cash inflows in overnight certificates of deposit.
- Performed financial audits for several independent service stations seeking credit.
- Processed several cash forecasting computer models and prepared visual aids for senior management presentations contributing to professionalism and effectiveness of delivery.

JAC OIL, INC. - Houston, Texas   1991

Environmental Affairs Summer Intern
- Researched and settled discrepancies with state regulatory agencies on differences between mutual records that dealt with underground storage tanks, piping, and leak detection methods.
- Aided in environmental audits conducted at company owned service stations, and made recommendations for improved safety and operation.

EDUCATION

Bachelor of Business Administration in Marketing - University of Houston, University Park - 1994
GPA (major): 3.65 - GPA (overall): 3.20 / Dean's List, Spring 1990, Fall 1990 & 1992

TECHNICAL SKILLS / LANGUAGE FLUENCY

MS Excel, Word, Windows, MS Works, Lotus 1-2-3, Harvard Graphics, IBM PC, Macintosh
Proficient Spanish

33) NAME
Address
City, State Zip Code
Home #
Alternate #

OBJECTIVE

General Management

SUMMARY

Over seven years experience in a variety of positions including management and supervision, sales and quality control, coupled with an MBA. Have demonstrated excellent planning, organizational and communications skills, contributing to organizational goals.

PROFESSIONAL EXPERIENCE

PRODUCTS CORPORATION - Seymour, Indiana   1993 - 1994

Department Supervisor
- Established computerized standards and samples for production.
- Supervised, trained, and motivated 18-25 hourly auditors resulting in efficient operations.
- Implemented statistical techniques to track and reduce spoilage, resulting in improved quality control.
- Reduced staffing needs by 25% within a 15-month period by increasing productivity.

INTERNATIONAL SALES - Albany, New York   1992

Sales Representative
- Developed a complete marketing strategy for the division's new product line, resulting in a 40% increase in sales.
- Launched and administered $1.5 million annual sales venture which resulted in increased profits.

J & J PLASTICS COMPANY - Rotterdam, New York   1990 - 1992

Quality Manager
- Established the initial plant quality standards for production through initiating and implementing procedures for new quality department.
- Resolved customer complaints at customer assembly and research locations resulting in improved customer relations.
- Achieved annual cost savings exceeding $300,000 by changing raw material suppliers and packaging designs.
- Maintained quality levels through production audits and quality circles.

COMMUNITY ACTION PROGRAM - Schenectady, New York   1987

Program Director
- Planned and implemented first summer energy conservation/food nutrition festival which resulted in excellent community participation and increased awareness of program goals.
- Performed public relations, obtained city permits and recruited exhibitors resulting in a successful festival.

EDUCATION

MBA, Syracuse University, School of Management - 1996 - GPA 3.66
BS, State University of New York, School of Business - 1990 - GPA 3.43

286

OBJECTIVE

Computer System Consultant

SUMMARY

Expertise in system programming, consulting, software quality assurance and system administration. Recent BS in Computer Science included eighteen semester hours of C-language programming. Bilingual in French.

PROFESSIONAL EXPERIENCE

INDEPENDENT CONSULTANT - San Antonio, Texas   1992 - 1993

Computer System Consultant

- Developed automatic record-keeping system which increased efficiency and accuracy of records.

- Designed accounting portion of system which increased accuracy of billing.

SOFTWARE WRITERS, INC. - Houston, Texas   1991 - 1992

Summer Employee (1992)

- Authored test scripts and performed software tests which identified problems; reported errors to developers and tested corrections which increased quality of product.

Part-time Employee (1991)

- Created C-language variable cross referencing tool utilized in code verification which rapidly provided testers with information needed on code to be tested.

- Maintained data and created charts reflecting department quality and accomplishments which manager presented to NASA in progress meetings.

- Designed detailed test procedures which found errors in software enabling developers to correct the problems prior to software release.

- Installed and performed system administration duties for a UNIX system required for running test scripts which located software errors.

OTHER EXPERIENCE

GIRL SCOUTS OF AMERICA

- Controlled expenditures creating savings of 15% of total budget while meeting all troop goals.

- Formulated and implemented detailed plans, leading girls to meet all program objectives.

- Maximized profits by accurately accounting for all product and income of troop cookie sales.

EDUCATION

B.S. Computer Science - Trinity University
San Antonio, Texas - 1993
(GPA - 3.5/4.0)

TECHNICAL SKILLS

Languages:
C, Lisp, Assembly, SQL, Prolog

Systems:
Unix, DOS, Windows, VM, MVS, OS/2, MacIntosh, Amiga

Applications:
Excel, DB2, FoxPro, dBase, Microsoft Word

PROFESSIONAL AFFILIATIONS

Upsilon Pi Epsilon (Computer Science Honor Society)

LANGUAGE FLUENCY

French

AWARDS, SCHOLARSHIPS AND HONORS

National Merit Scholar
National Merit Scholarship
Trinity University President's Scholarship
Dean's List

288

35) NAME
Address
City, State Zip Code
Home #
Alternate #

OBJECTIVE

Management Training Position

SUMMARY

Held several positions which developed work skills while completing BA with double major in Economics and Government.

PROFESSIONAL EXPERIENCE

LAW OFFICES OF WESTCHASE - Houston, Texas   1993 - 199_

Law Clerk

- Entered, edited and revised information on computer system ensuring accurate client and case data.
- Summarized, filed, and couriered depositions to and from courthouse on a timely basis.
- Assisted in running all office support activities resulting in smooth operations.
- Participated in training new support staff which ensured continuity of service to attorneys and clients.

REPUBLICAN PARTY OF TEXAS - Austin, Texas   1994

Phone Solicitor

- Canvassed state for political contributions to the Republican Party resulting in increased campaign funds.
- Prepared and mailed pledges which ensured support from contributors.
- Participated in project to canvass for the Oklahoma Republican Party, contributing to candidate recognition and voter involvement.

MEDICAL CENTER OF PINE FOREST - Houston, Texas   1990 - 1992

Pharmacy Clerk

- Filled prescriptions which ensured accuracy and customer satisfaction.
- Prepared I.V.'s, inventoried stock and distributed medications in hospital, facilitating patient care.

EDUCATION

University of Texas at Austin - Bachelor of Arts, 1996
Dual Majors: Economics and Government

TECHNICAL SKILLS

Familiar with BASIC, Pascal computer languages.

ACTIVITIES & HONORS

Lambda Chi Alpha Fraternity - University of Texas 1992-1994
Historian, 1994, Scholastic Committee 1992-1994

Moore-Hill Dormitory Government - University of Texas 1991
Scholastic Committee Chairman and Hall Representative
Youth Volunteer - Republican National Convention - Dallas, Texas 1991

Address
City, State Zip Code
Office #
Home #

OBJECTIVE

Law Clerk

SUMMARY

First year law student with strong writing, research, organizational, analytical and computer skills. Have held a variety of positions demonstrating the ability to work well independently, as well as with management. Have studied and travelled internationally.

PROFESSIONAL EXPERIENCE

WILLIAMS UNIVERSITY - Houston, Texas   1992 - 1993

Research Assistant

- Investigated and summarized legal and political history for article which was published in spring 1993 issue of Security Studies.

- Researched and reported on various law and economics topics contributing to other articles in progress.

PIZZERIA - Houston, Texas   1991 - 1992

Accountant's Assistant

- Prepared payroll, accounts payable, Alcoholic Beverage Commission reports, discount spreadsheets and sales summaries for daily operation of two restaurant locations, ensuring accuracy.

- Reconciled bank statements and produced general ledger sheets for financial reports, which improved management control.

LAW OFFICE OF FLOWERS AND ADLER - Houston, Texas   1989

Secretary

- Computerized all boilerplates which reduced duplication of effort and increased efficiency of attorneys.

- Managed all office activities resulting in smooth operations and scheduling.

COMPUTER CENTRAL - Houston, Texas   1988 - 1989

<u>Secretary</u>

• Utilized computer database system to manage incoming manuscripts and correspondence, resulting in improved document control and increased reader satisfaction.

• Authored return communication and preliminary evaluations of trial software for editor-in-chief, which reduced preparation time for monthly reviews.

EDUCATION

B.A., Rice University, Houston, Texas, 1993, GPA 3.9
Triple Major: Economics, Managerial Studies and Policy Studies

ADDITIONAL EDUCATION

Wharton School of Business, University of Pennsylvania
Philadelphia, Pennsylvania 1990-1991

International College at Cannes
Cannes, France 1990

ACTIVITIES AND HONORS

Phi Beta Kappa
Gaston D. Rimlinger Economics Prize Winner
Rice Program Council - College Representative
President's Honor Roll 1991-1993
Omicron Delta Epsilon
Delta Delta Delta Sorority - Scholastic Chair 1990-1991
National Merit Scholar
Hill House Dormitory Government - University of Pennsylvania 1990-1991
Social Planning and Budget Committee Secretary, Community Outreach Representative
Lead role in <u>The Enemy Within</u> - 1990
Commencement Speaker - Memorial High School
National Honor Society
State Debate Champion - 1989

TECHNICAL SKILLS

Westlaw, Wordperfect, MSWord, Wordstar,
Multimate dBase III, Lotus 123, Excel, Basic,
MS-Dos, Typing 65 WPM

37) NAME
Address
City, State Zip Code
Home #

OBJECTIVE

Mechanical / Environmental Engineer

SUMMARY

Completed degree in Mechanical and Environmental Engineering and gained substantial experience in the design and construction of a hybrid electric vehicle during my senior design project. Experienced with computers utilizing AutoCAD, Lotus 123 and FORTRAN. Have experience on campus and in commercial environments.

PROFESSIONAL EXPERIENCE

UNIVERSITY MICROCOMPUTER LABORATORY - Santa Barbara, California   1993 - 1994

Computer Lab Consultant

- Conducted orientations and short courses tutoring professors and students in the use of computer software which increased their proficiency.

- Counseled numerous computer lab users on various software applications increasing the efficiency and effectiveness with which they completed their projects.

- Assisted in the installation of new system software which enabled users to improve their productivity.

- Investigated and successfully repaired a harmful computer virus which had caused users to lose data.

- Identified and resolved computer network and printing problems enabling users to safely use the system with fewer crashes.

AMERICAN SOCIETY OF MECHANICAL ENGINEERS (ASME) - Santa Barbara, California1993 - 1994

Co-Chairman of University Chapter

- Directed the human powered vehicle project which placed sixth out of forty entries in the 1994 ASME human powered vehicle races.

- Organized several picnics and other activities which resulted in successful participation by ASME members.

- Recruited numerous students to join ASME, expanding participation and contributing to a more dynamic organization.

292

COMPUTER CITY, U.S.A. - Diamond Bar, California   1990

<u>Maintenance</u>

- Performed general maintenance functions efficiently resulting in increased satisfaction of both management and customers.

EDUCATION

MBA - anticipated completion date - 1996
University of Houston, Houston, Texas

BS, Mechanical and Environmental Engineering - 1994
University of California, Santa Barbara, California

ADDITIONAL EDUCATION

Senior Design Project - Hybrid Electric Vehicle
Technical Writing Course

PROFESSIONAL AFFILIATIONS

American Society of Mechanical Engineers (ASME)
Student Member and Co-Chairman

COMPUTER SKILLS

Applications:
AutoCAD, Lotus 123, WordPerfect, Excel, Word

Operating Systems:
DOS, Windows, UNIX, X-Windows, MacIntosh

Languages:
C, FORTRAN, BASIC

LANGUAGE FLUENCY

Working knowledge of German (speaking, reading and writing)

Address
City, State Zip Code
Home #
Alternate #

OBJECTIVE

Training Position in Marketing/Sales

SUMMARY

Recent college graduate with strong writing, interpersonal, research and analytical skills. Have held positions in various industries providing customer service and counseling, as well as, managing operations efficiently.

WORK EXPERIENCE

PAPER WORKS - Austin, Texas   1996 - Present

Assistant Manager
- Managed inventory control resulting in accurate records and timely ordering.
- Developed and set up in-store promotion displays.
- Acted as liaison between public and word processing department which reduced interruptions of processors and ensured customer satisfaction.
- Performed general office duties resulting in efficient operations.

WOMEN'S COUNSELING AND RESOURCE CENTER - Austin, Texas   1994 - 1995

Peer Counselor - Internship
- Provided individual short-term counseling which helped women in the Austin community.
- Developed counseling skills through supervision and training from professional psychology staff.
- Provided information and referrals which met client needs.
- Evaluated and referred clients to therapist and therapy groups for additional long-term counseling, ensuring that their needs were met.

CLARK COUNTRY INN - Clark, New Jersey   1993 - 1994

Assistant Dinning Room Manager
- Resolved customer complaints resulting in increased satisfaction.
- Trained new employees on use of new computer system resulting in more efficient operations.
- Scheduled and supervised staff of ten waiters and waitresses which ensured coverage and high quality services.
- Worked closely with resident manager which improved overall operation of dinning room.

SCOTCH PLAINS SAVINGS & LOAN ASSOCIATION - Scotch Plains, New Jersey   1991 - 1993

Bank Teller
- Interacted professionally with customers while accurately processing their transactions.
- Provided customers with information concerning various types of accounts and other banking services which contributed to increased business.

EDUCATION

BA, English, Minor in Marketing - 1996 - GPA 3.2
University of Texas at Austin

294

SUPPLEMENTAL INFORMATION

TECHNICAL SKILLS

Computer Literate
Word Processing
Typing - 55 wpm

ACTIVITIES AND HONORS

Member, Chi Omega Sorority
Longhorn Cheerleader
Newspaper Staff

OBJECTIVE

Financial/Accounting Position

SUMMARY

Over three years experience in accounting and related areas coupled with an MBA with a concentration in finance. Have demonstrated ability to communicate effectively with internal and external contacts, as well as to supervise other personnel in achieving organizational goals.

PROFESSIONAL EXPERIENCE

EASTERN UNIVERSITY - Syracuse, New York   1995 - Present

Graduate Assistant

- Counseled students in the preparation and revision of high quality resumes and cover letters.
- Initiated contact and acted as liaison between students and corporate recruiters in job placement activities for university business students resulting in interviews and placements.
- Compiled publication materials for the School of Management Placement office facilitating student access to materials.

BUFFALO SAVINGS & LOAN ASSOCIATION - Buffalo, New York   1992 - 1995

Auditor-in-Charge (1993-1995)

- Planned and executed financial and operational audits.
- Wrote executive summaries of audit findings for senior management which provided adequate information for decision making.
- Trained and supervised four staff auditors which ensured coordination of audit assignments and effective performance.

Staff Auditor (1992-1993)

- Performed audit procedures accurately on $2 billion lending portfolio.
- Coordinated internal audit projects with external auditors facilitating completion.
- Assigned to the task force responsible for conversion to a public corporation contributing to the team goals.
- Performed two-month temporary assignment to New York City division to evaluate operations resulting in recommendations for improved procedures.
- Awarded corporate merit bonus for exemplary performance in the audit department.

EDUCATION

MBA Finance - December 1995
Syracuse University, Syracuse New York
Overall GPA: 3.4; Major GPA: 3.8

BS Accounting - May 1992
Canisius College - Buffalo, New York

TECHNICAL SKILLS

Working Knowledge of SAS, Lotus 1-2-3, dBase III and Waterloo Basic

296

SUPPLEMENTAL INFORMATION

ACTIVITIES AND HONORS

National Association of Accountants, Buffalo Chapter
Association of Graduate Business Students
Boys Club Volunteer
Internal Revenue Service (Volunteer Income Tax Assistance)
Syracuse University Graduate Scholarship & Graduate Assistantship

Address
City, State Zip Code
Home #
Alternate #

OBJECTIVE

Human Resources Position

SUMMARY

Four years experience in a variety of environments with an MBA in Personnel Management. Have demonstrated excellent interpersonal skills in customer service, personnel and recruiting functions.

WORK EXPERIENCE

COLLEGE STATION UNIVERSITY - College Station, Texas   1996 - 199_

Placement Center

- Assisted liberal arts students in utilizing the placement center which contributed to achievement of their placement goals.
- Communicated with liberal arts recruiters resulting in an increase in visitations to the campus and interviews of students.

AEROSPACE, INC. - Houston, Texas   1995

Personnel Management Specialist

- Coordinated hiring, promotions, and performance evaluations resulting in improved employee relations.
- Performed special projects as assigned which contributed to increased visibility of human resources within the organization.
- Developed a program using dBase II resulting in significantly improved tracking of manpower needs.

BRYAN BANK OF TEXAS - Bryan, Texas   1993 - 1994

Customer Service

- Performed various bookkeeping duties which ensured accurate and timely accounting reports.
- Utilized bank computer to assist in efficiently handling customer transactions.
- Interacted with bank customers resulting in professional and effective customer relationships.

EDUCATION

MBA, Personnel Management - 1996 - GPA 3.2
BS, Psychology - 1993 - GPA 3.8
Texas A & M University, College Station, Texas

TECHNICAL SKILLS

Computer Literate, Word Processing - WordPerfect
Typing - 60 wpm

41) NAME

Address
City, State Zip Code
Home #
Alternate #

OBJECTIVE

Management Training Position in Sales, Marketing or Public Relations

SUMMARY

Four years experience in counseling, merchandising, sales and marketing with a BA in psychology. Have demonstrated excellent interpersonal and communication skills coupled with high self-motivation and willingness to work hard.

WORK EXPERIENCE

MANAGEMENT CONSULTANTS - Houston, Texas   1994 - Present

Marketing Assistant

- Researched and contacted corporations which supported on-going business development.

- Interacted with clients to meet their administrative needs resulting in very effective client relationships.

- Provided a variety of office and clerical support services which maintained efficient office operations.

- Greeted potential clients providing a positive and personalized image for the organization.

SPORTSWEAR WAREHOUSE - Houston, Texas   1994 - 1996

Sales

- Served as sales and marketing assistant for specialty sportswear retailer, resulting in increased sales responsibilities delegated by the merchandising manager.

- Designed and implemented store window displays and in-store attractions that enhanced the decor of the store and increased sales.

- Recognized for outstanding sales performance.

SELF-EMPLOYED - Atlanta, Georgia   1995 - 1996

Model

- Performed as free-lance model for major fragrance manufacturers.

- Represented products at major department stores resulting in increased sales.

REGIONAL HOSPITAL - Athens, Georgia   1996

Internship: Psychiatric Ward

- Monitored patients' attitude changes and progress, and reported findings to hospital counselors which facilitated their care.

- Organized free time activities resulting in improved patient quality of life.

- Assisted staff in counseling patients contributing to their progress.

CLOTHING SPECIALISTS - Atlanta, Georgia   1994

Sales

- Served as sales and merchandising assistant for specialty clothing retailers contributing to effective operations.

- Conducted floor sales and achieved top sales recognition at both stores.

- Designed and implemented in-store displays.

CAMP NAKANAWA - Crossville, Tennessee   1993

Counselor and Entertainment Director

- Served as camp counselor, aquatic instructor and entertainment director for exclusive girls summer camp, providing effective staff and operations support for the administrators.

EDUCATION

BA, Psychology - 1996
University of Georgia, Athens, Georgia
Paris Abroad Program: Study of French Language, History and Art - June 1995
Hollins College, Paris, France

ACTIVITIES & HONORS

Texas Children's Hospital Volunteer; Member of L'Alliance Francais
Kappa Alpha Theta Sorority; Dean's List Academic Achievement;
Psychology Club; French Club, Communiversity, Greeks Against Mismanagement of Alcohol;
Intramurals; KAO Social, Dance, Charity, and Pledge Committees

42) NAME
Address
City, State Zip Code
Office #
Home #

OBJECTIVE

Senior Executive Management

SUMMARY

Over thirty-five years experience in executive line and staff management of a wide variety of organizations worldwide. Worked at senior executive levels in both Government and private sectors. Experience includes planning, project development, design, construction, operation and maintenance of infrastructure facilities. Have demonstrated ability at the P&L level to (1) develop and implement strategic business initiatives, (2) build winning engineering, construction, sales, and management teams, and (3) manage business opportunities to achieve superior financial results.

PROFESSIONAL EXPERIENCE

DEVELOPMENT E&C, INC. - Houston, Texas   1991 - 1995

Vice President, E&C Environmental (1994-1995)
Assumed control of Environmental Remediation Operations, a start-up organization, in September, 1994, to turn around a loss in excess of $1 million.
- Reduced overhead and saved $1 million in overhead costs.
- Led management team that developed a strategy, mission statement, business plan and budget in about one month.
- Implemented business plan which will yield at least $2 million by end-1995, a turnaround of about $3 million, bottom-line, in less than a year.

Vice President, E&C Civil (1991-1994)
Recruited by company to implement quality improvement and turnaround the Worldwide Civil Engineering portion of this infrastructure-oriented, engineering and construction unit. The organization had offices in the U.S. (Texas, Florida, Louisiana and California), U.K. (London) and Hong Kong.
- Developed, through participative management, basic strategy/mission statements for various offices.
- Created alignment and buy-in among senior managers and widely dispersed employees of organization.
- Sold Hong Kong operation back to its Chinese founder, eliminating about a $1.5 million annual loss.
- Reduced the London operation from 1200 to 800 people, moving the bottom-line results from break-even to a profit of several million dollars a year.
- Eliminated several non-profitable offices in the U. S. operation, focused on infrastructure projects and engineering oversight, reduced overhead and moved from an annual loss position to a bottom line of $3.4 million in 1994.
- Created a more cohesive, dynamic, forward-looking group that made $4.4 million in 1993 and $7.7 million in 1994, a turnaround in excess of $10.0 million in less than 3 years.
- Directed company's efforts to win Department of Energy's Superconducting Super Collider Installation Contract (approximately $1 billion over a 6-year period) for installation of 10,000 sophisticated magnets and attendant utilities in 54-mile long tunnel under construction in Waxahatchie, Texas. As prime contractor, enlisted two Fortune 500 firms as subcontractors to compete with two other Fortune 500 primes. Company was well on its way to winning this job when the Federal Government decided to cancel project.

PACIFIC ENERGY COMPANY - San Francisco, California   1989 - 1991

Vice President and General Manager
- Successfully managed the firm's flagship project, a 240 megawatt geothermal power production facility on the China Lake Naval Weapons Center, near Ridgecrest, California, through transition from near-final construction through start-up to full operation.
- Exceeded gross revenues goal of $180 million by $4 million in 1990, the first full year of production, and stayed well within the $46 million operations budget while training and leading the 180-person work force through the challenges of start-up.

301

AEROSYS CORPORATION - Washington, D. C. 1988 - 1989

Vice President, Government and Aerospace Division
- Organized and managed business development and representational office in Washington, DC.
- Spearheaded efforts which led to award of a NASA contract to a Joint Venture between company and two other Fortune 500 firms for design/manufacture of the Advanced Solid Rocket Motor (ASRM) for the U. S. Space Shuttle. This $1.4 billion endeavor was to be financed by the Joint Venture and the ASRM sold to NASA as part of the Government's privatization emphasis.
- Maintained liaison with offices of selected Congressmen and Senators, the Departments of Defense and Energy, Environmental Protection Agency and selected aerospace and engineering/construction firms with offices in the Washington, DC, area.

CORPS OF ENGINEERS, UNITED STATES ARMY 1956 - 1988
Served with distinction at all officer levels of the Army. Achieved rank of Major General after 32-years of progressive leadership and management experience in results-oriented, highly diversified organizations worldwide.

Commander, North Pacific Division - Portland, Oregon (1987-1988)
- Successfully led/managed this 2500-person regional organization (5 Northwestern States, including Alaska) through several sensitive, politically-charged situations. (Average annual operating budget approximately $300 million). Duties equivalent to CEO of medium-sized private enterprise firm.

Director, Engineering & Construction - Washington, D.C. (1984-1987)
- Selected from the group of twelve engineer Major Generals in the Corps in 1984 to direct the worldwide operations of the Corps of Engineers. (Average annual operating budget of about $5 billion.) Duties equivalent to COO of a large private enterprise firm.

Commander, Missouri River Division - Omaha, Nebraska (1981-1984)
- Successfully directed this 2800-person, regional (9 Northern and Midwestern states) activity in planning, development, execution, operations, and maintenance of a large multi-million dollar water resource and military design and construction projects. (Average annual operating budget in excess of $400 million). Duties equivalent to CEO of medium-sized private enterprise firm.

Director, Facilities Engineering and Housing - Washington, D.C. (1980-1981)
- Directed the Department of the Army operations and maintenance activities at all Army installations worldwide ($2.6 billion annually) and design, construction and maintenance of all Army family housing ($900 million annually). Duties equivalent to COO of a large private enterprise firm.

Director of Facilities Engineering and Housing - Fort Bragg, North Carolina (1978-1980)
- Selected to manage 800-person organization responsible for master planning, operation and maintenance of all facilities (air field, streets and roads, major hospital, power distribution, water treatment and distribution, etc.) at Army's largest and busiest installation. Earned acclaim as Army's finest Facilities Engineer. Equivalent to Director of Public Works, city of 70,000 people.

Commander, 20th Engineer Brigade - Fort Bragg, North Carolina (1977-1978)
- Selected from group of 300 engineer Colonels to command this elite Brigade of 2000 combat engineer soldiers/paratroopers. Developed highest possible state of combat readiness to provide engineer support on worldwide contingency and deployment missions, including deployment of 500 troopers and selected heavy equipment to help the State of Massachusetts dig Boston out of the snowstorm of 1978; received Humanitarian Service Medal for this operation.

Prior Experience (1956-1977)
- Served stateside and overseas, peacetime and wartime, in command and staff positions, and consistently in jobs that demanded a keen understanding of people and a bias toward action.

EDUCATION

M.S., Civil Engineering - Princeton University, Princeton, New Jersey - 1961
B.S., General Engineering - U.S. Military Academy, West Point, New York - 1956

302

OBJECTIVE

General Management

SUMMARY

Over fourteen years of leadership and management experience in both corporate and military positions. Business analysis and evaluation skills have been progressively developed and enhanced through a corporate strategic planning position in Fortune 500 Company, an officer in a rapid growth company, a Masters of Business Administration and a West Point economics teaching assignment. Excellent interpersonal skills are evidenced by participation on corporate strategy teams, mentoring cadets and soldiers, and excelling in numerous responsible assignments.

PROFESSIONAL EXPERIENCE

CD ENERGY SERVICES, INC. - Houston, Texas   1993 - Present

Project Manager
Serve as officer and engineer for $30,000,000 pipeline engineering company. Responsible for pursuing business development leads to expand business and develop new business opportunities.
- Participated in various management decisions and strong company growth. 1995 net income is projected to exceed total net income for the past 5 years combined.
- Evaluated a number of different business opportunities, including start-ups and potential acquisitions resulting in increased revenues.
- Performed engineering and engineer support for company projects, including analyzing hydraulics of pipeline expansion that spanned the Andes; provided hands-on and billable engineering and inspection support on a pipeline in Lake Charles, Louisiana over a 4-month period; served as project manager evaluating river crossing replacement options for client; initiated business opportunity which has potential to lead to a $50,000,000 pipeline project in Pakistan.
- Started new line of compression services for company which is extremely technical and different from company's traditional business. Established and maintained business relations, recruited key staff, directed project execution, financial performance and project management which represents $2 million of outstanding bids.
- Upgraded company's systems including computer, software, and phone systems, and directed company expansion of office space, resulting in significantly enhancing operational efficiency.
- Recruited key officers and staff for company including engineering manager, controller and chief financial officer, manager of business development, an environmental engineer and the manager of compression services.

SIMPSON & CARLTON, INC. - Houston, Texas   1992 - 1993

Corporate Business Analyst
Assigned to the office of Corporate Business Development of a $3,500,000,000 corporation with 8 business units. Assessed market potentials and analyzed competitors, developed and implemented strategy with single or multiple business units, conducted internal consulting assignments, coordinated with unit business development staffs, and participated in the corporate decision making process.
- Analyzed a critical and sensitive issue for company which had precluded it from participating in a $1,100,000,000 market, resulting in recommendations from this work, the company clarified its policy, altered its marketing campaign and authorized several business units to operate in new markets.
- Initiated and coordinated a future planning exercise which developed powerful long term visions for the company and strongly influenced the strategic perspectives of the three largest business units in the company.
- Evaluated the existing strategic implementation plans for the 3D Computer Aided Design (CAD) system. Provided recommendations to top management on the economics of these systems and developed recommendations at the corporate level for implementing a broad based solution.
- Wrote and distributed a technical analysis of potential engineering strategies based upon 45 interviews with the top global managers in the company. This analysis established a standard for future such analyses throughout the company.

- Participated on a team that developed strategy for a 4000 person, global engineering organization. This strategy led to a major organizational realignment and focus.
- Produced and circulated a corporate position paper on legal, operational, and market implications of employing union labor in a construction environment. Under direction of the Chief Operating Officer of the company, this paper became required reading for all business unit managers.
- Supported unit business development activities through networking with professional contacts which led to a potential buyer for a $3,000,000 subsidiary and also identified a strong sales opportunity with a major international client.
- Analyzed sophisticated financial transactions involving nontraditional project finance techniques. Assisted managers in understanding the detailed implications of these actions which facilitated the corporate financial decision making process.

UNITED STATES ARMY   1981 - 1992

<u>U.S. Military Academy Economics Instructor</u>, West Point, New York (1991-1992)
One of 15 instructors selected from 150 highly qualified officer applicants to teach.
- Taught 110 cadets fundamentals of international trade theory, microeconomics, and macroeconomics and was identified by the department head as one of the best instructors in the organization.
- Reorganized the staff for a nationally acclaimed student conference to achieve greater efficiency.

<u>Company Commander</u>, Fort Stewart, Georgia (1988-1989)
Rebuilt a 140 person engineering organization required to deploy to a hostile environment on short notice. Maintained $4,000,000 of assigned equipment.
- Won award as best company out of 135 in highly competitive unit service and logistics competition.
- Led company to become recognized as one of the best in the battalion after the rebuilding of management systems and a strong emphasis on a quality program in all operations.

<u>Battalion Maintenance Officer</u>, Fort Stewart, Georgia (1986-1987)
Responsible for the maintenance program for a 850 person unit and for monitoring the employment and utilization of 70 mechanics and $40,000,000 of equipment.
- Led this battalion to achieve one of the highest vehicle availability rates.
- Advised the commander on the status of all maintenance operations and programs.

<u>Civil Engineer</u>, King Khalid Military City, Saudi Arabia (1984-1986)
Supervised the construction of $30,000,000 of commercial construction with the U.S. Army Corps of Engineers in Saudi Arabia. Also negotiated claims and changes with international contractors.
- Identified $4,000,000 savings for the Saudi government as a claims negotiator.
- Directed a multi-cultural training program for Saudi engineers.

<u>Battalion Personnel Officer</u>, Colorado Springs, Colorado (1983-1984)
Director of the personnel program for a 1000-person unit. Managed a human resource center and a staff of 21 soldiers. Served as the special advisor to the commander on all actions.
- Selected as the most junior officer ever assigned to this position in this battalion.
- Overcame a staff shortage in the personnel center to achieve superb personnel support.

<u>Engineer Platoon Leader</u>, Colorado Springs, Colorado (1982-1983)
Led a 35-person combat engineer platoon and maintained $4,000,000 of assigned equipment.
- Described by the battalion commander as the best Platoon Leader in the battalion.
- Graduated from the prestigious U.S. Army Ranger School which is achieved by less than 0.5% of those in the Army.

EDUCATION

MBA, Stanford University, Stanford, California - 1991
BS, United States Military Academy, West Point, New York - 1981

PROFESSIONAL REGISTRATION

Registered Professional Engineer (In the States of Texas, Louisiana, Florida, New Mexico and Virginia)

Address
City, State Zip Code
Home #

OBJECTIVE

Corporate Aviation

SUMMARY

Eight years experience as a Naval Officer and jet pilot. In depth management and training experience obtained while involved in various assignments. Made extensive use of Navy computer system in performance of duties.

PROFESSIONAL EXPERIENCE

UNITED STATES NAVY   1984 - 1992

Advanced Jet Flight Instructor (1989-1992)

- Responsible for the training of student Naval jet pilots. Involved in depth one of one simulator and in-flight instruction and critical analysis of student performance. Annual pilot training rate of 100 pilots demanded maximum airborne efficiency and instructional effectiveness.

- Standardization check pilot in all phases of flight training. Awarded designator of Master Training Specialist by the Chief of Naval Air Training in recognition of extensive experience and responsibility.

- Organized and chaired committee responsible for the development of new advanced flight training manuals. Effectively coordinated the efforts of the Navy's three advanced flight training bases.

Training Wing Standardization Officer (1990-1992)

- Designed and maintained a computerized instructor qualification matrix which resulted in a more efficient method of tracking qualifications and a decrease in man-hours required to generate reports.

- Developed an innovative tracking program for ensuring three training squadrons and 150 instructors complied with all Naval flight training procedures. Resulted in zero discrepancies in a major Naval inspection.

- Personally reviewed and rewrote the training wing standard operating procedures instruction which resulted in a significant increase in training productivity and safety.

Training Wing Student Control Officer (1991-1992)

- Oversaw daily operations of the base's Automatic Training Support System (ATSS) and associated personnel. Managed personnel responsible for entry of time critical data entry into the Navy's Central Database.

- Maintained Training Wing's database of students under training, reducing student training assignment time and increasing efficiency of tracking and reporting.

S-3A Viking Pilot (1987-1989)

- Pilot in command of the Navy's sophisticated carrier based anti-submarine jet which required extensive knowledge of all aircraft systems, avionics and procedures. Squadron awarded Battle "E" for operational excellence while deployed abroad USS Roosevelt in the Mediterranean.

Maintenance Department Division Officer (1988-1989)

- Officer in charge of squadron's electronic maintenance division. High tempo operations routinely required the maximum possible productivity, efficiency and quality control.

- Officer in charge of squadron's line maintenance division. Effectively managed and coordinated efforts of a division required to maintain 13 aircraft with the manning of a ten aircraft squadron.

- Developed and oversaw program to ensure all shipboard squadron and personal electronic equipment tested safe each month. Resulted in zero discrepancies during shipboard safety inspections.

Educational Services Officer (1987-1988)

- Developed and operated a computerized database of all enlisted personnel eligible for advancement exams. This more efficient method of tracking resulted in a significant increase in enlisted advancement.

- Designed innovative and comprehensive rate training program for squadron's enlisted personnel. Resulted in a 43% increase in total members advanced, and zero failures among members taking exam.

Student Naval Aviator (1984-1987)

- Naval jet flight student involved in an intensive three year training syllabus requiring the mastery of four naval training aircraft. Named to the Wing Commander's list for academic excellence during intermediate and advanced flight training.

EDUCATION

Bachelor of Science - Boston College, Chestnut Hill, Massachusetts - 1984

ADDITIONAL EDUCATION

Naval Jet Flight Training - 1986
Aviation Officer Candidate School - 1985

TECHNICAL SKILLS

IBM and Compatible Personal Computers
WordPerfect 5.1

306

OBJECTIVE

Veterinarian Assistant

SUMMARY

Over two years experience as an administrative assistant in a veterinary hospital and professional office environment. Have demonstrated excellent interpersonal skills with the ability to work well with all levels of corporate staff, management and customers. Have excellent computer skills with extensive experience in Leading Edge Word Processor, The Veterinary Assistant, WordPerfect (DOS and Windows), Avery Label Manager, The Print Press and working knowledge of Paradox, Lotus 123 and Harvard Graphics. Additional one year experience as a customer service clerk in a retail environment.

PROFESSIONAL EXPERIENCE

LOVING ANIMAL HOSPITAL - Houston, Texas   1994 - 1995

Receptionist
Served as receptionist and part-time veterinarian assistant for Veterinary Hospital, greeting customers, performing administrative duties, and assisting doctors and technicians in administering care for animals.

- Prepared and mailed weekly notices to patients which reminded them of services needed for pets' health, and generated monthly "past due" notices which ensured payment for services rendered.
- Answered telephones in a friendly and professional manner responding to questions, inquiries and concerns, ensuring that customers' needs were met.
- Scheduled appointments and surgery, meeting the needs of the patients while maintaining a feasible schedule for doctors.
- Assisted doctors as needed with animals ensuring that procedures were completed and patients received required care to ensure recovery.
- Consoled customers that had pets euthanized providing comfort in time of grief, while obtaining a release for the service in a professional manner.
- Maintained and updated client information files and completed filing in a timely and accurate manner which ensured patient information was readily available when needed.
- Maintained cleanliness of reception area, waiting area and examination rooms which contributed to patients' comfort and improved efficiency.
- Set up new patient information files, completing information data sheets thoroughly and accurately and creating labels.
- Checked patients in and out, totalling charges for services rendered, explaining services, receiving checks and cash, and processing credit card charges, ensuring that charges and receipts balanced at the end of each day.
- Performed and maintained inventory on supplies including pet food, medicine, vaccinations, etc., which ensured that items were immediately available as needed.
- Prepared and mailed welcome letters to new homeowners in the area which increased company visibility and resulted in new business.
- Provided relief kennel support walking animals, cleaning cages, administering medicine and caring for pets boarded on weekends and holidays.
- Typed correspondence, letters and notices for doctors using Veterinary Assistant computer program.

OUTPLACEMENT CONSULTANTS, INC. - Houston, Texas   1993 - 1994

Administrative Assistant
Provided part-time support, while attending high school, assuming a full time position upon graduation. Developed excellent interpersonal, communication and clerical skills while working in fast-paced office environment providing administrative support to staff and clients as well as serving as relief receptionist to approximately 30+ executives and professionals.

- Served as relief receptionist answering telephones for two companies consisting of thirteen lines with over thirty-five extensions. Screened calls for principals of company and transferred calls or took messages for appropriate individuals, ensuring that all calls were handled in a prompt and professional manner.
- Trained client on basic techniques and use of Lotus 123 which enabled her to gain an interview for an administrative assistant position requiring basic knowledge of Lotus.
- Provided front office support, greeted clients and welcomed guests in a professional manner and notified proper individuals of their arrival, which contributed to company's professional image.
- Conducted research at the City of Houston library, updated list of materials available for use in conducting an effective and efficient job search.
- Performed administrative duties for 30+ executives and professionals which consisted of word processing resumes, cover letters, envelopes, consulting proposals, invoices and merging multiple letters in a timely and accurate manner.
- Collated materials for seminars ensuring that an adequate number of hand-outs and support documentation were available for consultants to effectively make their presentations.
- Performed miscellaneous duties which included organizing library materials, distributing newspapers, posting job leads and organizing job opportunity boards, preparing coffee and following up on delivery of lunches which contributed to efficient and effective office services.

PLANET ARTS AND CRAFTS - Houston, Texas   1992 - 1993

Cashier
Served as a part-time cashier for large retail craft store performing various duties which ensured customers' shopping convenience and satisfaction.

- Answered telephones, responded to inquiries and transferred calls to appropriate departments in a timely manner resulting in improved customer satisfaction.
- Operated manual cash register and assisted customers with their purchases which included regular price and sales items, ensuring that totals charged to customers were accurate.
- Assisted customers with directions in locating specific items and checked availability of items when not readily available on display, which contributed to increased sales.
- Processed credit memos and/or refunds for customers returning merchandise previously purchased, reviewed sales slips and verified receipt of proper credit.
- Assisted in cleaning facilities and restocked merchandise which resulted in organized and readily available merchandise.

EDUCATION

Pre-Veterinary Medicine - Sam Houston State University, Huntsville, Texas - Currently Attending
Alief Elsik High School - Alief, Texas - Graduated 1994

TECHNICAL SKILLS

Leading Edge Word Processor, The Veterinary Assistant
WordPerfect 5.1 (DOS and Windows), Lotus 123 (WYSIWYG), Avery Label Manager
The Print Press, Harvard Graphics, Paradox, Typing (50 wpm)

308

OBJECTIVE

Quality Control

SUMMARY

Over twenty-three years of high technology manufacturing experience, including twelve years in quality control and auditing, for the process and electronic chip manufacturing industry.

PROFESSIONAL EXPERIENCE

COMPUTERS INCORPORATED - Houston, Texas   1969 - 1992

Surface Mount Center (SMC) Line Operator/Test Operator (1986-1992)

- Operated Panasonic and Fuji Pick-and-Place and TRC Machinery in building boards and integrated chips.

- Determined materials needed and prepared requisitions for supplying material to eight SMC production operators for building integrated circuits, which contributed to achievement of customers' specifications and delivery objectives.

- Determined program and loaded computer to test different types of devices for all customers resulting in the maintenance of quality and quantity production objectives.

- Determined packaging, routing and labeling, entered data into computer and performed final testing and packing of the shift's production, assuring specifications and customer delivery objectives.

Quality Control Auditor (1979-1986)

- Monitored machine operators at their etching and alignment machines during their job operations, assuring performance to product and process specifications.

- Conducted continuous audit of machine and process equipment controls for factors such as humidity, temperature, water character, acidity formulation and running rate which resulted in attainment of process and product objectives.

Quality Control Inspector (1974-1979)

- Inspected slices (chips) under a microscope to assure proper orientation, contamination, correct alignment of the slice.

Pre Cap Inspector (1969-1974)

- Inspected bonded integrated circuits (chips) for bridging gold wires and gold bonded balls to detect contamination and other foreign particles, and recommended process and production adjustments to increase yields and meet critical specifications.

EDUCATION

Nursing/Assistant Certificate - 1964
International Business College, Houston, Texas

Jack Yates High School - 1963
Houston, Texas

ADDITIONAL EDUCATION

WordPerfect 5.1 - ExecuTrain, Houston, Texas - 1993

Overview of PC - ExecuTrain, Houston, Texas - 1992

CERTIFICATES AND AWARDS

Certificate: Understanding Semi-Conductors - 1982

Certificate: SPC: Statistical Process Control I & II- 1989 & 1990

Certificate: 5 Gold Star Accomplishment for
Contributing Total Quality Improvement in the SMC Area

Perfect Attendance Award Annually for Years 1988 - 1991

Merit Bonus Raise for High Quality Performance and Attendance -1992

47) NAME
Address
City, State Zip Code
Office #
Home #

OBJECTIVE

Product Development/Technical Service Technician

SUMMARY

Over twenty years experience in process operations, instrumentation and electrical control systems, quality control lab, product development, ISO 9000 certification, and customer technical service support. Have demonstrated ability to work effectively in teams, supervise and train personnel. Expertise includes process/product quality improvements, trouble shooting process and process control systems which has contributed to bottom line results.

PROFESSIONAL EXPERIENCE

INDEPENDENT CONSULTANT/CONTRACTOR - Houston, Texas   1995 - Present

Contract Application Development Technician
- Performed repairs and maintenance to Foxboro, Rosemont, Fisher, Honeywell and Bailey transmitters, PLC controllers, Allen Bradley and Modicon systems, and programmed new processes within existing equipment. Received extensive training on Foxboro I/A, Honeywell DSC and Honeywell Triconics system controllers and smart transmitters which tie in with each system.

HBM CHEMICAL COMPANY - Pasadena, Texas   1979 - 1995

Application Development Technician (1991-1995)
- Co-developed an Ultra High Molecular Weight-Polyethylene injection moldable and initiated the use of an additive package resulting in the development and marketing of a new specialty resin which is projected to increase product sales by 200 thousand pounds or $300,000 in 1996.
- Identified and tested additive packages and resin combinations which are scheduled to be introduced into the market in the near future and are projected to increase annual product sales by a minimum of 500 thousand pounds or $750,000.
- Identified improvements to core product; including quality changes to process equipment and operations. Identified and recommended improvements to redesign packaging equipment which will reduce off-grade resins by 500 thousand pounds or $500,000 annually.
- Identified and recommended improvements to the packaging and sales of off-grade materials by several different avenues which were later instituted by the management team resulting improvements in core competencies. Received "Quality Award".
- Identified and initiated new system which saved time, money and man power by reducing resins, containers and storage systems used for required sampling and testing.
- Conducted polymer testing, customer complaints research, satisfied customer technical requests, served as back-up for data systems manager, and trained new technicians in quality control and process polymer testing which improved operations.
- Updated and edited existing lab procedures to comply with ISO 9000 format for ISO certification, and developed ISO procedures for customer specifications, packaging and transportation of resins, customer technical service and complaint procedures, calibration and maintenance schedules of lab equipment, testing and data base procedures.
- Received several "Quality Awards" for achievements, either initiated or identified, by the management team for improving the quality of the business unit which increased resin production and sales.

Instrument and Electrical Technician (1985-1991)
- Performed repairs, preventive maintenance and calibrations on instrumentation and electrical systems within styrene monomer manufacturing unit, utilities, high density polyethylene and ultra high molecular weight polyethylene production plants.
- Designed and updated Piping & Instrumentation Drawings (P&ID's) prints, and installed new control systems from P&ID's which included electrical, analog, digital and pneumatics.

311

- Supervised contractors and coordinated activities during high maintenance periods, and trained new I&E technicians on all four processes, safety requirements and required documentation.
- Participated in numerous "Quality Action Teams" representing the I&E Department, regarding issue directly affecting the department, and received quality awards for problem solving during these activities.

Process Technician (1979-1985)
- Participated in start-up of new Styrene Monomer Process Plant, receiving cross-training in all jobs related to daily operations resulting in assignment to cover any job on all 4 shifts when needed.
- Directed operations in absence of supervisor and participated in the development of operational policies and training of new technicians on processes and safety requirements.

LATIMORE INDUSTRIES - Pasadena, Texas   1974 - 1979

Process Technician
- Performed process operations using a propylene oxide and glycol process.

WILLIAMS CHEMICAL COMPANY - Freeport, Texas   1971 - 1974

Process Technician
- Performed process operations using batch and continuous operating processes for Agro-Chemicals.

EDUCATION

AA in Instrument and Electrical - 1988
San Jacinto Junior College - Houston, Texas

AA in Business Finance - 1970
San Antonio Junior College - San Antonio, Texas

Plan to complete Bachelor of Science - University of Houston, Houston, Texas

ADDITIONAL EDUCATION

In-house Courses:

Injection Mold Machine Operations and Maintenance	DOT Certification
Injection Molding Tool Design	Quality Technical Service Operations
Plastics & Petroleum Testing (ASTM, ISO)	Digital Computer Interfaces
Foxboro Spec 200	Rosemont Smart Instruments
	Maintenance and Repairs
	Honeywell TDC 3000

HARDWARE/SOFTWARE SKILLS

UNIX	WordPerfect	Microsoft Office
LAN	FoxPro	Lotus 1-2-3
IBM Mainframe	Novell	Microsoft 2D Drafting
MS Work	Excel	

TECHNICAL SKILLS

Maintain, Operate and Repair:
Laboratory Testing Equipment (Wet and Physical Testing)
Blending Equipment (Extruders, Mixers)
Instrumentation (Analog, Digital and Pneumatic)
Electrical Control Systems (High Voltage AC & DC)
Process Analyzers (O_2, N_2, Hydrocarbons)
Process Systems (Valves, Meters)

PROFESSIONAL AFFILIATIONS

Society of Plastics Engineers (SPE)   American Chemical Society (ACS)

312

48) NAME
Address
City, State Zip Code
Office #
Home #

OBJECTIVE

Political Consultant

SUMMARY

Over ten years experience in political and international trade consulting, government affairs and communications for academic organizations. Creative problem solving, regulatory networking and analytical skills have been used to expand the energy market, manage political issues and develop proactive approaches, resulting in increased corporate presence in, and influence over, governmental policy-making. Designed corporate strategies to deal with government-generated opportunities and threats. Maximized corporate access to governmental and private sources of information conveyed in textual and electronic forms resulting in more efficient corporate decision-making.

PROFESSIONAL EXPERIENCE

INDEPENDENT CONSULTANT - Houston, Texas   1989 - 199_

Communicated political analyses to a variety of audiences for purposes both in person and in writing.

- Analyzed governmental expenditures, appropriations and decision-making for draft dissertation, broadening political, economic and financial expertise.

- Evaluated quantitative data on personal and a mainframe computers, and using a variety of personal computer software, resulting in increased computer literacy and more effective reports.

- Examined domestic and international events, and submitted articles to local newspapers and national magazines resulting in practical applications of political science.

- Assisted in formation of political organization at grassroots level and lobbied state regulators on the organization's behalf.

- Redesigned government courses to prepare students for advanced placement tests, resulting in increased number of college credits awarded.

- Formulated summer courses for basic college introductory courses in political science.

UNIVERSITY OF HOUSTON - Houston, Texas   1985 - 1989

Lecturer

Presented fundamental and sophisticated methods of political analysis to audiences.

313

- Designed series of presentations for, and conducted seminars on, *American National Government* and *State and National Government* at both honors and regular levels, resulting in exposure of undergraduates to new and challenging material.

- Researched and designed, and led seminars on, *Minority Group Politics* and *Political Parties and Interest Groups* for upper level students, resulting in increased organizational and electoral expertise.

- Served as a panelist reviewing and presenting reviews on papers at professional conference, appeared as speaker in a variety of on- and off-campus venues and wrote published reviews of political science books.

- Directed students in individual readings courses and advised both departmental majors and students matriculating in courses taught on a variety of issues.

- Gained approval of prospectus on a dissertation, and researched U.S. budgetary activity across years from 1865 to 1935 for dissertation.

UNIVERSITY OF HOUSTON - Houston, Texas   1981 - 1985

<u>Graduate Fellow</u>

Prepared papers and reports on many domestic and international political topics.

- Studied broad range of substantive, quantitative, and methodological topics in politics and government, researched national, state and local governmental trends and completed all course work required for Ph.D. in political science.

- Assisted in research of Acting Dean of Social Sciences through verification of citations and editing of text.

- Served as teaching assistant in large survey courses on American government and international relations by attending classes and leading tutorials.

- Supervised national telephone survey and coordinated two-week on-campus seminars supported by the Mellon Foundation.

EDUCATION

M.A., Political Science
University of Houston - Houston, Texas

B.A., Political Science
University of Houston - Houston, Texas

49) NAME

Address
City, State Zip
Office #
Home #

OBJECTIVE

Administrative Assistant

SUMMARY

Over twenty years experience in a wide variety of corporate social and executive administrative responsibilities utilizing strong interpersonal and communication skills. Possess excellent team skills and ability to work productively with little or no supervision.

PROFESSIONAL EXPERIENCE

TECH ELECTRONICS, INC. - Boston, Massachusetts   199-

Administrative Assistant
(Temporary Assignment in Engineering Department)

- Performed secretarial duties including word processing, payroll entries, answering telephones, taking messages, and distributing mail, contributing to efficient operations.

Receptionist
(Temporary assignment in main lobby and Human Resources Department)

- Directed customers, vendors, applicants to appropriate destination and assisted visitors in a professional manner.
- Handled telephones and assisted with Human Resource projects, compiling information and data entry which ensured that accurate information was readily available.

SEOUL, KOREA   1991 - 1992
As wife of Tech Electronics - Korea President, hosted and entertained company and official visitors.

- Belonged to and participated in Seoul International Women's Association, American Women's Association, Seoul Christian Women Society meetings, and fund raising activities, contributing to a positive company image.
- Entertained and escorted visitors around to selected sites for cultural, food and shopping tours, facilitating positive relationships.

ADELAIDE, AUSTRALIA   1988 - 1991

- Participated in the Australian Red Cross Organization, contributing to the community goals and needs.
- Volunteered at a local hospital information desk and addressed emergency room physician notification letters, ensuring professionalism and patient satisfaction.
- Toured visitors around South Australia and entertained corporate visitors, facilitating a comfortable environment for guests in unfamiliar surroundings.

CANADIAN CANCER SOCIETY - Toronto, Canada

<u>Volunteer</u>

- Supported the Canadian Cancer Society by assisting in the office regularly and participating in annual fund raising campaigns, which contributed to achievement organizational budgets and goals.

VERSAILES MEDICAL CENTER - Versailes, Kentucky

1980 - 1984

<u>Administrative Assistant for Clinical Associate Program</u>

- Handled all administrative assistant duties for 4 facility members and students ensuring professionalism and effective operations.
- Assisted in preparations for National P.A. Exams and P.A. State Convention held in Lexington, Kentucky, which ensured smooth running programs within budget.

TECH ELECTRONICS, INC. - Attleboro, Massachusetts

1975 - 1980

<u>Statistical Clerk</u>

- Served as Statistical Clerk for Quality Assurance Department Manager. Compiled weekly, monthly and annual reports, both domestic and international, ensuring accuracy.
- Provided secretarial support for department manager and 2 supervisors.

EDUCATION

Continuing course work in Human Resources and Introductory Word Processing - 1983
University of Kentucky - Lexington, Kentucky

Graduated - Coshocton City High School, Coshocton, Ohio

PROFESSIONAL AFFILIATIONS

Australia Red Cross - Volunteer
Canadian Cancer Society - Volunteer
United Way - Volunteer

TECHNICAL SKILLS

WordPerfect, Lotus
Typing: 30 WPM

316

Address
City, State Zip Code
Office #
Home #

OBJECTIVE

Strategic Change Management Consultant

SUMMARY

Twenty-five years experience in program design and implementation with focus of strategic management, policy development, training, and service delivery. Strengths are in strategy formation, process design, human factors management, and training which achieve strong organizational performance. Demonstrated skills in organizational assessment, strategic planning, management and leadership development, and the creation of training programs which develop strong team performance. Excellent personal skills in group facilitation, providing feedback, training presentation, platform speaking, writing, and editing.

PROFESSIONAL EXPERIENCE

CHANGE MANAGEMENT - Houston, Texas   1986 - Present

Provide consultation and training to organizations seeking to manage strategic change. Client list includes Bowling Green State University, University of South Carolina-Spartanburg, Tarleton State University, the Southern Association for College Student Affairs, and the Association for Student Judicial Affairs. Plans formulated and major goals achieved within allotted time frames.

- Designed, implemented, and evaluated over 50 training programs, group development experiences, workshops, and management development activities which guided learners in the identification of issues and the formulation of goals and solution strategies. These modules incorporate experiential exercises, simulations, role plays, case studies, presentations, and group discussion to deliver training which is sensitive to differences in learning styles and temperaments.

- Conducted organizational assessment, established three-year performance agenda, and guided implementation of significant turnaround strategy for a credit union resulting in growth of assets, 183%; membership, 282%; loan volume, 302%; payroll deduction, 570%; and a 42% decrease in delinquencies.

TRAVIS-McGEE UNIVERSITY - Houston, Texas   1988 - 1995

Associate Vice President and Dean of Students, and Adjunct Associate Professor of Management
Divisional executive responsible for 34 professional and 60 support personnel in the design, implementation, and evaluation of service programs and associated staff development and training functions. Budget responsibility exceeded $2.3 million annually. Service goals were achieved 90+% in every year.

- Led strategic direction, policy development, personnel supervision, program design, implementation, and evaluation for institution serving 9500 clients.

317

- Directed group process re-engineering and organizational downsizing to achieve 20% reduction in operating costs over a two-year period with minimal reduction of service.

- Designed and implemented customer service training program for over 800 employees in an education industry service group, resulting in increased performance and customer responsiveness.

- Trained 125 participants in leadership skills focused on group development, formation of work team values, and synergy (two years). Training objectives achieved with 4+ ratings (5 point scale).

- Managed major upgrade of health and psychological services, pharmacy services, and special clinics with resulting increase of 20+% in patients served, and 150% increase in revenues.

HAWKING STATE UNIVERSITY - New Orleans, Louisiana   1975 - 1988

<u>Assistant Vice President for Student Affairs</u>
(Promoted from Assistant to Vice President, and Instructor)

- Established Center for Leadership Development with modules in personnel assessment, leadership training, and leadership skill development. Served over two hundred clients with highly positive ratings.

- Supervised three departments with twelve professional staff and 50 support personnel. Met or exceeded all performance goals annually.

- Directed design and implementation of all student-client orientation programs and professional staff development. Achieved high ratings on all implemented programs.

- Taught courses in higher education administration, leadership development, residence staff training, and peer advisor development. Course rating always exceeded 4.0.

CALUMET UNIVERSITY - Delaware, Ohio   1970 - 1975

Positions held during this period were Director of Campus Programs, Director of Residence Life, and Coordinator of Residence Programs.

EDUCATION

Ph.D., Management & Organizational Behavior
Louisiana State University - 1986

M.A., Economics
Ohio University - 1970

M.Ed., College Student Personnel Administration
Ohio University - 1969

B.A., Economics
Oakland University - 1968

Index

About the Authors

Kenneth M. Dawson is Chairman of Dawson & Dawson Consultants Inc., a Houston-based firm which has provided a comprehensive range of services in Outplacement, Inplacement®, and Corporate Excellence since 1977. He has held top management positions in leading corporations and has provided a diverse range of professional consulting services to senior executive management in a wide variety of corporate settings. In addition to his business background, Mr. Dawson is a widely respected speaker, author, management instructor, and counselor who has taught and consulted with executives, managers, and employees representing a broad range of Fortune 500 companies.

During his management and consulting career, he has successfully conducted hundreds of executive seminars, workshops, and speaking engagements covering a comprehensive range of business subjects in numerous organizational settings. A Marine Corps veteran, he received his undergraduate degree in psychology prior to completing two graduate degrees with honors.

Sheryl N. Dawson is President of Dawson & Dawson Consultants, Inc. Her extensive business, management consulting, and assessment background, coupled with an MBA, provides to the firm's clients a broad perspective for professional career development. Her counseling abilities not only apply to career transition situations including spouse relocation assistance, but to internal career development as well. Having managed transition programs for a wide range of industries, affecting all levels and functions of employees, she contributes an added depth of understanding and expertise to enhance the success of companies and their employees who are transitioning.

Also responsible for business development, marketing, financial planning, and administration of the firm, she offers additional expertise in the start-up, organization, and operation of independent business and consulting practices. She has written numerous articles on human resource related topics and is a frequent guest on radio talk shows around the country. As author, speaker, and consultant, Mrs. Dawson represents the firm to a diversity of industry groups and associations.